Life in 1...
London

About the Author

Mike Hutton is a London-history author. His previous books include *The Story of Soho* and *Life in 1940s London*. He lives on the borders of Leicestershire and Northamptonshire.

Praise for Mike Hutton's *Life in 1940s London*:
'Well researched and well paced, this scrupulous account is occasionally hilarious, often touching, and all the better for the author's personal recollections.' Brian Sewell

Life in 1950s London

MIKE HUTTON

AMBERLEY

First published 2014
This edition first published 2015

Amberley Publishing
The Hill, Stroud
Gloucestershire, GL5 4EP

www.amberley-books.com

British Library Cataloguing in Publication Data.
A catalogue record for this book is available from the British Library.

ISBN 978 1 4456 4965 8 (paperback)
ISBN 978 1 4456 2133 3 (ebook)

Typeset in 10.5pt on 14.25pt Celeste.
Typeset by Fakenham Prepress Solutions, Fakenham, Norfolk NR21 8NN
Printed in the UK.

Contents

Contents

Introduction
A City of Contrasts

My father gave me a white fiver on my twenty-first birthday. It was the only one I ever owned. Its very size conveyed its worth, so large that it had to be folded to fit in my wallet. Even its texture was different, creating a vague sense of decadence. It belonged to a bygone era, not the modern decade that beckoned. The black-and-white £5 notes had not been issued for the past two years, but were still legal tender as I set off to pick up my Italian girlfriend from Hampstead underground in the August of 1959.

Sporting my new Italian-style suit bought from Cecil Gee in Shaftesbury Avenue and a shorn 'college boy' haircut, I really felt I represented the new, confident face of 'Young London'. Gone were the duffle coat, cavalry twills and the floppy hair, reminders of an earlier, austere age. Thoughts of the dark days of war were dispelled as those of my generation dashed ahead, embracing what we hoped would be a brighter future.

Foreign voices were still relatively rare in London, although increased affluence had led to an influx of exotic au pair girls. Even so, the lovely Paula was viewed with outright envy by some of my friends. Soho remained London's most cosmopolitan area, although Clerkenwell had traditionally been home to a sizeable Italian community which had increased again since the end of the war. Despite the arrival of the first West Indians, black faces and those from the subcontinent were still seldom seem in central London.

I travelled with Paula by tube to the bright lights of the West End. My outward self-confidence was only superficial. Too late I realised I should have taken her to a small, romantic French or Italian restaurant in nearby Soho. Instead I opted for the Cumberland hotel. While hardly the most prestigious hotel in London, it did at least offer a degree of glitz and surface glamour. My fiver paid for our three-course meal and the bottle of expensive wine. The problem was the Crème de Menthe. Paula flashed me a winning smile, her lips dyed green for a moment, as I looked in horror at the bill. I desperately rummaged through my pockets for the few extra shillings required. I realised that I had no money left to leave as a tip. The waiter hovered, staring accusingly at the plate. My white fiver lay covered in an assortment of copper coins. Should I imperiously tell him 'I assume service is included' and leave, or make a dash for the gents? To my shame I scuttled out ahead of Paula, sensing the feeling of rage being silently transmitted by the aggrieved waiter. I had much to learn. I only managed one more date with Paula before she kicked me into touch. Who could blame her?

My sense of rejection didn't last long. London was too hectic and exciting to dwell on failure. A quiet revolution was under way. Perhaps for the first time in London's long history, the young were emerging as an influential group. Not in the political sense, but as an economic group to be targeted. There was full employment and the young had money to spend – and they did. Most was invested in entertainment and, particularly, on fashion. While their parents were generally careful and predictable in their buying habits, the young felt liberated and they unleashed a tide of spending that retailers were quick to respond to. Working-class parents looked on in horror as their sons ditched their cloth caps, greased their hair and strutted round in Teddy Boy suits. Dress still defined your class, but less so than in previous generations. Middle-class parents were not spared the general angst felt about their young. They grumbled away at their sons as they opted for two-buttoned jackets and tight-fitting trousers. They even knotted their ties incorrectly. Dads were bemused to find their well-brought-up offspring sitting in the bath for hours in order to shrink blue denim jeans, a material previously only worn by manual labourers. T-shirts completed the look in an attempt to mimic Marlon Brando or James Dean. The world had gone mad. Where were the tweed sports jackets, Kangol hats and cravats?

It was becoming increasingly difficult to tell which side of the social divide young women came from until they opened their mouths. Gone were the twin set and pearls. Skin-tight sweaters were now all the rage, loved by young men and the young women built like Marilyn Monroe or Diana Dors. Curves were accentuated by circular skirts that were held out by yards of layered nylon petticoats. Considered worse still was the 'art school look', all sloppy sweaters and skin tight trousers. Now the young congregated in coffee bars and listened to rock music blaring from jukeboxes. A new confidence bordering on cockiness among the young was disconcerting to their elders. The pubs were largely left for the older generation to grumble into their beer or port and lemon. Most pubs remained rather dingy and the young opted for the bright lights and hubbub of the coffee bars, now seemingly situated on every street corner.

The new sense of affluence was spreading out in ripples, reaching all but the very poorest. Even they managed to buy or rent a television set so as to lose themselves for a few hours, escaping the problems of modern life. This newfound affluence had somehow crept up with few being able to pinpoint when it all began. For the time being there seemed to be no going back. More people were buying cars. Ford even started an advertising campaign extolling the virtues of a second family car. Four bedrooms, three children and two cars were on the aspiration map. So London was now a city for the young, but also one of increasing wealth and consumption. A walk through the West End highlighted the changes underway. For those of us who grew up in times of darkness and constant shortages, it was still a thrill to see the windows of the stores brimming with an endless choice of goods. More people were now taking annual holidays and some even defying 'Spanish tummy' by venturing abroad.

For all its surface well-being, the West End was not typical of the rest of London. It was also a city of poverty and deprivation. Swathes of it had still not recovered from the battering it took during the war. It was not just in the East End that people lived in squalor. Large families were often cooped up in a couple of rooms with little sanitation. Since the introduction of the welfare state, nobody went around without shoes as they had done before the war, but some children still slept four or five to a bed. Shocking living conditions and traditional male dominance still led to occasional outbreaks of domestic violence.

London is in a constant state of change, illustrated by areas previously regarded as slums becoming fashionable and other respectable neighbourhoods sliding into squalor. In 1959, I had just started working in an Islington that few would recognise as the gentrified area it is today. Camden Passage was not lined with fashionable restaurants and antique shops, rather by run-down outlets given over to mending bicycles or radios and a greasy spoon café.

By now most of the bomb sites in central London had disappeared. Like missing teeth in a gaping mouth, they had been filled. Gone were the weed-strewn open cellars that taunted and haunted passers-by. They were mostly replaced by ghastly slabs of concrete and glass. Across central London and the City, cranes thrust themselves skywards, the noise of jackhammers and rebuilding dwarfing for a moment the constant roar of traffic. The ancient skyline of London was undergoing significant change and pointing the way to massive redevelopment.

London has always embraced greed. It is a greedy city, constantly pushing outwards to satisfy its need for growth. It spawns greedy men whose sole motivation is money. For centuries, speculative developers have built swathes of residential London. Many, thought to be jerry-built, still stand today, although the Georgian bricklayers and Victorian carpenters who branched out into property speculation are largely forgotten. Their 1950s cousins had grander plans and larger projects to fulfil. The cranes and piledrivers pointed the way to vast riches, but not for the crane drivers or the labourers. These new moguls had mostly enjoyed a comfortable war and were now about to capitalise on London's misfortune. Their modern disciples are still with us today and money is still their god.

London has always been a city of temptation as well as opportunity. It caters for the weak willed. It tempts, it lures. Outwardly prudish and sanctimonious armies of hypocritical men kept London's vice trade buoyant. It was 1959 before street girls were prohibited from soliciting. Some felt that their withdrawal to flats and dodgy clubs reduced the attraction of areas such as Mayfair, Soho and Paddington. The 'oldest trade' merely retrenched, and soon telephone kiosks were festooned with all manner of outlandish services available. Generally, attitudes to sex and nudity had changed since Vivian Van Damm first introduced London to static naked ladies. The first strip club had opened in Soho in 1957 and Paul Raymond was already stretching the bounds of accepted decency at his Revue Bar in Walkers Court.

Organised crime also bubbled away. Huge amounts were being made from prostitution and, increasingly, pornography. Strangely, it was rare for normal residents or visitors to the capital to encounter trouble. The criminal gangs tended to restrict their violence to each other.

There was, of course, a softer, more caring side to London. Although the Church held far less influence than previously, it was still active in helping those down on their luck as well as fulfilling the more mundane tasks of christening, marrying and burying parishioners. Visiting St Patrick's church in Soho on Christmas Eve was an eye-opener. Here, swarthy-looking hoods and peroxide-blonde street girls sought a little easing of their consciences as the collection plates overflowed with high-denomination notes.

So here was London at the end of a momentous decade. An ever-changing, restless mixture of good and evil. A city of contradiction, of learning and ignorance rushing towards an uncertain future. It was also a city of talent, represented by its medicine and arts. It had some of the world's greatest teaching hospitals, and theatres in and around Shaftesbury Avenue that rivalled Broadway.

On New Year's Eve in 1959, I went to Trafalgar Square with some friends to see in the new decade. There were fireworks and we sang the national anthem and 'Auld Lang Syne'. Some, unable to resist, jumped into the illuminated fountains. Nelson looked down impassively from his column. He had seen it all before: the celebrations, rallies and demonstrations. Ten years earlier, the mood was doubtless more subdued. Just as we look in the mirror and don't see any changes in our appearance day by day, so it is living through an entire decade. Particularly when young, you wonder if anything is going to change. Of course it does and so do you. Only by looking back do you realise how immense those changes were and that what you have witnessed is a slice of London's uncontrollable history.

1
Real Austerity

Bleary-eyed revellers glanced at their alarm clocks, rolled over and went back to sleep. The first day of the new decade luckily fell on a Sunday, and those who had found something to celebrate could now enjoy a day off work in which to recover. It was 1974 before New Year's Day was declared a national holiday. The first working day of a new year witnessed a glum-looking army going through the motions at work and longing for it to end. Normally a new decade is greeted with a renewed sense of optimism, but as 1950 dawned it was difficult to raise much enthusiasm. The damp, overcast day reflected a London set in monotone, desperate to discard its gloomy image but seemingly unable to do so. This was a deeply conservative, even prudish time in our history, but with a population sensing change.

The following day, London resumed its normal pattern. From the main-line train stations an endless stream of commuters are spewed out onto the crowded streets of central London and the City. The legions of typists, secretaries and shop assistants are joined by office boys, clerks and managers. Some have folded newspapers tucked under an arm and carry important-looking briefcases. They march as if choreographed to their place of work. They stream across bridges bringing travellers from the southern suburbs to mingle with other commuters from all corners of the capital and beyond. For the most part it is a dowdy army, dominated by banks of blacks, browns and greys. Most of the men wear a hat, those city-bound sport bowlers, with the occasional 'topper' marking out the wearer as someone of influence. The bankers and brokers opt for black or navy overcoats and well-cut suits. The clerks and general office staff are also tidily dressed. Their clothes tend to be well worn and shiny and most wear stiff, starched shirt collars. These are normally worn for a couple of days before being collected once a week by a company that specialises in cleaning these symbols of middle-class respectability.

Away from the City there are homburgs and trilbies and, of course, cloth caps, although these tend to be confined to factory neighbourhoods. London still remained a major, but declining, centre of manufacturing. The women and young girls obviously set out to lighten the mood with their outfits, but there is little sense of style or high fashion. It is unfair to criticise this constrained generation too harshly as clothes rationing remained in force until 1954 and money was short. Even the youngest heading for work that day would have experienced the hardships and possibly the horrors of the Blitz, which still left its scars some five years later. Much rebuilding was already underway, but bomb sites continued to pepper the capital. So it is that shabby gabardine raincoats, shiny suits, owlish spectacles and laddered stockings accurately mirror the London in which these people live and work.

The Blitz had changed the London landscape more than at any time since the Great Fire. Some felt the bombing had ripped at its very heart. Vast swathes had been flattened. Many beautiful and historic buildings had yielded, along with countless tenements and ordinary homes. The skyline had been changed forever. Both the City and the East End had been devastated. It is astonishing that so many landmarks survived. Some were damaged, but were soon restored to their former glory. St Paul's Cathedral continued to stand proudly, despite much of the surrounding area being destroyed in the firestorm of December 1940. Elsewhere in the City, the Bank of England, Mansion House and the Royal Exchange endured despite the carnage. Westminster Abbey and Buckingham Palace also sustained damage, but survived. The area around Piccadilly Circus was heavily bombed, as was Trafalgar Square, with the National Gallery being damaged but already repaired and intact. All of them were symbols of London's survival, as were the Tower of London, the Kensington Museums and the Tate Gallery. Perhaps the most astonishing survival was that all the bridges spanning the Thames still stood proud, despite having been prime targets for the Luftwaffe.

Across London, office blocks and high-rise flats proved practical but ugly replacements for what had stood before. In the East End, slum clearance added to the destruction. Initially, few really welcomed their new modern homes. There was a feeling of resentment at the fracturing of a long-held sense of community. From Croydon in the south to Hendon in the north and across the West End, few areas escaped and there was now a desperate need for new housing.

London felt constrained and less assured, the theatre of the street somehow muted. London needs to be rich, self-confident and arrogant. Before the war it had presented itself to the world with a certain swagger. True, it had been as chaotic as ever, crowded and dirty, yet the pomp and grandeur it projected created the overwhelming impression. It needed to re-establish itself as the greatest city in the world. The Square Mile in the City of London still dominated the global banking industry and the world of insurance. Its docks, which had suffered so badly during the Blitz, still handled a sizeable percentage of the nation's imports and exports. London remained a centre of academic and medical excellence. It enjoyed a thriving cultural life, with theatres that rivalled Broadway. Yet this grand old city was like a patient recovering from a major operation. Much in life revolves around confidence, and this had been further weakened by our declining influence in the world. Managing a shrinking empire was difficult and expensive. The country had security commitments ranging from the oil states of the Middle East to Malta and Cyprus. It had also entered into the Korean conflict, and all of these commitments were denying us the financial strength to deal with the many problems at home.

Austerity is a word often bandied about by modern politicians, although today's privations bear little relation to what was being endured in 1950. It seemed quite preposterous that food rationing had already been abolished in Germany, while in Britain almost everything remained on ration. How was it that we had been victorious and yet life for most was getting progressively tougher?

After five years of socialist rule, the electorate appeared to be in truculent mood. With the unexpected landslide victory of 1945, the Attlee government had felt confident enough to introduce the most radical social welfare reforms in British history. Despite all the advantages offered by a raft of measures, including free healthcare and secondary education, there was little sense of well-being. Free milk and school dinners, together with new unemployment and sickness benefits, were soon taken for granted. The nationalisation of key industries split opinion, and all of these measures had to be paid for by higher taxation. Many of the changes were directed at helping the working class and were resented by those who were ostensibly better off but didn't feel it.

On 10 January, Clement Attlee announced that the general election would take place on 23 February. There was a feeling that, despite the astonishing changes the government had made to British life, an ungrateful public would punish Attlee in much the same way they had their wartime hero Winston Churchill. The socialists had previously needed the support of middle England to win, but it was they who felt undervalued in the quiet revolution that had been going on all around them.

Food, or rather its scarcity, had become a major preoccupation. People spoke nostalgically about the food they had enjoyed before the war. Ten years of enforced diet had provided a lean but resentful population. Due to a breakdown in negotiations with Argentina, meat was in short supply despite already being severely rationed. A diet dominated by enforced rationing restricted individuals to one egg a week and under two ounces of cheese. An allowance of six ounces of butter and just two pints of milk called for continued ingenuity in the kitchen. Despite the restrictions, a diet low in sugar and fat, but high enough in protein, was perfectly healthy and being overweight or obese was a rarity. Carrying on a wartime tradition, many people tended allotments and fruit and vegetables formed an important part of the diet. Joan Clarke, living in Barking, had looked enviously at photographs of her father eating a banana when he was stationed in the Far East. She kept on about it so much that her mother, in desperation, used to mash parsnips and cover them with banana essence to keep her quiet. The first banana I ever ate I shared with a friend whose father was serving in Palestine. By the time it arrived in London it was just a blob of blackened goo, but we solemnly ate it and declared it delicious.

Early in the election campaign there was a feeling that the Tories would be returned, although the result was likely to be close. Despite some rowdy scenes from the hustings, it was a strangely muted campaign. The BBC went to enormous lengths not to show any bias. All programmes were vetted in advance to make sure that no political influence, no matter how oblique, was aired. Party political broadcasts enjoyed huge audiences. Three days prior to polling, the *News Chronicle* published a Gallup poll that gave Labour a lead of 1.5 per cent, but few put much faith in the prediction.

By the evening of the election, the West End was packed with crowds gathered in Trafalgar Square, while a huge screen was erected above the Criterion theatre in Piccadilly Circus to relay each result as it came through. Many in the crowd were students, wearing their statutory duffle coats with college scarves flung carelessly over one shoulder. The college or university scarf was another symbol of establishing social standing in British society. Whether it be town or gown, or cloth cap and bowler hat, clothes continued to announce social standing in class-ridden Britain. Party rosettes worn that night did illustrate that, in politics at least, there was a degree of social cross-fertilisation.

The elite of British society, meanwhile, gathered at London's swankiest hotels, longing for a respite from what they reckoned to be socialist vindictiveness. Since 1945 they had been subjected to the most punitive taxation ever imposed in Britain. Someone had to pay for all the social welfare changes, and, with a standard rate of income tax levied at 47.5 per cent, those at the top were hit with a surtax of an eye-watering 98 per cent. Real incomes for the wealthiest had halved since 1939. Inflation had also eaten away at their spending power and they were even pursued to their graves, with death duties applied at 75 per cent of their retained assets. The government, like that of today, was desperate to raise additional revenues. Across the country, grand houses were sold off, abandoned or demolished. London mansions were sold as some of the aristocracy decamped to smaller or less prestigious addresses. This was made more necessary as there was now such difficulty in finding suitable servants. Few girls fancied the thankless work anymore, and set off for better-paid jobs in shops, offices and factories.

Shaking off the smell of mothballs, the rich and influential donned their evening wear. Their wives fished out the family jewels and off they set for Claridge's and the Ritz with the hope that the Tories would win and set about getting the country back on its feet. Over a thousand people gathered in the Great Room at the Grosvenor House, waiting anxiously for the first results. Those staying overnight were whisked to their rooms by four new Waygood-Otis lifts, claimed to be the fastest elevators in the world. Not to be outdone, Lord Camrose, the proprietor of the *Daily Telegraph*, hosted a party for 2,000 guests at the Savoy. Claridge's put on a cabaret for their gilded clientele, hosted by a young Tony Hancock. Across London, champagne corks popped. Early results made the bubbly taste distinctly flat. Long faces replaced the bonhomie. In Piccadilly each result was greeted by a chorus of exuberant cheers, mixed with boos and hooted derision. Radio programmes were constantly interrupted with the latest results. An astonishing 84 per cent of the electorate had voted, dispelling rumours that the voters had become apathetic. Many stayed up late into the night, but it was becoming obvious that the outcome was too close to call and would possibly be decided by the final few constituencies to declare. While Labour had gained a comfortable early lead, most declared seats had come from their traditional urban strongholds. The morning results from rural constituencies were likely to favour the Tories. I remember sitting with my parents trying to decide which party I would have supported if I had been old enough to vote. My father was a confirmed socialist, while my mother was the bluest of blue. As the morning progressed, the champagne started flowing again at the Dorchester, where the Rothermeres were hosting a party. Here was proof that the Labour government had not managed to get their hands on all upper-class money. The super-rich have always found a way to protect their wealth. Now it was time for the accountants to weave their magic.

By Friday evening, with only a few results outstanding, it was obvious that Labour would win with the narrowest of overall majorities. There was some talk of a coalition, but the Cabinet decided to carry on in government. Not only would life continue to be extremely difficult for most, but it was obvious that there would have to be another election before long.

Labour conducted a post-mortem as to why they had lost so much support. Boundary changes explained some of the shift, but a major concern was the defection of the middle-class voters from the suburbs and shires. A combination of high taxes and rationing restrictions had left them feeling aggrieved. They also felt miffed by their perceived loss of status as more resources were targeted towards the underprivileged. Middle England was convinced that they represented all that was best about the country. They considered themselves hard-working, honest and thrifty, and yet they felt neglected and unloved. They viewed the upper classes as lazy, immoral and condescending, and the workers as feckless, boorish and vulgar. In many respects there was empathy between the toffs and the working class in that both tended to despise those in the middle.

Class, or perception of it, pervaded every corner of British life. It was a question of convenience that three main groups had been established, but class in Britain was far more complicated than that. It could be divided into endless sub-sections. It had been our class system that had so shocked American servicemen stationed in Britain during the war. For them it was the huge social divide between the officers and other ranks which they found laughable and counter-productive. It illustrated the depth of snobbery that haunted and stunted our post-war recovery.

Discussion of money had long been considered vulgar by the aristocracy, but circumstances were changing. They still tended to set themselves apart. Now they felt like an endangered group, fighting to protect their inherited wealth. Making them feel equally uncomfortable was the arrival of a new breed of self-made men, the nouveau riche who had made fortunes during the war, invariably sporting loud suits and grey shoes and accompanied by brassy blondes wearing fox furs. Their loud, common voices had started to invade London's best hotels and, alarmingly, even some of its exclusive clubs. These establishments had previously been the preserve of people with breeding who knew how to conduct themselves. It was obvious that even the staff resented the interlopers, but these people, these take-over tycoons and property developers, needed to be watched. They might someday even need to be courted. Life had changed. It was a harsher, more aggressive environment. The establishment had to adapt if they were to flourish and survive.

It was not just the social elite who despised the new manifestation of commercial success. Men who had seen action and had enjoyed a 'good war' from lower down the social scale often found themselves being subordinate to a man who had avoided war service altogether. Having to take orders from someone who wouldn't have made the rank of corporal was galling. This frequently led to resentment and frustration. Despite all the changes taking place, the 'old school network' still flourished. It was frequently a case of who rather than what you knew that led to job opportunities. Some of those who had witnessed the horrors of war close up found it impossible to settle down in civvy street. Men returned altered beyond recognition, given to mood swings and sometimes even violence. Others just opted out of what they considered to be a rat race. A neighbour of my parents had been a submarine commander during the war. Previously he had held an executive position in the City. Haunted by his war experience, his drive and ambition had seemingly been torn from him. He settled for selling insurance from door to door. Each morning he would set off on his bike, seemingly content. Having been a high flyer, he now just conveyed a sense of placid calm. At home, his attractive wife missed the parties and the high life of the Mess. She resented this new incarnation she lived with. It was a recipe for disaster, cut short by his early death.

So London in 1950 was a place few youngsters today would be able to relate to and is not viewed with much affection by those of us who were around at the time. It was a place that encouraged conformity, particularly from the young. Most wore school uniforms, the girls in gymslips and bobby socks and the boys, even into their early teens, having to wear short trousers. Wearing a school cap was also the norm. It would be a few years yet until the teenage revolution was unleashed on an unsuspecting public. Many women chose to stay at home because running a home was a full-time job.

There were Hoovers, of course, but few washing machines and not many families owned a fridge. Food shopping, therefore, tended to be done daily. By the time cooking and cleaning was completed it was time to change and get ready to welcome the man of the house home after a tiring day's work. Generally speaking, across the classes, the man wasn't expected to help in the house. Very few homes had central heating, and open coal fires helped heat the living room. The kitchen was usually fired by a coke-fed boiler. In winter, it was up to bed with a stone hot-water bottle and often waking to find the windows frozen from the inside.

Of course, this was a London with no computers, iPads or mobile phones. In fact, most people didn't even have a phone in their homes, using instead the red telephone boxes situated on almost every street corner. There was no texting and people still relied a great deal on contacting each other by letter. The Mitford sisters, John Betjeman and Evelyn Waugh, among many others, fired off letters most days. Winston Churchill, writing to his wife from Hyde Park Gate in April 1950, tells of a visit from his son Randolph and daughter-in-law June, during which he sensed tension in their relationship. Although Clemmie was in Italy at the time, the couple often wrote to each other even when only separated by a few miles.

This was a London with very few black or brown faces. A place where foreigners generally were seldom seen or heard, except in areas like Soho. Here, there were many foreign restaurants. You could dine at Casa Pepe in Dean Street for 5s plus a house charge of 1s 6d. The maximum price restaurants were allowed to charge remained at 5s, although cover charges and wine could send the bill soaring. *What's on in London* advertised La Belle Meuniere in Charlotte Street or Rules, London's oldest restaurant, if you fancied more traditional fare. Dancing was on offer at the Trocadero or Fischer's in Bond Street.

There were no official nightclubs in the London of 1950, but this was circumnavigated by joining 'day clubs', which organised reputable bottle parties. Ciro's in Orange Street was the most lavish, costing a hefty ten guineas, while the slightly less reputable Murray's in Beak Street charged five guineas with concessions for overseas visitors. These clubs normally closed at midnight, but night owls were catered for at the Embassy, Astor and Coconut Grove. There, bottle parties started at 10.00 p.m. and wove their way to a tipsy four o'clock in the morning. The Larder in Vicarage Road, Kingston upon Thames, was ahead of the game by offering takeaway meals.

This was a London where abortion was illegal, as was homosexuality. The relative tolerance shown towards the gay community during the war was in reverse by 1950. Although there remained a few discreet bars and pubs where 'queers' were tolerated, many lived in real fear of arrest, although a blind eye was turned to the famous, particularly among the theatrical fraternity. It was a time of considerable police corruption, particularly in central London.

Away from the main roads, London was a place where boys could play cricket and football in the street with little interference from traffic. A place where girls skipped and played hopscotch. It was a place where people queued outside cinemas and there were only a few thousand households who had a television. It was a place where plimsolls, not expensive trainers, were worn, of Bakelite wirelesses and heavy penny coins. There were workmen's cafés on every street, including even the fashionable areas of the West End. For a treat you could be taken to a Joe Lyons Corner House. It was the nearest that most of us ever got to perceived luxury.

Each floor had its own themed restaurant, some with a band playing in the background. There were many more Lyons teashops where you were served by a 'nippy'. These outlets were pretty basic, and you sat on uncomfortable bentwood chairs while you drank your stewed tea. In 1950, for a special treat, youngsters were taken to London Zoo to see Brumas, the only polar bear to be bred in captivity in Great Britain. The country needed to trumpet every achievement, no matter how obscure.

This was not a London for today's demanding consumers. London was dull, down at heel and in need of a boost. For once the government was planning one. It was to offer the first chink of light pointing the way forward. A chance for Londoners to cheer up collectively and to forget the real austerity that had been grinding them down for so long. For a short time, anyway.

2
Festival Time

It was obvious that he was not well. Onlookers were shocked by his gaunt appearance. Surrounded by his family, he stood on the steps to St Paul's Cathedral to announce the opening of the Festival of Britain. The public had been led to believe that the king had fully recovered from the ill health he had experienced two years previously. His voice was firm, with little hint of the stammer that sometimes plagued his public appearances. Although there were festival events taking place throughout the British Isles, attention inevitably was centred on London. The festival had been planned to take place exactly one hundred years after the Great Exhibition staged in Hyde Park. The venue for the modern festival was significant. The choice of a derelict site on the south bank of the Thames was intended to highlight a modern, forward-looking Britain, but it inadvertently emphasised Britain's decline. Instead of an affluent West End setting for a country that a century before had been at the height of its world power, the South Bank setting indicated a near-bankrupted nation seeking a new start among desolate bomb damage.

This uneasy feeling of inferiority was emphasised by a tribal division that had always been noticeable between Londoners living either side of the Thames. An unfounded sense of superiority existed widely among those living to the north. This perception probably originated in Roman times and has been endorsed for centuries since. Roman legions moving north had set up camp on the south bank of the Thames and with them came camp followers, including prostitutes to give comfort to the legionnaires far from home. This set a precedent for the area that continued for hundreds of years. Following the Battle of Hastings, much of this land was awarded to King William's brother-in-law before eventually falling under the jurisdiction of the Bishop of Winchester in the twelfth century. He did little to change the nature of the area and was happy to collect rents from the brothels that thrived there. The terrain was marshy and unwelcoming. It became a district where felons and even murderers could find sanctuary. If they managed to escape capture for a year and a day they became free men.

As the centuries progressed, other attractions started to flourish along the Thames's southern banks. Theatres sprouted, offering entertainment, and from Tudor times bloodthirsty animal sports became hugely popular. Bear gardens and cock-fighting pits were attended by raucous crowds, who often wagered huge sums on their particular favourite. There were dog fights with badgers, and even horses were pitted against each other. Top attractions would be an occasional lion or leopard, imported specifically to rip apart a smaller but fearsome opponent. Both Samuel Pepys and John Evelyn made visits to a bear garden, which they recorded in their diaries. They wrote of dogs being tossed into the crowd by enraged bulls. It was obvious that bear- and bull-baiting was not to their taste, and Evelyn wrote, 'I most heartily weary of the rude and dirty pastime'. A reputation for enjoyment, no matter how cruel or crude the sport, stayed with the neighbourhood, which became increasingly busy and crowded; London Bridge was constantly thronged with travellers, wagons and carts crossing the Thames.

It is doubtful whether any of this dubious history was uppermost in the government's mind when the South Bank site for the festival was chosen. Initially, it was thought the area was too small, but Herbert Morrison, the Deputy Prime Minister, whose job it was to oversee the project, was convinced it would be a great boost for South London and its much maligned population. Born in Brixton, Morrison was a Londoner and proud of it. There had been talk of a festival for years, but the general concept was brought into being by Gerald Barry, the editor of the left-leaning *News Chronicle*. Morrison appointed him director general, along with a committee featuring civil servants, architects and a leading theatre manager.

From the summer of 1950, people strolling along the Victoria Embankment could gaze across the river and witness a wasteland being transformed into a series of strange shapes. Despite a constant shortage of raw materials, regular trade disputes and threatened strikes, the skyline was being redefined. Workmen scrambled over scaffolding and steel pillars like acrobats at the circus. By the end of the year, the 'dome of discovery' was crowned with its metal roof. The site was like a giant stage with hundreds of 'extras' moving, running, shambling, as if in need of a professional choreographer. From the seeming chaos, order slowly emerged. By March, a suspended cigar-shaped creation appeared as if floating unaided. The vertical feature known as 'the skylon' remains the abiding image of the festival. It served no real purpose other than pointing the way forward into the unknown. From an initial sense of apathy, interest in the festival began to bubble. Herbert Morrison was certainly caught up in the general excitement that he was central in creating. Much of the press and some Tory MPs referred to the festival as 'Morrison's Folly' and dubbed him 'Lord Festival'. The objectives were the very British formula of creating a platform for public education and mixing it with popular culture. Morrison referred to 'putting a mirror in front of ourselves for our benefit and for that of the outside world'. It was an attempt to explore Britain's past and peer into its future across the arts, science, technology and industrial design.

An attempt was made to create a continental atmosphere. Striped awnings and umbrellas dominated the open-air cafés and restaurants. Futuristic chairs and tables of bonded board with spindly wire legs helped create the illusion. Unfortunately, the bags of chips and candyfloss on offer hardly rivalled the culinary delights of France or Italy. No matter, it was a start. For the British public it was time to forget the problems of the Korean War and the escalating cost of rearmament by devoting a few hours to pure enjoyment.

Morrison admitted to being overcome with emotion at the opening ceremony. A full orchestra backed by massed choirs performed 'Land of Hope and Glory'. Maybe a salute to our imperial past, but to a public restricted to eight pennyworth of meat a week and rising inflation, hope was unfortunately more appropriate than glory.

The following day began wet and miserable as an enthusiastic but bedraggled public streamed through the turnstiles. Deep pools formed on the paths, sodden flags clung to their posts and the café awnings sagged under the weight of water. Despite the atrocious weather, the initial impression was still one of shock. For most, it seemed like entering a foreign and unfamiliar land. A public that had been denied much in the way of colour and new home décor for the past decade took a deep breath. Sculptures by Henry

Moore and Barbara Hepworth fought for attention among designs made from plastic, wood and aluminium, together with buildings consisting of great walls of glass. Even the wastepaper baskets and conical metal lampshades turned their backs on the past. A new look was being created to rival the shock that Dior had brought to womenswear in 1947. The new buzzword was 'contemporary'.

The River Thames formed a memorable backdrop for the festival. Morrison and his advisors had been vindicated. Overlooking some of London's most iconic landmarks a new Britain was presenting itself, however falteringly. From the towers of Westminster, travelling east to the majestic dome of St Paul's, London embraced and welcomed the changing landscape. While at the time of the Great Exhibition Victorian Britain splattered the world's map with imperial red, two world wars had left Britain crippled by debt. It was time for the country to reinvent itself. Perhaps it would become less involved in world politics? Not yet. There were still influential British politicians who wanted us to retain our imperial power. There were still a few convulsions to be endured.

My first view of the festival was at night from the Victorian Thames Embankment, staring over the shiny water, past the boats chugging by like ghost ships. In the distance was the illuminated Skylon, hanging like an invader from outer space. Later in the summer I went to the exhibition on a school trip with a class of spotty thirteen-year-olds. Our first stirrings of interest in girls were emerging. Although there were hordes of them milling around – all gymslips, bobby socks and ponytails, they dismissed us with disdain. Rebuffed, gloomily we made our way to the nearest pavilion, chatting in voices that lurched from alto to baritone. Girls would have to wait. It was time to improve our minds. Here was a public lesson devised by the great and the good for our further enlightenment. An extended lecture to improve the public's understanding. Looking back now the whole concept strikes as being somewhat condescending, but a public starved of going out to enjoy themselves came in their droves. Eight and a half million stared at the exhibits. Most felt the experience was interesting, if not exactly exciting.

The dome of discovery gave a flavour of what was on offer. It was split into separate sections, illustrating Britain's contribution to world progress. The living world covered biological discoveries, exploring the story of living things in relation to their environment. There were exhibits that covered animal behaviour, embryology and the development of the brain.

Another gallery was devoted to the sea and Britain's contribution to the development of charts, maps and instruments, together with a study of the ocean bed. The polar section attempted to show the effects of extreme weather conditions. I found the earth gallery the most interesting with its explanations of what could be discovered just by digging. Mineral resources rather passed me by, but I found the work of the archaeologists fascinating. So on we trooped to the area covering the physical world, which explored the spirit of scientific discovery, including the groundbreaking work of Newton and Faraday. For centuries the land had been central to British life, and this was not going to be ignored. The section devoted to the earth covered not only British farming but also the contributions the country had made overseas. Our expertise in the development of crops and irrigation had been particularly significant throughout the Commonwealth. A section devoted to the sky had visitors gazing upwards trying to understand British weather patterns, but the most popular area of the dome was a glimpse into the future.

It was not just schoolboys who were fascinated by outer space. A journey into the unknown through the science of astronomy set minds racing. The prospect of the amazing developments awaiting the world had the crowds gazing with studied intent.

A major theme of the festival was the seemingly unlikely marriage of science and the arts, yet it had been echoed a century before by Prince Albert at the Great Exhibition. The most obvious example on the South Bank was the building of the Festival Hall. Designed by members of London County Council's own architectural department, it was the first significant post-war building in London. Built to seat 3,000 people, its design proved controversial. It was described as a leg on a cradle, while Sir Thomas Beecham likened it to a chicken coop. The concert hall offered light and space, a style that was unique at the time. The opening concert concentrated on music by British composers. Handel was afforded honorary status as his work was played alongside examples of Vaughan Williams, Parry and Elgar. Built on the site of the old Lion Brewery, the Royal Festival Hall became the lasting legacy of the festival, standing alone once the rest of the buildings had been demolished.

Herbert Morrison had always wanted the festival to be fun rather than purely educational. The creation of the festival gardens and funfair downriver at Battersea provided the perfect background. Occupying the northern area of Battersea Park, the gardens were approached through a line of trees on a variety of raised wooden walkways linked by three houses. There were water gardens and fountains to admire in an attempt to offer a tranquil setting in a space invaded by huge crowds. As the weather improved during June, knotted handkerchiefs provided protection from the sun, and heavy jackets were discarded. British men were visibly uncomfortable in hot weather. Casual leisurewear was not available to most and the combination of belts and braces was prevalent – a thick leather belt securing heavy cloth trousers with elasticated braces on show as a backup. Aertex shirts were popular among the younger men, but it was left to the ladies to create some sense of style and colour.

A major fairground attraction was the Far Tottering and Oyster Creek Railway. The engines featured crazy funnels, including a frying pan and weathercock. The three locomotives were designed by the artist Rowland Emett. Nellie was probably the favourite, but the Wild Goose and Neptune still managed to pull the customers in. The Battersea funfair was a huge draw for the young. There were the usual roundabouts, dodgem cars and rifle galleries, but the fair offered one overwhelmingly popular attraction. The big dipper was a spectacular, frightening rollercoaster. Girls squealed while their boyfriends tried to maintain a masculine calm as thousands of day trippers were hurled down the largest rollercoaster in Britain. While the festival was an overall success, Morrison encountered a puritanical backlash when he attempted to keep the funfair open on Sundays. The Sunday observation zealots were having none of it and the only concession he was able to offer the public was to halve the entrance price for the festival gardens on Sundays to one shilling.

Although some commentators ridiculed the festival, suggesting it showed more of the country's perennial weaknesses than its strengths, most of the public disagreed. Opinion polls conducted shortly after the festival's closure suggested the population attending were impressed. Even some of the newspapers and politicians who had been sceptical reluctantly acknowledged that overall the event had been a success. A very British success, drawing extremes of interests and culture briefly together in what everyone hoped would be a better future. As it turned out it was the final throw of the dice from a government who had chosen to challenge long-held perceptions of British life, but who had finally run out of steam. With a wafer-thin majority and problems both at home and abroad, another general election beckoned.

Life in 1951 didn't solely revolve around the festival. On New Year's Day, the BBC introduced a programme reflecting the life of country folk on a three-month trial. By Easter the programme had been switched to the prime listening slot of 6.45 p.m. on the *Light Programme*. To the consternation of many, their favourite programme *Dick Barton, Special Agent* was killed off. Despite the furore that followed, *The Archers* obviously uncovered some hidden need in the British public and, of course, the soap of all soaps continues today, albeit with storylines that would have shocked a 1950s audience.

In April the mood in London was lightened by the staging of the first Miss World competition. The brainchild of Eric Morley, a young Londoner, the event became controversial over the years as it was thought to demean women, but back in 1951 the curvaceous Miss Sweden, Kiki Haakonson, met with the general approval of a British public desperate for a little glamour in their lives. Meanwhile, the proponents of women's liberation and political correctness awaited their turn to take centre stage.

The summer of 1951 was further enlivened by the arrival of Sugar Ray Robinson, middle-weight champion of the world and global superstar. He came with a retinue of staff and his pink Cadillac convertible, transported from the Continent, where he had been going through the motions with a series of non-title bouts and exhibitions. He was considered to be the greatest pound-for-pound boxer alive. His tour of Europe was to be concluded with a fight against a British boxer called Randolph Turpin. Robinson, who had all the trappings of a present-day pop star, admitted he had never even heard of Turpin. 'Randy' Turpin's elder brother Dick had become Britain's first black boxing champion the previous year. Robinson was in for a shock. Randy had been a cook in the Merchant Navy, a tough career choice in the days of virulent colour prejudice. Later, he had taken on all comers as he learnt his trade in fairground boxing booths.

The excitement swirling around Robinson led the management of the Savoy hotel to ask him to leave, as the huge crowds gathered outside were annoying their other guests. Mounted police were required to control the crowds when Robinson arrived at Jack Solomons' gym in Soho for the weigh-in. He was again attended by his retinue, which included his hairdresser and a dwarf who was retained as his court jester. It was here that Robinson had his first misgivings. While he had been swanning around Europe living it up and taking plaudits, Turpin had been training as never before. He carried not an ounce of surplus flesh and, more importantly, not a speck of fear for his illustrious opponent.

The bookies were in no doubt as to who would win and neither were the pundits. It soon became obvious that they were wrong, however, and this would be no walkover for Sugar Ray. Turpin stuck to his plan of simply out-fighting the American, but taking no risks in seeking a spectacular knock-out. He steadily built up a points advantage, although those listening to the radio commentary may have been led to believe otherwise. By the fifteenth and final round the crowd at the Earls Court arena were on their feet singing 'For he's a jolly good fellow'. Robinson was gracious in defeat, but he knocked Turpin out in a return bout held in the States. From then on Turpin's life went into a gradual decline until his suicide in 1966 at the age of thirty-seven.

A week before the Festival of Britain officially ended on 30 September, King George VI had part of his lung removed. Crowds gathered outside Buckingham Palace as the news spread. The bulletin issued by his doctors stated 'that anxiety must remain for some days'. The king had recovered sufficiently by the end of the year to broadcast his normal Christmas message, which had to be pre-recorded because of his condition. It was obvious he was seriously ill, and the country began to anticipate a new chapter in their relationship with the royal family. The king was a very popular monarch, whose quiet, unassuming manner was generally applauded by an extremely pro-royalty public. His decision, together with the queen, to stay in London during the Blitz had reinforced this bond, and there was growing concern about his condition.

By the end of the year it was obvious that the Labour government was exhausted. Earlier, Aneurin Bevan, Harold Wilson and John Freeman had resigned in protest at prescription charges being introduced for spectacles and dental care in Hugh Gaitskell's budget. Another Socialist giant, Ernest Bevin, died in April 1951, just a month after being appointed Lord Privy Seal. These were body blows to the Attlee administration. Attlee was also unwell. Eventually, he called for an election to take place on 25 October.

Polls suggested an easy Tory victory. There were divisions within the Labour Party, but there was a feeling that they had achieved much of what they had set out to do. The Tories ran a more engaging campaign, but the thought of the country being run by a seventy-seven-year-old Winston Churchill hardly pointed the way to a brave new world. Once again, the early results favoured the Socialists, although eventually the Tories were returned with a majority of sixteen. This was in spite of the fact that Labour gained more votes than the Tories. A significant fall in support for the Liberals was telling, as was the first-past-the-post system that saw Labour mainly increase their vote in constituencies that they already held.

Four days after the election, Clementine Churchill wrote to her husband from Chartwell. She asked him not to be angry with her, but she was anxious that her son-in-law, Duncan Sandys, should not be considered for the key post of Secretary of State for War. She thought it unwise for him to work immediately under her husband. If anything went wrong it could prove delicate and tricky, she concluded. Winston obviously listened to his wife, as Sandys was subsequently appointed to the lesser position of Minister of Supply.

Having secured a notable victory, Churchill became the second-oldest prime minister in British history – rather at odds with Britain's desire to offer a new modern face to the world. No matter, he held a huge family party at Chequers and departed on New Year's Eve to meet President Truman. The fact that he chose to travel in a leisurely manner by sea, aboard the *Queen Mary*, emphasised the gap between a Britain stuck in the past and one wanting to create a modern and dynamic future.

Not to worry – the contemporary look of the country was being upheld by thousands of housewives. Victorian furniture, jardinières and lace tablecloths were being hidden away or despatched to the salerooms. There was a huge row at home when my mother sold our grandfather clock to an Irish 'knocker'. Anything vaguely contemporary was snapped up as bright primary colours began to dominate the terraced houses, flats and suburban semis of London. This faltering step was soon to be enveloped in an impenetrable, cloying fog as London succumbed to the Great Smog.

3

The Year of the Great Smog

Britain in the 1950s was overwhelmingly deferential. Doctors, schoolteachers and policemen were figures of respectability and authority. Youngsters were particularly wary of the local bobby, who was quite likely to give them a clip round the ear if they were caught misbehaving. Deference reached its peak in the attitude that was adopted towards royalty. At times this could spill over into outright sycophancy. After the trauma of the abdication of Edward VIII, the royal family had steadily gained in popularity. There was a genuine affection for the shy, stammering king. His two attractive daughters brought more than a touch of much-needed glamour. A royal family they certainly were, but they were one that was embraced by the public and were thought to represent the values of the country overall.

On New Year's Eve in 1951, a frail-looking king stood on the tarmac at London airport waving goodbye to his eldest daughter. Princess Elizabeth and her husband were bound for a state visit to East Africa. Since the king's operation for lung cancer four months previously, the couple had taken over a number of official overseas visits. Although it was known that the king was seriously ill, news of his death at Sandringham on 6 February came as a surprise. The previous day he had been out shooting on the estate and had planned more sport for the following day. He was found dead in the morning, having suffered a severe coronary thrombosis. He was only fifty-six and he had ruled for sixteen years.

There was a general outpouring of public grief, but this was far more measured than that which was witnessed generations later with the death of Princess Diana. The difference illustrates how much the public mood has changed. Sixty years ago the British stiff upper lip still held sway. Only foreigners wailed and blubbed in adversity. Public exhibition of emotions was generally looked upon with suspicion across the social divide. Victory, defeat, joy and despair were all expected to be treated with restraint.

A saddened Elizabeth and her husband flew home from Kenya. On 11 February the king's coffin was transported from Sandringham to lie in state in Westminster Hall. The mood in London was sombre as over 300,000 people paid their respects by filing past the coffin. The king's early death was attributed to the stress he had suffered, particularly during the war. It was also noted that he had been a heavy smoker, but the discovery of the full consequences of smoking was still in its infancy. It was two days after Elizabeth's father's death that the accession proclamation was read out to the public by the Garter King of Arms at St James's Palace. This was repeated in Trafalgar Square, in Fleet Street and at the Royal Exchange.

From around the world foreign royalty and politicians gathered for the funeral. Into this rarefied gathering was pitched a wild card in the figure of the Duke of Windsor. The former king had arrived on the *Queen Mary* two days before the funeral. He was not accompanied by his wife, who had not been invited. There were old scores to settle and a degree of mutual animosity between the two royal families. Edward had only learnt of his brother's death from journalists while wintering in New York. His mood darkened further when he was told that his £10,000 a year allowance that had been granted by his brother was going to be withdrawn.

Early on the day of the funeral, large crowds were already gathering. The weather matched the general mood, being overcast, damp and misty. Big Ben chimed a mournful fifty-six times as the mile-long cortege set off from Westminster Hall. Schoolchildren were given the day off. I watched the slow journey on a television that my parents had only bought a few weeks before. The coffin on the gun carriage was draped in the royal standard. Also on the coffin were the Imperial State Crown, the orb and the sceptre, together with insignia of the Order of the Garter. There was just a single white wreath from the king's wife, now the queen mother. The first carriage contained the new queen, the queen mother, Princess Margaret and the princess royal, all dressed in black, their faces covered by veils. They were followed on foot by the dress-uniformed dukes of Edinburgh, Gloucester and Windsor, and the young Duke of Kent in morning dress. The route along the Mall passed Marlborough House, where the late king's mother, Queen Mary, looked on. Despite her being 'as tough as nails', according to the Duke of Windsor, there must always be a particular sadness at seeing your child die before you. The cortege made its slow journey past St James's Palace to Piccadilly and on to Hyde Park and Marble Arch. It then left these famous landmarks for the nondescript surroundings of Edgware Road and Sussex Gardens before arriving at Paddington station. Pomp and colour were provided by the Household Cavalry and the band of Scots Guards. As always on state occasions, the staging of the event was faultless. The coffin was taken by train to Windsor, where the king was buried in St George's chapel. As prime minister, Churchill said in his eulogy, 'for the fifteen years George VI was King, never at any moment in all the perplexities at home and abroad, in public or private, did he fail in his duties. Well does he deserve the farewell salute of his governments and peoples ...'

A period of court mourning was announced to run until the end of May, so the excitement at the prospect of a new Elizabethan era had to be put on hold for a while yet. Despite this, it was impossible to quell the anticipation entirely. There was a groundswell desire for a great British revival. With a fresh government and a new, young monarch, surely there was room for optimism. New stamps were issued in 1953 featuring a stunning profile of the new, young queen, created by sculptor Mary Gillick. Already an established artist in her seventies, her design was selected from a field of seventeen. It showed the queen wearing a wreath rather than a crown. It captured perfectly the longing for a fresh and better future. The image was also used both for British coinage and across many countries of the Commonwealth.

Newspaper editors were not slow in realising that a royal story could add thousands to their circulations. It was strange that a country which had started on the journey toward equality should embrace the pinnacle of privilege so completely. It appeared that almost all were royalists now. Who could ask for a better cast to feature at the beginning of a long-running saga? There was a beautiful young queen married to a ridiculously good-looking prince. General casting at MGM or Warner Brothers would have struggled to find more glamorous stars. A strong family image was endorsed by the couple's young children, particularly the blonde, photogenic Princess Anne. Add to that the sultry film-star looks of the queen's younger sister, Princess Margaret, and the inches of newspaper column that could be filled seemed endless. Over the years, Margaret created numerous headlines, most of which were confined to continental papers as Buckingham Palace advisers filtered what they deemed suitable for British consumption. So a perfect royal family was projected and celebrated. It was only the queen's voice that grated. Surely nobody, no matter how posh, spoke like that. She had not just swallowed a plum, rather a whole bowlful!

With excitement about the forthcoming coronation mounting, the souvenir industry geared itself up to meet the expected demand. An official souvenir committee was set up in an attempt to regulate the type and quality of products on offer. Pennants for cyclists and a range of pottery from Stoke-on-Trent, along with other tasteful memorabilia, passed muster, but the committee drew the line at panties embroidered with a crown. Meanwhile, hours of discussion and argument took place at County Hall while the London County Council deliberated on what free gift should be given to the schoolchildren under their jurisdiction. The merits of a pottery beaker or a plastic pencil were earnestly and endlessly debated. Work was also underway at the coronation HQ who had set up in Berkeley Square, as every detail for the great day was pored over.

Despite a population desperate to throw off the shackles of austerity and hoping to enter a new golden age, fate had decreed that more setbacks had yet to be endured. The summer of 1952 heralded a series of disasters, some manmade and others through the force of nature. On 15 and 16 August the south of England was deluged by a tropical-type storm. London was largely spared, but along the coast of Devon floods left a death toll of thirty-four. Within weeks a disastrous crash at the prestigious Farnborough Air Show resulted in thirty-one of the crowd being killed. It was as if the country was being blighted by continual bad news. While compulsory identity cards had been abolished earlier in the year, it was one step forward then another back as a one-shilling charge was introduced for prescription drugs. The autumn weather reflected the mood. Fog clung to London most mornings, like an unwelcome colleague at an office party. It dirtied the buildings and soiled clothes. It was depressing. It was also dangerous.

On 8 October 1952 disaster struck in London. Harrow & Wealdstone station witnessed the worst rail crash ever experienced in England, which claimed 112 lives. Only a dreadful crash at Gretna Green in Scotland back in 1915 recorded more fatalities. Doubtless, the patchy fog once again hanging over London had contributed in part to the horrific accident. More puzzling was why the driver and fireman of the Perth to London express had ignored two warning signals. It was at 8.20 a.m. that the locomotive had ploughed into the back of a stationary commuter train travelling from Tring to Euston. Due to the foggy conditions the commuter train was running seven minutes late, while the Perth express was over an hour behind schedule and travelling at about sixty miles per hour in an effort to catch up. Almost immediately, another express travelling at the same speed in the opposite direction smashed into the existing carnage. This train was heading northwards to Liverpool and Manchester and carried roughly 200 passengers. Only seven people were killed on this train, with twenty-three perishing on the Perth express. Over sixty people died on the commuter train, while people standing on the platform were killed by debris and, horrifically, by passengers being hurled from the trains. Others crossing a bridge linking the platforms were killed as carriages were concertinaed skywards. Nearby residents quickly appeared on the scene to help, as did a passing detachment of US airmen. Heavy-lifting gear was brought in, but it was hours before the last survivors were rescued. The horror of the crash led to British Rail accelerating the introduction of automatic danger signals.

Surely it would now be possible to put these traumas aside and look forward to a brighter new year? No. Unfortunately, another killer was waiting to strike. A silent enemy. One who was difficult to avoid and who chose its victims from among the very young, the old and those suffering from bronchial weaknesses. It was an insidious enemy, creeping under doors and through cracks in window frames. Since the Industrial Revolution, London in winter had been characterised as a city shrouded in fog. Writers and artists have faithfully recorded 'pea-soupers' and 'London particulars'. It had long been a city of belching chimneys and the acrid smell of coal in the air. The blackened coalman humping a hundredweight sack on his shoulder was a regular sight in London streets, his wagon pulled by a giant carthorse that dwarfed the sturdy little horses assigned to milkmen.

Nobody took undue notice when a fog started to form on Thursday 4 October. By the following morning it became obvious that here was a super fog. An impenetrable fog. The weather had been unusually cold, which led to huge numbers of coal fires being lit. There was no wind to help shift the smoke and a static anti-cyclone caused the cold, sulphurous air to stay trapped under a layer of warm air. The fog merged with clouds of chimney smoke and exhaust fumes to cloak the world's greatest city in an all-enveloping, dirty and smelly embrace. By Friday London had ground to a virtual halt. Cars were left unattended as their drivers lurched away. Buses were stranded and only the tubes continued to give a near normal service. Huge numbers of commuters were unable to get to work and shops closed. Visibility was reduced to just a few feet. I remember getting hopelessly lost just a few feet from my parents' house. The effect was most disconcerting, not even being able to see your own raised hand in front of your face. Smog masks flew off the shelves of those chemists that remained open. The foul air still managed to seep through the protective gauze. It attacked your throat and your eyes smarted painfully. A school friend, whose family ran one of London's best-known undertakers, would boast later that he had to step over coffins that lined the staircase to his bedroom as the funeral parlour was full. Initial predictions of 1,000 deaths a day attributed to the smog were later found to be a massive understatement.

William and Ann Marlow were unlucky enough to choose the Saturday of the smog for their wedding day. The bridesmaids' car was lost on the way to the church and the bride's white dress quickly acquired a sooty black sheen.

By Monday, if anything, the smog had tightened its sulphurous grip. Theatres closed as audiences struggled to see the stage. There was no escape. The smog pursued you even in your home and up to bed at night. Blowing your nose was like a mini chimney fall. You didn't only feel grubby – you *were* grubby. Despite coughing, desperate spluttering and wheezing, most Londoners survived. However, 12,000 people died as a direct result of the smog and a further 100,000 were taken ill. The attrition rate over only four days was frightening. If these fatalities had been caused by a series of air crashes or a terrorist bomb, it would rate as one of the worst disasters ever to befall the capital, and yet seemingly Londoners hardly paused to give the problem much thought. Obviously the wartime mantra of 'keep calm and carry on' still applied. It did, however, have a profound effect on the attitude of the authorities. Price concessions were given on smokeless fuels, also the use of gas fires helped until central heating became the norm. Progress, as ever, was slow and it was 1956 before the new clean air policies finally came into full effect.

Despite constant setbacks, London was slowly clawing its way back to some sort of pre-war normality. It was proving more difficult than many had thought. Here was a population which, for those aged forty or over, had endured two world wars. Almost every family would have been affected by loss or injury to loved ones or suffered damage to their homes. Every teenager could only remember their city as one of gaping cellars, jagged walls and ghostly ruins. Major streets, like Cheapside, savaged by blast and fire, were now barely recognisable. Londoners, by nature and reputation, tend to be cocky and confident, but it was taking some time for them and their city to reassert themselves.

The country was still trying to play a major role on the world stage. The announcement that we had a nuclear capability helped further the illusion, but most would have preferred to see more resources devoted to a better standard of living at home. There continued to be tiny indications of change, such as with the abolition of the utility furniture scheme. There was a longing to break out of the stranglehold of uniformity and to be able to express personal taste. That required money and a choice of goods for sale, but both were still in short supply. In 1951 the average wage for a man was £13 per week. Women could only expect £8 per week on average, an amazing disparity which many employers were happy to exploit. Life expectancy was much lower than today. A state pension of £1.50 per week was supplemented by an additional £1 for a married couple, but the cost to the Exchequer was far less proportionally than it is today, as there were only half the number of pensioners receiving benefit. Back in 1952 only a third of the population were homeowners. This was more to do with tradition and availability rather than cost. With an average house price of less than £2,000 equating to roughly £48,000 at today's prices, a major shift in home ownership was inevitable.

Television was also about to make a huge leap forward. It would be sparked by the coronation, but already detector vans were scouring the streets seeking out those among the few hundred thousand who had a set but who hadn't paid their licence fee. The programmes were mostly pretty dire, and subject to constant technical problems, during which time a film of *The Potter's Wheel* was often shown. A speeded-up London to Brighton train journey in four minutes was also a popular interlude that kept viewers amused when programmes were frequently not available for screening on time. December saw the first showing of the children's series *The Flower Pot Men*. Today, this and other programmes seem ludicrously amateurish. The amazing potential that the embryonic medium was going to have over the coming years was slowly taking shape.

The year was brought to a close by the first Christmas speech given by the queen to the Commonwealth. Christmas celebrations at home were curtailed while a whole nation listened intently to her bland message. It was to this young woman that the country would turn to the following year. They would marvel at the pageantry of her coronation and use it as a launching pad for their own increasing aspirations.

4

A New Elizabethan Era

C-Day had finally arrived. The coronation was to be a day of ritual, religion, pomp and glamour. It was to be a production of Hollywood proportions, involving a cast of thousands, all planned down to the minutest detail. In March, with delicious timing, old Queen Mary left the stage. She had let it be known that her death should not lead to a postponement of the coronation. It was, however, symbolic, for she had represented the buttoned-up past. The new royal cast was infinitely more exciting. Coronation fever gripped London in a fond embrace. The West End was exposed to miles of scaffolding and the noise of carpenters' saws as temporary viewing stands appeared along the route. People queued for weeks before the great day to be taken round the route by bus. In Kensington Gardens, a tented village sprung up to accommodate close on 20,000 troops who were to add to the grandeur of the day.

The crowds lining Trafalgar Square and extending down Whitehall were perhaps a dozen people deep by daybreak. Most had camped overnight, defying the persistent drizzle. With my sister I had taken the first tube of the morning up to the West End. We enjoyed a privileged vantage point from her office, overlooking Nelson's Column and the Whitehall Theatre. Below, bedraggled spectators waved sodden Union

Jacks, while water dripped from the hats of the troops lining the route.

The crowd that stretched before us was very different from those that gather today for grand state occasions. Although many had travelled from the provinces and there was a smattering of foreign tourists, overwhelmingly this was a crowd made up of Londoners. They were outwardly loud and humorous but, depending on age, had been brought up by Victorian or Edwardian parents, or at least imbued with the values of those times. Their lifestyle and aspirations were very different from those enjoyed today. Things that we take for granted would have been a revelation to them. Cars were only owned by a tiny minority and central heating was almost unheard of. Many houses still lacked a bathroom and a visit to the lavatory involved a trip to the end of the garden. Forget mobile phones – most people didn't even have a land-line. Making a call usually required a walk to the nearest kiosk. Refrigeration during a hot summer was confined to a bucket of cold water to help keep milk from curdling. There were no rolling news programmes, but newspaper sales were at levels that modern-day editors could only dream of. There were no celebrities, only 'stars', many of whom continued to use public transport without being pestered by fans. Life was more contained and restrained. In 1953 the term 'teenager' still had little significance, although it had first been coined in the early 1940s. The youth revolution had a short while to wait yet. Youngsters from across the social scale were expected to ape their parents in appearance. This generation of youngsters was brought up to work hard, observe convention and have relatively modest aspirations. There was not the modern obsession with money. There was no rich list, nor were there constant references to earnings or the value of property. Discussion of money or wealth was considered intrusive and not a little vulgar. Of course, there was a degree of envy and 'keeping up with the Jones's', but discussions regarding personal finance tended to be confined to family and close friends.

Sex for many women was something to be endured rather than enjoyed. Today's laddish behaviour would have caused outrage and ostracism. For most a women's place was confined to being a homemaker – her days were dedicated to cooking, cleaning and bringing up the children. There was little sign of sex equality, 'women's lib' or political correctness. Domestic violence directed at wives and children was commonplace. This tended to be centred in areas of deprivation. Appalling living conditions were still common in vast swathes of London. Abuse was not wholly confined to working-class areas, however, and young children were often subjected to corporal punishment, both at school and home. The rhyme 'Glory, glory, hallelujah, teacher whacked me with a ruler' was at the soft end of the punishments to be endured by the young; a swishy cane was the most feared and was administered to a hand or the backside. Against this background it is not surprising that relationships floundered, but rarely ended in divorce. Sexual repression and misunderstanding led to London having the greatest number of prostitutes in Europe.

Few girls leaving school went on to university and the range of jobs open to them was limited. Depending on their qualifications, they tended to opt for factory or office work. Typing, clerical and secretarial work were popular, as was the retail sector. Nursing was still looked upon as a vocation and their ranks were largely filled by young women from solid middle-class backgrounds.

The influence of the BBC was enormous. Its output tended to underscore a rather prudish outlook on life. They controlled what they felt was suitable for public consumption. The nation's straight-laced 'aunty' knew best. There was no mention of sex or swearing and even innuendo was frowned upon. The BBC projected a sanitised world represented by people with beautifully modulated voices. Regional or Cockney accents were assigned to working-class characters in drama, where inevitably the villains were foreign. Jokes in pubs and music halls were directed towards mothers-in-law, foreigners and effeminate men. To be seen as different in early 1950s London was a sin. To some, Britain was constrained and repressed, to others, well ordered and civilised. People were easily shocked and quick to condemn. Outward displays of anger or emotion were frowned upon. Life was not as frantic. There was less pressure and lower expectations of financial success. There was not the modern obsession with looks and self-image. Simple enjoyments assumed a greater importance in life. A visit to the cinema or even the prospect of getting a new book from the lending library created excitement and expectation. Was this crowd we look down on from our perspective over sixty years on boring and lacking in ambition? Possibly, but in spite of all the downsides of life in the fifties, the impression was one of relative contentment. What you haven't had, you don't miss. Compared with what had gone before, the only way was up and the coronation shone a light towards a brighter future.

An estimated three million people had gathered along the route, while a further twenty million crowded around their newly acquired television sets. Most screens were fourteen inches or smaller, so friends and neighbours sought prime positions across the nation's living rooms. There was unseemly jostling in some of London's swankiest hotels as the rich and famous elbowed their way closer to the tiny screens set up in ballrooms and restaurants. The writer

James Lees-Milne donned his best blue suit and made his way by public transport to Brooks. He complained that the windows at his club had all been left open and it was bitterly cold. No doubt the waiting crowds agreed as the thermometer plummeted and the rain continued unabated. Sodden newspapers proclaimed the conquest of Everest by Edmund Hillary and Sherpa Tenzing. What a shame they weren't British, but a New Zealander would have to do! The nation's collective chest swelled a little further.

Westminster Abbey opened its doors at 6.00 a.m., as it was going to be a major undertaking to shoehorn some 8,000 guests into the pews. There had been severe doubts expressed by powerful establishment figures as to the wisdom of allowing television cameras to witness the historic event. With these overcome, the BBC and the world's press waited to swing into action. Introduced by Jean Metcalfe, a team of reporters, including Wynford Vaughan Thomas, Richard Dimbleby and cricket reporter Rex Alston, described the unfolding scene of pomp and pageantry. The early part of the procession to the abbey was low key. The Lord Mayor of London set off from the Mansion House, while the Speaker started from the House of Commons. Dukes and duchesses, along with minor royals and sundry VIPs, were despatched by car. Colonial rulers were accompanied by an escort of military police. Things were hotting up. The crowd was now in full voice as the newly knighted Winston Churchill led a procession of Commonwealth prime ministers. At last a splash of colour as each leader had mounted escorts drawn from their respective armed forces. Union Flags now formed a sea of movement as carriages bearing the dukes and duchesses of Kent and Gloucester swept by escorted by the household cavalry on their gleaming black mounts. We were nearing the top of the bill. The queen mother rode in the Irish State Coach sporting a crown bearing the fabulous Koh-i-Noor diamond. A jewel first mentioned in ancient Mesopotamia around 5,000 years ago, it had endured a tortuous journey to eventually find its home in the House of Windsor. Its ownership is still disputed today, and it was thought to bring ill fortune to its owner. On coronation day no one seemed to care. Finally, we witnessed the gleaming gold and glass State Coach carrying the queen and the Duke of Edinburgh. How we all cheered. I felt quite overcome with emotion, and yet I couldn't understand why.

At the abbey, some hungry peers had already eaten sandwiches, which they had craftily hidden away under their coronets. Nobles slightly down on their luck had been allowed to trim their robes with rabbit skin rather than the traditional ermine. One publicity-seeking blue-blood, the Marquis of Bath, had earlier defied the Earl Marshall by arriving at the abbey in his own coach-and-six. These minor distractions were now cast aside as the young queen alighted at the abbey. For those watching on television the darkness of the day did nothing to dim the startling clarity of the pictures. A fairytale feeling was evoked as the queen's ladies-in-waiting struggled to lift the heavy woven velvet cloak to enable her to walk freely. The crowds now had a long wait for the service to be completed. It was magnificent, a combination of tradition, pomp, searing music and a hint of showbiz set against the glorious towering backdrop of the abbey. Here was a stage production in which Britain excelled. The nation looked on, totally enthralled. The choirs of St Paul's, the Chapel Royal and St George's Windsor joined an orchestra conducted by Sir Adrian Bolt in performances of the work of largely British composers, both old and contemporary. Britten and Vaughan-Williams stood alongside Parry and Elgar, while Handel gatecrashed the party with Zadok the Priest. During the service the Archbishop of Canterbury walked to the four sides of the abbey to ask the congregation if they accepted their queen. In response to their affirmation the queen gave a slow half-curtsey. This is the only time that the monarch has been known to undertake a curtsey herself. Placing a heavy crown on a young head while being watched by millions was never going to be easy. For a moment it seemed to tilt forward slightly. At that moment the gathered princes and peers donned their coronets and a twenty-one-gun salute boomed out from the Tower of London.

It was time for the nation to put the kettle on. The religious service still had some way to run, but for most people it was the joyful procession back to Buckingham Palace that was most eagerly anticipated. Wearing the Imperial State Crown and holding the orb and sceptre, the new monarch appeared from the nave out of the Great West Door. It was time to marvel at the spectacle of thousands of troops and military bands, which even the dismal weather could not dim. There were colour and pageantry, skirling bagpipes, beating drums and an outpouring of emotion experienced by those present. The most popular guest was Queen Salote of Tonga. Despite the rain she insisted on her carriage being open. The plume of feathers she wore in her hair were reduced to a single stem, but she waved, her smile as large as her huge personality, and the British public loved her. Beside her sat the tiny, rather bemused figure of her husband. In typically acerbic form, Noel Coward, when asked who it was sitting next to her, replied, 'her dinner'.

As we gazed down on Trafalgar Square, the procession appeared never-ending; as the noise of one band faded away so the strains of another was heard approaching. Successions of troops were loudly applauded. Most popular were the Gurkhas and the fierce-looking Indians and Pakistanis. For all the might and colour of the forces drawn from around the world, it was the queen that most wanted to see in the magical gold coach designed for George III's coronation, drawn by six bays with grooms in eighteenth-century finery. It disappeared from our view down the Mall, which was decorated with huge glittering crowns suspended in the sky beneath golden arches. Later a massive crowd gathered outside the palace and, as the queen appeared on the balcony, the people were deafened by the roar of the RAF fly-past.

It was party time in London. Thousands of street parties were held despite the weather. Safely sheltered from the continuing drizzle, the rich and famous enjoyed special celebration dinners in the most prestigious hotels and fashionable restaurants. Moët et Chandon released a 1953 vintage as their Coronation Cuvée while Tío Pepe introduced their exclusive Coronation Dry Sherry. It seemed everyone was determined to have a good time. The coronation had produced a sense of overall celebration and pride. Later, crowds were able to stand and cheer again as the queen attended a service of thanksgiving at St Paul's Cathedral. There was a rare mood of camaraderie and nationhood similar to that evoked by the celebrations to mark the end of the war. The first performance of Benjamin Britten's 'Gloriana' was performed at the Royal Opera House. Commissioned to celebrate the coronation of a new monarch, it explored the relationship between the first Queen Elizabeth and the Earl of Essex. Unfortunately, it was not rated a hit and received very mixed reviews.

Much more to the general public's taste was the running of the Derby. By 6 June the Downs at Epsom were bathed in sunshine and huge crowds had gathered to enjoy the fair, the side-shows and the boxing booths, as well as the racing. As is so often the case in life, if the true story of that day had been written as a novel, few would have believed it. Gordon Richards had been champion jockey twenty-five times, but in twenty-eight attempts he had never won the Derby. It had just been announced that he was to be knighted in the Coronation Honours List. He was a jockey who seemingly gave his all, no matter what horse he was riding and, as such, was much admired by the public, who were willing him to win in this, his last Derby ride. A downside to Richard's illustrious career was perceived by some as an inability to pick the right horse to ride in big races. Despite this he had won thirteen Classics over the years, but never the epic Derby. His luck changed months before the race was run. He was riding out on Newmarket Heath on a much favoured horse when he was overtaken and left trailing by a huge bay with a white blaze. The horse, Pinza, had been bought at Tattersalls by Sir Victor Sassoon for 1,500 guineas. It was sent to the trainer Norman Bertie, who had previously been head lad to the legendary Fred Darling. As a two-year-old the colt had won a couple of races but had also been well beaten on other appearances. An injury early in the year prevented his entering into full training until the spring. When he eventually appeared in the Newmarket Stakes, he won with ease and was made one of the favourites for the Blue Riband Classic.

The 1953 Derby was thought to contain a vintage crop of horses. There was the queen's Aureole, the joint favourite Premonition and a crop of highly fancied French horses. The experts doubted Pinza's ability to handle the undulations of the Epsom course. Being so large he sometimes gave the impression of being uncoordinated. At the crack of dawn on race day Richards sneaked his mount on to the course and rode him flat out round Tattenham Corner. He returned to the stables a happy man. He was convinced that here, at last, was the mount to bring him glory at the very end of his career. Twenty-seven horses lined up at the start. Richards always had Pinza well placed, and as they descended round Tattenham Corner into the straight he shook the reins and gave the horse its head. With its huge stride it quickly opened up a sizeable gap, with the queen's horse giving chase. Many had hoped that she would triumph in her coronation year, but Pinza's win by four lengths was one of the most popular in the race's history. The sense of drama and poignancy continued when Fred Darling, Pinza's breeder, died a few days after the race.

It was perhaps inevitable that a new cast of young royals would launch a soap-box drama that continues unabated today. A simple gesture during the coronation was picked up by a journalist and sent the rumour factory into overdrive. The glamorous Princess Margaret was seen flicking a speck of fluff from the jacket of Group Captain Peter Townsend. A simple gesture, but one that suggested a familiarity not normally associated with members of the royal family. It launched an ongoing discussion about the changing face of the monarchy. How much could it change? How much should it change? As news of the affair became more widespread, the old establishment set itself implacably against the romance. A starry-eyed public longed for a royal wedding based on love rather than rank. Newspaper sales soared. Was this to be another state snub to a commoner? Would Margaret, like her uncle Edward, renounce her title and line of succession for this good-looking, distinguished man some sixteen years her senior, but, significantly, also a divorcee?

Who really knows when it all started? Peter Townsend arrived in the royal household as equerry to the king. He accompanied the royal family on a trip to South Africa in 1947. By the time Margaret's father died it appears they

were already in love. Margaret had been extremely close
to the king and she was devastated. Her highly emotional
state and the fact Townsend was appointed as equerry to
the queen mother ensured they were constantly in each
other's company. He helped her through her grief and the
die was cast. He later described her as 'a girl of unusual
intense beauty, confined as it was in her short, slender figure
and centred on her large eyes, generous sensitive lips and
a complexion of a peach.' She was at times a mimic and
outgoing, while at others remote, cutting and imperious.
This was a heady brew and gave her a power she used to
intoxicate many men for years to come. With newspaper
articles becoming ever more numerous and pointed, the
couple were forced to break cover. The queen had always
been close to her younger sister and had sympathy for her
situation. The queen mother did not. She was totally opposed
to the relationship. The old school courtiers closed ranks.
When Townsend informed the queen that he wanted to
marry the princess, courtier 'Tommy' Lascelles exploded 'You
must be either mad or bad!' Prime Minister Churchill didn't
agree, stating, 'What a delightful match. A lovely, young royal
lady, married to a gallant, young airman safe from the perils
and horrors of war.' Churchill's power and influence were in
decline and Townsend was duly conveniently despatched to
Brussels as air attaché. It was hoped that an enforced parting
would cool the relationship. Under the Royal Marriages
Act, permission to marry had to be granted by the queen.
By now Churchill had retired and the Cabinet under Prime
Minister Eden insisted they were prepared to present a Bill
of Renunciation to Parliament. This would, in effect, strip
Margaret of all her rights of succession, title and Civil List
entitlement. The couple were reunited again in the autumn
of 1955. Townsend insisted their feelings for each other

had not changed, but that he felt it unfair for Margaret to make such profound sacrifices. On 27 October she informed the Archbishop of Canterbury of her decision. Four days later she issued a statement: 'I would like it to be known that I have decided not to marry Group Captain Peter Townsend, mindful that Christian marriage is indissoluble and conscious of my duty to the Commonwealth. I have resolved to put these considerations before others.'

So the old guard had won. Service and responsibility before love. Or was it? A subsequent letter sent in 1955 to Prime Minister Anthony Eden, handwritten from Balmoral by Margaret, suggests she was undecided about the prospect of the marriage. The *Guardian* newspaper was scathing with criticism of the pressure brought to bear by the government on the young princess. The public was generally sympathetic towards her, in spite of having been denied a fairytale wedding. The whole drama symbolised an ongoing struggle between traditionalists and those who wanted change, in the form of a less stuffy monarchy and a Britain willing to shed some of the social shackles of the past.

5

The Social Pecking Order

'We have always been an aristocratic country and I hope
we shall always remain so, as they are the mainstay of this
country.'

King Edward VII

The English have long been obsessed by class. Its influence
still permeated each rung of society in the 1950s. Trying
to establish where you belonged in the complex scheme
of things niggled and irritated like a persistent gnat bite.
Foreigners, particularly Americans, were in turn confused,
amused and appalled by its consequences. GIs serving in
Britain during the war were staggered by the snobbery and
obvious distinction between the officer class and his men.
The pinnacle of this class consciousness was found in the
exclusive cavalry regiments. An American officer described
them as being 'the most mentally inert, unprofessional and
reactionary group in the British army'. He went on to suggest
that few of the serving American officers would have been
allowed to rise above the rank of NCO.

In 1956 the publication of *Noblesse Oblige* caused a
sensation. Edited by Nancy Mitford, it was, in effect, a guide
to the correct speech patterns of the upper classes. The 'U'
people were apparently easily distinguishable from the rest

of us, the 'non-Us'. Bizarrely, it was written as a linguistic exercise by Professor Alan Ross for Finnish students. It started with the assertion that there were just three classes: upper, middle and lower. How wrong could he be? For within those headings there existed countless sub-divisions. On stronger ground, Ross suggested that being upper class didn't necessarily indicate a person was 'better educated, cleverer or richer'. In essence, it was all down to breeding, in much the same way as a racehorse is judged, but, as we know, they throw up some very unexpected results. Ross was primarily concerned with language, both written and spoken. By implication he suggested that here was a social minefield that had to be negotiated. There were a thousand ways for the socially aspiring to be exposed. Not many of us have to address a letter or speak to a duke or even a knight of the realm, but in the case that you do be sure your pronunciation and vocabulary will not find you out. Regional accents, no matter how attractive, were considered dreadfully 'non-U'. On the other hand, to be 'refained' was worse still. Making 'ride' sound like 'raid' would have the well-bred making a dash for the exit. It was all so confusing because the toffs took the 'l' out of 'golf' to arrive at 'goff'. So what was the difference? But there was one, and unless you had been brought up in upper-class society you struggled. It was like learning a foreign language and the English are notoriously bad linguists. Asking for the toilet rather than the lavatory created a look on the faces of those who knew better, as if there was a blockage in the drains. If at a dinner party you asked your host to 'pass the cruet' it would likely have him choking on his claret. Relating to food, 'U' speakers eat lunch in the middle of the day and dinner in the evening. A lighter, less formal evening meal was a supper. 'Non-U' speakers tended to have their dinner in the middle of the day and then an evening meal. Belching is something we all experience on occasions. 'U' speakers would say 'I'm frightfully sorry', but a muttered 'manners' was an ultimate 'Non-U' faux pas.

Despite the royal family being at the top of the social pyramid, they were not immune from criticism. It was Nancy Mitford, no less, who nicknamed Princess Margaret 'Pigmy-peep-a-toes' because of her tendency to wear open-toed shoes that Nancy considered vulgar. Margaret, like so many, was often unsure of her place in society. At times she wanted to experience 'real life' through incognito visits to East End pubs, then at a moment's notice switched to her most regal and dismissive manner. James Lees-Milne was none too impressed when he was a member of a small party, including Margaret, attending a private dinner at Rules in Maiden Lane. He records 'she is physically attractive in a bun-like way, with trussed up bosom and hair like two cottage loaves, one balancing the other'. He reckoned she was '... cross, exacting, too sophisticated and sharp'.

For generations the upper classes had come up from the country and gathered in London's swankiest hotels to celebrate great state and royal occasions. During the war these bastions had been breached by all kinds of undesirables. In all but the sniffiest, the mantra was 'if you can pay you can stay'. This was illustrated by celebration events held for the new queen's coronation. All were well attended, but the place to be that night was the Savoy. Record numbers of visitors flooded into London for the great day. In the morning the hotel was awash with ermine and the jingle of spurs. There were Maharajas with jewelled turbans, princes with collars decorated with diamante and Commonwealth prime ministers in court dress. For once American film stars not invited to the abbey were just 'bit players' staring on at this moving wave of colour. In the evening the hotel staged 'the ball of the century', and all for just twelve guineas. The whole hotel was given over to the event. The 1,400 guests arrived through singing crowds that thronged the Strand. The official decorations had been designed by Cecil Beaton, with the restaurant being transformed into an Elizabethan pavilion. Hundreds of champagne corks were popped as pipers from all the regiments of which the queen was colonel-in-chief skirled away. Four dance bands provided music as the guests began to let their hair down. The upper classes, who generally despised 'new money', seemingly had no such qualms about wealthy Americans. The same blue-bloods, who were often anti-Semitic and viewed many inhabitants of the colonies as mere 'natives', mixed happily, for one night at least, with Indians, Pakistanis, black Americans and even Japanese people. Well, they were all relatively civilised. Winton Churchill arrived after the meal to great applause on the arm of the Pasha of Marrakech. As midnight sounded guests were showered with Elizabethan favours fluttering down from the ceiling. Then the princes, diplomats and generals grabbed the nearest ladies, who were wearing gowns created by Dior, Balmain or Hartnel, and formed a conga line. There they all were, acting no differently to the countless thousands gathered in pubs across London.

Of course they were different, these gilded few, separated from the masses by position, fame and wealth, either earned or inherited. Despite sky-high taxes, the upper classes were generally enjoying a surprisingly prosperous decade. They may have appeared unworldly, but they were not stupid and they employed expert advisers. Henry de Vere Clifton kept permanent suites at both the Ritz and the Dorchester because, as he said, 'If I am passing down Park Lane and feel tired then I've got somewhere to go.' A true eccentric, he was once driven to Brighton, where his chauffeur was instructed to fill large bottles with water. Later that night at the Ritz, he was able to take his bath in sea water, apparently giving him much satisfaction. The Ritz was going through a period of rather faded glory. Maybe this is why it was reckoned to offer the best value among London's grandest hotels. At the end of the 1950s you could stay in one of their smallest rooms for 50s a night, while a top suite would cost £25. Its Edwardian Baroque had slid into seediness, and the appalling food discouraged many. The hotel's main attraction appeared to be that it drew a certain section of London society, most of whom knew each other. The Ritz had become a club for those who avoided the glitzier hotels. It was a place for 'old money' and acceptable talents like Graham Greene and Evelyn Waugh. Perhaps it was value for money that led Paul Getty to take a suite in the Ritz. Known for his meanness, he assigned his mistress an adjoining room without a bath and even queried her making local telephone calls on his account. In a famous shot set up by a photographer for *Time Life*, he was pictured on his knees picking up pennies thrown there by an accomplice of the magazine.

While the Ritz and Claridge's often attracted establishment figures, the Dorchester and Grosvenor House tended to spread their net rather wider. They also invested in modernisation. Grosvenor House was the first to install a radio rediffusion service, giving a choice of the three BBC programmes. For a small fee television was also available. Their Great Room could accommodate a thousand guests, and after the war the Queen Charlotte's Ball returned to the hotel. Established back in the eighteenth century by Queen Charlotte, consort of King George III, it was resurrected in 1925 by the formidable Lady Howard de Walden. The ritual involved lines of young ladies dressed in virginal white following each other down the grand sweep of the main staircase behind a huge cake lit by electric candles, which was held aloft for all to see. Then, in a tradition utterly incomprehensible to most, each girl curtsied to the cake. Described as a mixture of the Nuremberg Rallies and the Dance of the Fairies, it was a laughable exercise and open to ridicule in the changing social climate of the 1950s. Still they came, these coiffured dolls of the aristocracy, landed gentry and, increasingly, interlopers who would never have made the cut before the war – the pretty, prissy, gorgeous, gawky, frumpy, lumpy and some who looked decidedly grumpy.

Earlier, in March, these same young women had curtsied to the queen and Prince Philip at Buckingham Palace. This was prelude to a whirl of parties and balls, which was essentially a posh marriage market where it was hoped that the young would meet a suitable life partner. By the late fifties, the whole debutante thing had become something of an anachronism. In 1957 Lord Altrincham described the charade 'as an embarrassing ritual which should have been quietly discontinued in 1945'. The death knell had already sounded when Princess Margaret was quoted as saying, 'We had to put a stop to it. Every tart in London was getting in.' Tarts or not, it was certainly true that these debutantes were no longer drawn from the establishment. Entry was increasingly obtained by wealth rather than lineage.

While wealth was celebrated in America, the English struggled with its implications. It had to be handled with care. A Calvinistic streak demanded discretion. Here the 'old money' aristocrats were grudgingly admired. Despite their wealth, many of them lived quite frugally in their rotting piles, confining their enjoyment to country sports and when in London hunkering down in their prestigious clubs. The new moneymakers – the property tycoons and take-over kings – attracted little admiration except from their like-minded operators. Conspicuously lavish spending drew criticism and derision from across the social spectrum, and none were more criticised than Sir Bernard and Lady Docker. She was an ex-show girl whose previous marriages to the president of Fortnum & Mason, followed by the boss of Henekey's wine merchants, had given her a taste for the high life. Her third 'hubby' was not about to let her down. Already the owner of *Shemara*, his luxury yacht, Sir Bernard, as chairman of the Daimler company, was ready to indulge her. His cars were variously covered in thousands of gold stars or silver plated complete with zebra skin upholstery. The couple were rarely out of the headlines as they launched into an uninhibited orgy of spending. Envy and awe at their antics was mixed with derision and outright amusement. Their behaviour was just not British. Docker, who had been a director of the Midland Bank for twenty-five years, had become an embarrassment and was asked to resign. Three years later his outrageous expense claims led to his removal from the board of BSA. The couple kept on spending and making headlines, usually prompted by Lady Docker's outrageous behaviour, before drifting from the limelight as their wealth declined.

The Dockers highlighted the fact that money alone would do little to puncture the snobbishness of the British class system. It was felt that they behaved no better than a working-class couple coming up on the football pools. Although generally damned, it was middle England that suffered most angst about their place in society. The rules were endless, the pitfalls always waiting to engulf them. Social events were a minefield, particularly when meeting new people. A casual reception could end up like a job interview. After the initial pleasantries the questions began. 'Tell me, what do you do?' Having embellished the importance of your own job for the enquirer, the more detailed social probing got underway. For a man old enough to have served in the war, your rank, regiment or squadron was required. Still trying to place you socially, it was not unusual to be asked which school you had attended. This could be very tricky territory. A friend of mine, a struggling actor, had passed muster with his very attractive girlfriend. When invited back to meet her parents in their Knightsbridge apartment, he made the mistake of wearing a Tonbridge school tie he had purchased in Burlington Arcade. His accent was fine. He looked the part, but sod's law decreed that the girl's brother had been to Tonbridge. No amount of trying to deflect the queries about his time at the school would do. He couldn't remember the headmaster's name, or even which house he had been in. Cue his exit, red-faced and embarrassed, and the end to a glorious romance.

Prying eyes were constantly on the lookout for imposters. To be 'U', even in a middle-class sense, you had to speak properly, not tie a Windsor knot or wear a two-buttoned jacket. Brown or suede shoes worn with a blue suit was very nearly a hanging offence, while a cravat was required when wearing an open-necked shirt. A real giveaway was how you held your cutlery. Many a knowing glance was exchanged when a knife was wielded as if writing with a pen. Still, the gaffs were there to be made. A young man requesting a whisky with coca cola would never make the grade. Worse still, a young lady drinking gin and orange or, perish the thought, port and lemon, was hardly likely to be suitable wife material for the son of the house. The list of no-nos stretched on, seemingly forever. Girls with too much make-up and plastic handbags were hardly the thing. Young men with long hair were suspect, particularly if expressing outlandish political views. Worse still were young girls who were too intelligent. No one liked a know-it-all – they must learn to defer to their elders, no matter how bigoted.

In the 1950s the 'old school tie' connection continued to be very important. Many of the middle-class job opportunities came about through family or friendly connections. It remained very much about who, rather than what, you knew. Influential contacts were an important ingredient of the middle-class social network. Old school or university friends and ex-forces colleagues could be a useful bridge for your children's careers. Politics provided perhaps the best proof of these incestuous connections when in 1955, 260 public-school-educated Tory MPs were elected to parliament. This was a well-connected social mafia whose influences extended far beyond Westminster into the Civil Service, professions, business and the military.

Keeping up with the Joneses was now as important as attempting to be a 'U' person. The upwardly mobile middle classes started taking holidays abroad. A suntan represented a certain standing, particularly during winter months – it had doubtless been gained on a skiing trip or a holiday in the Caribbean. More important still was a car, surely the ultimate status symbol. What could be better than ostentatiously washing it on your drive while your neighbours quietly fumed behind their net curtains? This all sounds so petty, but it was a time when many were out to change their perceived social status. Despite their best efforts, many were fighting a losing battle. With increased mechanisation, new supervisory jobs were created and there was a merging of blue- and white-collared jobs. Traditionally, middle-class wives had not gone out to work, but this too was changing. A combination of wanting more money of their own and the need to escape the boredom of household drudgery led to a desire for more independence.

There were other important changes taking place. A new type of working class was being created. For centuries, the poor in London had been confined to ghastly living conditions and a low life expectancy. By 1954 a report noted that the height and weight of children across London was now uniform. The welfare state, with its free medical attention, school dinners and better hygiene, was having a dramatic effect. Not so welcome was the continuous break-up of traditional working-class communities. Bomb damage had devastated large parts of the East End. Factories, as well as homes, had been destroyed, leading to a further exodus. With full employment, the working man was no longer generally happy to take on tough and dirty jobs unless he was highly paid. Social nuance had spread to the working class; no one wanted to be called a labourer. There was still a solidarity about the London working class, particularly those belonging to a union. They were also bound by their distinctive rules, language and humour. Life for most was improving, with universal paid holidays being one of the most welcome changes. More than half the population was now going away for a holiday. While some of the middle class flew off to Spain, most working-class families headed for the seaside on a charabanc. For many of the elderly, this would have been the first holiday of their lives.

A good indication of the improvement in the working man's life was reflected in the decline of the pawnbroker during the 1950s. Less than half those operating before the war were still going. Now the working classes joined with their middle-class neighbours in taking out hire purchase agreements for televisions and the increasing range of household appliances available. Many working-class jobs were also becoming salaried. Collecting a wage packet each Friday was a tradition in decline. The class gap was closing, albeit slowly. New housing in London also had the effect of blurring the lines. The housing shortage remained acute, and seventy-five per cent of all new home building was being undertaken by local authorities. One in four people across the country lived in publicly owned flats or houses. To some, the very term 'council house' carried an odour of 'second rate' and willingness to live on charity. Nonetheless, modern homes with subsidised rents drew many who considered themselves middle class on to council estates. Some maintained their perceived standards by paying their rent by cheque rather than cash. By such small and seemingly futile gestures, the whole crazy, complex class divisions were perpetuated. A Gallup poll conducted in 1954 recorded that roughly half of British people considered themselves to be middle class. More accurately, they were really stating that they were not working class. Many realised that their lives and the opportunities on offer were so different from those of their parents and grandparents. They refused to be stereotyped. Discarding their cloth caps, they were refusing to be locked into a restrictive life where everyone was supposed to know their place and stay there. In 1950s London it was becoming impossible to describe the social present in terms of the social past.

During the 1950s, all the classes (even if some didn't admit it) joined forces in filling in their football pools coupons. No matter how wealthy you were, £50,000 would always come in very handy. Here was a chance to dream. To win a life-changing amount of money. It was reckoned that sixty per cent of postal orders sold were sent to the pools companies. By 1955 the annual stake was estimated at a staggering £74 million. Each Saturday afternoon at five o'clock millions tuned into *Sports Report* to see if they had managed to predict eight score draws correctly.

A far more important issue had Londoners of all classes in general agreement. While they were happy to welcome au pairs and 'home helps' from across Europe, this did not extend to an influx of West Indians. Several thousand from the Caribbean had served with the RAF and at munition plants during the war. At the time, unlike the Americans, the British appeared to have little racial prejudice. West Indians sent back favourable accounts of life in the 'mother country'. There were jobs available and free education for the kids. Soon Londoners became aware of athletically built Jamaicans strolling along in groups. They wore bright blue suits with loud ties and trilby hats perched on the back of their heads. Since the first arrivals aboard the *Windrush* in 1948, their numbers had grown so that by 1956 they had reached a population of 26,000. This accelerated to around 150,000 by the end of the decade. These early arrivals had a dreadful time. A damp, cold, grey climate was matched by suspicious, unwelcoming Londoners. Matters were inflamed by the severe housing shortage. The new arrivals tended to fall into gaps left by the welfare state. They were confined to shockingly overcrowded accommodation and rack rents. Notices stating 'No blacks, Irish or dogs' were placed in windows of rooms to rent. As the black migrant moved in, so their white neighbours moved out. There were accusations of dirt, squalor and the sound of thumping music. There were tales of drug-taking and, worse, alarming details of their men taking up with white women. There were rumours that they were sexual predators who quickly had their girlfriends working the streets. Much of this was sensationalised. They were just young men and there were relatively few West Indian women who had joined them in London. Their increase in numbers played into the hands of right-wing bigots, and 'Keep Britain White' signs became commonplace.

A survey carried out by sociologist Anthony Richmond reckoned that over a third of Britons were extremely prejudiced against the immigrants. Iris Chapple, living in Brixton, confirmed this, but as a teenager she loved the smell of cooking coming from their crowded tenements, and particularly their rhythmic music. To her parents and neighbours the whole area had become an alien hell. The smell of marijuana was added to the list of negatives that helped form the damning stereotype of West Indians. Despite many working on the railways, underground or at the Royal Mail, they were reckoned to be lazy, arrogant and immoral. They were pushing white people out of their homes by their behaviour and turning previously respectable areas into ghettos. A major problem was the fundamental difference in temperament. Most West Indians were outgoing and laid back. They resented the grudging acceptance of the locals, which frequently spilled over into rudeness and casual, hurtful racism. In August 1958 this rising tension lurched into violence in North Kensington. Today, Notting Hill is home to film stars, hedge-fund managers and politicians. Sixty years ago those same swanky houses were divided into foul, overcrowded tenements. There had been spasmodic violence in the area earlier in the summer. Groups of white youths armed with iron bars indiscriminately attacked any black men they came across. Five were treated in hospital, but this was just a prelude for what was to come. The worse race riot ever seen in Britain was triggered by a domestic dispute. A young white Swedish woman was having a heated argument with her Jamaican husband outside Latimer Road tube station. A group of white young men tried to intervene and a scuffle broke out. By the following night hundreds of white youths rampaged through the streets of North Kensington, chasing young blacks and hurling petrol bombs into houses. Violence fanned out to Shepherds Bush, Paddington and Marylebone. The police had trouble in containing the riots, which went on intermittently until 5 September. Hundreds were arrested, including some blacks who had armed themselves for protection. It is no surprise to learn that the right-wing Union for British Freedom had recently been active in the area, and street meetings had been addressed by Sir Oswald Mosley.

Britain was appalled. Television beamed the unsavoury pictures of the riots around the world. Britain looked mean and spiteful and, after the recent Suez adventure, much diminished. West Indian politicians flew to London for consultations with the Prime Minister. Welfare organisations were strengthened and interracial committees formed. For the first time it was acknowledged officially that the country had a 'colour problem'. With resentment running deep on both sides, an uneasy truce got underway. London has always been a violent city, with Londoners likely to take matters into their own hands. Contrary to general belief they had never really welcomed newcomers, particularly foreigners. Gradually, though, each successive wave is assimilated and adds its own flavour to the cauldron that is London.

1950s London was a social melting pot. Set against great world events, its citizens fought for their own tiny place in the pecking order; some born and bred Londoners and others drawn from all parts of Britain. There were immigrants from around the world, all seduced and excited by the possibilities London offered. The blue bloods, snobs, chancers, conmen, all rubbing shoulders with an army of honest, hard-working people just wanting to make a living. The talented, lazy, and corrupt, the beautiful, cruel and deranged all thrown together, playing their part as the spear carriers in the life of the world's greatest city.

Two events held at the Savoy in the mid-fifties illustrated the continuing social differences in 1950s London. In one suite, the exclusive Eton Beagles were enjoying their annual dinner. Just along the corridor a rather more raucous occasion was underway. The charladies' ball, sponsored by *The Daily Mirror*, celebrated the work of the Mrs Mopps working across the capital. Between these two extreme groups the rest of us tried to make sense of a confusing and rapidly changing world.

6
Building for the Future

With roughly a third of London homes either damaged or destroyed during the war, there was a chronic shortage of property either to rent or buy in the early 1950s. The building of thousands of prefabs on cleared bomb sites had made little impact on what was an acute problem. House or flat hunting became something of an obsession and the shortages saw a considerable hike in prices. Classified columns in newspapers for properties had to be booked weeks in advance. A previously obscure publication, *Daltons Weekly*, tapped into the never-ending demand. Copies flew off the shelves of newsagents as the frenzied search continued. Corner shops also regularly displayed postcards with details of rooms to rent.

Patrick Abercrombie's 'Greater London Plan' suggested a solution. Ten new towns were to be built beyond an imposed green belt. Previously London's suburbs had been halted at where they had reached in 1939. New towns, including Harlow, Basildon and Hemel Hempstead welcomed thousands of former Londoners, but still the housing famine remained. With the return of a Tory government in 1951 the emphasis on house building continued with a renewed nod towards the private sector. Despite this, by the mid-fifties it was reckoned that three-quarters of all new home building had been undertaken by local authorities. Now, over twenty per cent of Britons were living in publicly owned properties. Living in a council property carried a silent social stigma in a class-ridden society, but these homes were generally a real improvement on what most had previously endured, with many having previously lived in Dickensian slum conditions. Vast new estates were being built all over London, often located close to what had previously been considered a desirable area. This caused tensions, but was part of an ongoing process in London where neighbourhoods either became gentrified or slipped down the desirability league.

The East End was changing. Slum clearance led to acres of working-class areas being torn down. It appeared that what the Luftwaffe had failed to destroy, the local authorities did. The population in Stepney in 1952 was half that prior to the war. The true Cockney was in decline, with only a quarter of the local population having been born within the sound of Bow bells. Slum tenements were replaced by high-rise flats that many found cold and unwelcoming. There was a loss of communal spirit, with residents locked away in their own little world. Trips to the local shops required using lifts which often didn't work. Vandalism and graffiti gave many of the blocks a depressing, run-down look within months of their being occupied. This was not what had been envisaged by the LCC who, in a brochure issued at the time, promised an estate made up of small high-rise apartments and larger, lower units with gardens intended for larger families. It boasted of good space standards, although in fact the rooms were small by pre-war standards, and seemed smaller still with ceiling levels lowered to save on building and heating costs. Increasing attempts were made to improve design and create an attractive environment. This culminated with the construction of the prestigious Alton Estate in Roehampton in 1959. The cost of building averaged out at just over £2,000 a dwelling, which represented good value, even allowing for the fact that the rents were subsidised.

At the beginning of the decade, £2,000 was about the average price for a three-bedroomed semi-detached house. It was possible to obtain a fixed-rate mortgage secured with a ten per cent deposit. With full employment, buying a house had never been more affordable. Improvement grants were available for older homes that needed modernising by the addition of a bathroom and toilet. Many older properties were converted into bed-sits. Renting a room was often the only option for youngsters with little or no capital. Freed from licencing, private and speculative building accelerated during the fifties. Working-class people, whose families had previously never owned any property, were now able to join the landed class. By the end of the decade almost forty per cent of mortgage purchasers were wage earners making less than £750 a year. These tended to be self-employed or aspiring blue-collar workers, many of whom were making a break from a past of poverty and deprivation. Of course, levels of desperately poor remained. In 1955 thousands of houses were condemned as unfit for habitation. Fourteen per cent of homes still had no inside toilet.

Increasingly, architects were being influenced by American and Scandinavian designers. The external appearance of buildings was now considered as important as the interior décor. A greater use of glass was underway, as was weatherboarding, while plastic guttering was introduced to replace traditional iron drainpipes. A modern-style detached house could cost upwards of £4,000 depending on size and location. Roofs were shallow-pitched, with the mock Elizabethan look losing favour. Still, Britons found it difficult to go in for cutting-edge design. There was just a shift from mock Elizabethan to mock Georgian. Despite early building restrictions and the lack of design flair, Londoners increasingly wanted to own their own homes. By 1958 twenty per cent were living in properties that had been built since the end of the war.

Diversity has always played a major part in London's architecture. In the grand squares of Mayfair and Chelsea the rich, powerful and influential were adapting to this strange post-war Britain. Many had dispensed with their servants. Below stairs had become eerily quiet, with the daily help now being the most frequent visitor. Across London in places like Camden and Islington, houses of similar design and distinction had fallen into disrepair and squalor. This was a blip in their long lives as they waited for future generations to restore them to their former glory. Today they are worth millions and are home to bankers and wealthy Russians in a London constantly reinventing itself. In Kensington, ancient cage-like lifts shuddered their way up and down in service flats, where largely elderly residents hung on to a lifestyle of faded opulence. From the slums of the East End and Paddington to the faceless high-rise flats and rows of new-built semis, London sought a new face to show to the world. Fate and circumstance conspired to offer no grand plan for the rebuilding of the capital. The desperate need for housing after the devastation of war only produced an ugly, incoherent mishmash. The chance to create a grand design for the city was lost. Any thought of this was soon surrendered to the lure of quick money. Enter the property kings, the Cottons, Samuels and Clores. Old buildings were replaced by giant slabs of tower blocks capable of showing a healthy financial return. The moguls' power and influence seemed endless until the property tycoon Jack Cotton came up with a plan to redesign Piccadilly Circus. This really could have resulted in the famous song lyrics becoming reality – 'Goodbye Piccadilly, farewell Leicester Square.' In 1959 Cotton proposed building a thirty-floor tower on the site of the former Café Monico. It would feature shops, offices, restaurants and banks. The building was to be covered in a vast array of advertising displays. Despite obtaining the backing of the LCC, this was a project too far for the British public. Piccadilly was one of London's iconic landmarks, known across the world. Despite defending his scheme, for once the money men were defeated by the ferocity of the public's opposition. Messy, crowded, chaotic Piccadilly Circus was saved intact for generations to come.

Meanwhile, less powerful builders were creating new homes for Londoners. 'Small' was the watchword. Most 1950s homes contained fewer rooms but they tended to be more flexible. Victorian and Edwardian houses usually offered a generous entrance hall and high-ceilinged rooms, which created a feeling of space. Kitchens often extended into a scullery and washroom. Many of these features were still evident even in the rows of suburban semis built before the war, but circumstances required the average 1950s house to utilise space more sparingly, with open-plan making its debut in British housing. The kitchen and scullery were merged, as were the living and dining rooms. Alternatively, kitchen-diners became increasingly popular.

New technology created a raft of products set to change domestic life. Formica advertised itself as 'the surface with a smile.' Housewives were offered 'three ways to transform your kitchen with jewel-bright clean-at-a-wipe'. The publicity blurb spoke of the excitement of carefree colours which this new laminated surface could bring. No more wooden draining boards collecting germs. For under £100 the kitchen worktops could be transformed and be heat resistant.

Many of the new technological changes centred on the kitchen. By 1958 most kitchens featured plastics in one form or another. Food was already being packaged in plastic film, while polythene bags were becoming commonplace. They were joined by their cousins, polystyrene, polyethylene and polyester. Plastics were always tough and often colourful. They were now making a valid contribution to an easier life for the housewife. While the Aga had been introduced in the 1930s, it was, and still remains, a huge favourite. It had the added advantage of heating water, keeping the kitchen warm as well as providing hobs and ovens for cooking. Their 1950s advertisements claimed that 'the Aga never goes out. No drudgery of any kind – no bother. No switches, no knobs. The thermostat does all the coaxing and adjusting for you, keeps ovens and hotplates at exactly the right cooking temperature, always.' All this for prices ranging from £90 to £123. By the mid-fifties a refrigerator was at the top of most housewives' wish lists. Prestcold offered three models to choose from and Frigidaire conjured up visions of luxurious American kitchens as depicted in Hollywood movies. The iconic brand was now available at a price of £99 19s. You could purchase the 'family Frigidaire, the very thing millions have been waiting for'.

With the fridge safely installed, the desire for a truly modern kitchen assumed still greater urgency for many. Enter the 'must have' fitted kitchen – and with it a new industry was created. Mass production methods had the effect of lowering prices. English Rose was just one of many companies who entered this lucrative market. Here was a clean, efficient, space-saving method to reduce work. English Rose sent out consultants who explained a planning service that showed the customer how the kitchen would look when installed even before they purchased. A scaled, coloured drawing was made to illustrate the finished article. Simple, but totally new and the first step, English Rose claimed, to 'a life of freedom from kitchen drudgery'.

What was the event that finally changed a Britain shackled to austerity into a forward-looking nation of change? Some reckon it came in 1954 with the final abolition of wartime rationing restrictions as meat became generally available. Others think it was the Festival of Britain with its emphasis on technology and design, but arguably the watershed came in 1953. In the year of the coronation, hundreds of thousands threw caution to the winds and bought a television. Watching the grandeur of coronation day stayed in the memory, but that single purchase changed our lives and the way we lived. Long-established customs were ruthlessly cast aside as that small flickering box became the centre of attention. No longer was the fireplace the focal point of the room. Meals, which for centuries had been eaten at a table, were now taken on a tray in front of the hypnotic screen. Conversations were restricted, as were visits to the pub. Panic spread to the cinema industry. Queues no longer formed outside cinemas waiting for the second sitting. Across London hundreds of picture houses closed, and not just the flea pits. A new strategy was urgently required to tempt the public back. Sales of draught beer slumped as canned beer found favour. We were being transformed into a stay-at-home nation. Television swept all before it. A classless medium that engulfed and mesmerised us.

With money being tight, many newly-weds had to initially accept hand-me-down furniture and fittings when setting up their first home. Inhibiting as this was, they were able to express their own taste with the interior decor. Being let loose with a paintbrush meant even the gloomiest interiors can be transformed. Paint manufacturers like Walpamur

reacted to market demand by extending their range of
water paint to include new vibrant colours. By 1957 *Home
and Gardens* magazine was offering their own extensive
paint colour swatches. With wallpapers no longer having
selvedges that needed to be trimmed, intrepid DIY addicts
met with very mixed results as they attempted to transform
their homes. Were the young having second thoughts about
contemporary décor? Sales of Regency striped wallpaper
were at record levels. For the more established married
couples it was out with old-world, Jacobean-styled furniture.
Get rid of the Tudor beams and leaded lights. Distempered
walls shouted pre-war. They had to go. Walls were now to be
lovingly cloaked in pre-trimmed wallpaper, with three walls
of one design and on the fourth a plain, contrasting colour.
Fitted carpets did away with the need to polish floorboards.
Progress was being made, but those huge leather armchairs
had to be despatched to the auction room. Asprey in New
Bond Street continued to offer silk brocade furniture suitable
for the owners of country mansions, but it was Heals that
offered comfort and design for a wider audience. Shopkeeper
Ian Henderson in Sloane Street edged a little closer to the
contemporary. A Nigel Walters futuristic chair with rubber
foam upholstery and wire legs was on offer for £9. In Regent
Street, a black, iron tripod candlestick was available from
Liberty for £11 3s and still strikes a futuristic chord even
today. Contemporary furniture with its clean uncluttered
lines combining metal and wood was well suited to mass
production. G-Plan, manufactured by E. Gomme Ltd in High
Wycombe, became the most successful British producer of
well-designed, light oak, inexpensive furniture. Backed by a
wide-ranging advertising campaign, it was possible to build
up a collection gradually, piece by piece. The customer could
also visit the company showroom and see the furniture in

a room setting. The concept was so successful that profits soared and the company was floated on the stock exchange in 1958.

Changes in the home were now marching to a modern tune. With the open fire no longer the main focus of the living room, alternative forms of heating were being contemplated. The latest gas and electric fires were fitted where once flames and smoke held sway. Central heating, featuring those comforting, chunky radiators, were installed in some of the swankiest homes. Multi-point contemporary lighting cast a surgical glare over proceedings. The hissing, wall-mounted gas lamps were now but a fading memory. Suddenly there was a craze for pot plants. Living rooms became mini jungles with cacti and trailing greenery fighting for attention. Another exotic touch was added by caged birds, who chirruped and tinkled their bells to the background noise of the television. By 1956 it was estimated that six million of our feathered friends bathed seed manufacturers and pet shop owners in a warm glow of appreciation.

Bedrooms were not immune to the revolution taking place in many homes. Old, hulking wardrobes were destined for the rubbish dump. Enter fitted bedroom furniture and with it the dawning of another major industry. Do-it-yourself had arrived and with it the sales of electric drills, saws and paintbrushes soared to stratospheric levels. For those with deeper pockets, Harrods devoted much of its third floor to a range of furniture galleries offering (they claimed) infinite choice. It was time for lumpy old beds to be transferred to the guest room. Staples offered 'beds complete with spring interior mattresses at a reasonable price'. Hardly the most engaging advertising slogan. Never mind, competitor Dunlopillo featured a very stylish-looking young lady sitting decorously on a bed while a salesman says, 'Madam, you're missing one of the best things in life until you sleep on a Dunlopillo mattress.' She looks as if she believes him. She might also have invested in 'Earlywarm' all-wool Witney blankets. Made of the softest pure wool, a mid-1950s advertisement trumpeted that 'these blankets had been famous through fifteen reigns'. Finally, in the bedroom, the linoleum lining the floor harked back to times best forgotten. Rugs or a carpet now brought a hitherto unknown warmth and cosiness to this most private of spaces.

For many, a bathroom was a little known luxury. Gone was the metal bath tub set out on the parlour floor in front of a roaring fire. There were stories of people new to such luxury filling their bath with coal, but most just rejoiced in the new-found pleasure of having a long soak. Bathroom suites were still mainly white, although some colour was introduced towards the end of the fifties. Although space continued to be an issue, toilets were always situated in an adjoining room away from the bathroom. Heated towel rails were another welcome addition to a room where it was possible to escape from the rest of the family. It was now possible to buy attractively designed towels, usually in a range of pastel colours. Waxing lyrical, Zorbit, a leading supplier of towels, stated their selection was 'typifying to the full the modern trend towards more tasteful living', capturing 'the lightness, gaiety, elegance, colour and design which is now of such significance in the new, more graceful phase of interior decoration'.

It was the young, first-time buyers who were setting the pace of modernisation. Their parents were not so easily swayed by trendy new innovations. They distrusted much of the change swirling all about them. They hated the music blaring out from coffee bars. They failed to understand the love of all things foreign. Youngsters were eating weird foreign food, their sons wearing Italian-style suits and now furnishing their homes with ghastly, uncomfortable Scandinavian furniture. Across society the generation gap had never been greater. What was wrong with meat and two veg, Bing Crosby and the moquette three-piece? With unemployment registering at just under two per cent, it was not just the young who had buying power. The sale of traditional furnishings still featured prominently in the leading department stores.

Sweeping and cleaning were as much a part of 1950s life as they are today. The Hoover was virtually unchallenged, apart from by traditional carpet sweepers such as the Metoluk, which traded under the slogan 'the deeper sweeper'. Gardening remained an obsession with many, even in crowded London. For those living in flats or tower blocks, window boxes were a worthwhile substitute, offering a summer blaze of colour. Petunias were particularly popular, with Firechief, Bluebedder and White Double Caprice combining to bring a hint of the countryside to dirty old London. Weekly talks on the radio by Fred Streeter had armies of gardeners descending on Woolworths each spring to buy their seeds to plant. Many turned over parts of their gardens to vegetable patches and council allotments were also available in many areas. Gardening was one of the most popular leisure activities, particularly at the weekend. Towards the end of the decade, car ownership grew and Sunday morning was devoted instead to sponges and buckets of soapy water.

Our home represents one of the most important factors in our lives. We devote time, effort and money to its upkeep. It represents our tastes and, to an extent, our standing in the community. In the fifties, tastes were changing as an increasing range of products became generally available. In 1953 the Design and Industry Association held an exhibition at Charing Cross underground station. Two rooms of identical size were furnished, one in traditional style and the other featuring contemporary design. The cost of completing the rooms was identical. The public were asked to vote on which display they preferred. Over 30,000 took the time to vote. A distinction was recorded between men and women, but also those over or under thirty-five. The finding threw up an almost equal divide. Young people found the traditional décor 'dark and depressing'. Older voters were equally dismissive of the contemporary room, insisting it was 'neither cosy nor comfortable'. There was also a sizeable majority stating they had spent more on traditional furniture rather than contemporary, but that was in 1953 and, as in music and fashion, tastes were changing fast.

Today in the twenty-first century we are seeing antiques, which until recently had been much in vogue, sidelined as minimalist décor holds sway. Fashion is fickle, so look in the garage for any old G-Plan you may have. Retro 1950s is already experiencing something of a renaissance.

7
School Days

Childhood is all too fleeting for today's savvy children. At too young an age they are assailed by dangers and temptations that previous generations never had to deal with. Luckily they are spared a brooding black cloud that appeared on every youngster's horizon in the 1950s. Primary school was a lengthy preparation for the dreaded eleven plus examination. Here was a three-part test that was likely to have long-term implications on the rest of your life. The exam had been introduced in 1944 and was designed to identify the academically gifted who would be suited to a grammar-school education. Those failing were designated to attend secondary schools whose aspirations were generally lower and targeted towards more technical skills.

The examination was tough and one that many of today's youngsters would struggle with. The exam was in three parts, testing for numeracy, literacy and general knowledge. The arithmetic test had, of course, to be undertaken without the use of calculators. What's more, workings out had to be written out to show how the conclusion had been reached. In addition, the student was asked to complete a series of mental arithmetic tests. The English exam involved the testing of grammar, punctuation and the writing of an essay. The general knowledge section was designed to assess the students' ability of problem solving. None of this was easy.

Many children still didn't fully understand the difference between grammar schools and secondary moderns, despite the promptings of parents and teachers. The exam brought an abrupt end to a carefree childhood. Despite taking the exam in the familiar surroundings of their regular classroom, it was impossible to ignore the tension as the youngsters stared apprehensively at the face-down paper on the desk in front of them. In a sense it was something of a lottery as many bright children who suffered from examination nerves failed, while seemingly less-talented students passed. Uppermost in many youngsters' minds was that they were soon to be separated from the friends they had made since starting school at the age of five. It was a harsh and abrupt lesson that left many talented children feeling a sense of failure so early in their lives.

For those who passed, the tension continued by having to attend interviews. Parents could select up to three schools in order of preference. For many youngsters, entering a grammar school for the first time was forbidding. Masters swept by wearing flowing gowns as pupils in smart uniforms stood aside. Here, it appeared, discipline was paramount. Assembly halls were lined with boards listing past students who had obtained entrance to Oxbridge colleges. All very intimidating. Once a child had finally established a place, making new friends became the priority as did getting used to being at the bottom of the heap as a first-former. There was a third option for those with money or whose parents were prepared to make a huge financial sacrifice. London had over twenty prominent public schools. While most of those catered for boys only, there were also exceptional girls' schools, including St Paul's and North London Collegiate

School. Gaining entry to all these establishments was also extremely competitive. They set tough entrance examinations in the search for the most gifted students. Some stretched a point by taking on a dull or difficult child if the parent was prepared to donate, say, a new boat for the first eight, or a refit of the school's gymnasium. Otherwise, the less-gifted offspring of the rich were consigned to a number of private establishments across the country. Their aim was to turn out children with manners, who knew how to hold their knives and forks and, for the girls, how to curtsey to royalty. Some public schools, while turning down the most bone-headed of applicants, could be influenced by a child's sporting potential. It was considered important to turn out rounded individuals rather than just academic successes.

So, while childhood for this generation was extended more than it is for today's streetwise children, there were other formidable problems for them to overcome. Discipline at all types of schools was so severe that it sometimes lurched over into brutality and sadism. I remember an occasion when I owned up to talking in class. I had to make my way to the front of the room to take my punishment. Our minute Scottish chemistry master peered down at me from his desk perched on a raised dais. Leaning forward, he instructed me to 'put out my tongue'. He then dipped a pair of forceps into a glass jar on his desk containing some white crystals which were being used in the experiment he was conducting. He gave my tongue a hearty tweak and told me to sit down and keep silent in future. By the time I arrived home my tongue was red and slightly blistered. My indignation at my treatment was not shared by my mother, who seemed to think it served me right. The incident illustrates the huge shift in attitude towards the punishment of children, and what was then a perfectly normal parental response. Most parents endorsed any of the teachers' actions. Authority was to be respected and obeyed. Severe punishment at school was not unusual. Many children growing up in the 1950s were beaten by their teachers. At my school prefects were also allowed to administer the cane. We were also subjected to having our hands whacked with a ruler and we became adept at ducking flying chalk or blackboard cleaners hurled at us by exasperated teachers. Catching the projectiles only increased the masters' rage. Amid all this you had to deal with bullying, sometimes from your peers but more often from older pupils. Boys tended either to toughen up or deflect aggression with humour. Being the form clown led to popularity, providing you were prepared to take the endless punishments and threats of being expelled.

Girls were generally more agreeable and any bullying tended to be more subtle, although where it did take place, it was no less upsetting. Discipline was particularly fierce in the convent schools across London. School uniforms were considered to be a great leveller. Boys often continued to wear short trousers into their early teens. Generally, girls were required to wear gymslips and bobby socks. In an age of genuine austerity most families were short of money and it was usual for uniforms to be bought several sizes too large to allow the youngster to grow into them. School dominated most children's lives. Few would subscribe to it being the happiest days of their lives, but many were influenced and inspired by teachers they encountered. It is those teachers who lit the spark that often shaped future lives.

In an age where people were still categorised by class, it is perhaps not surprising that schooling underlined these differences. Public, grammar and secondary modern schools created divisions that carried on into adult life. It was not just academic qualifications that pointed the way to success. The 'old school' network was still alive and well, often excluding talented youngsters from less privileged backgrounds. Attending a public school in a working-class area of London, I had some sympathy for the lads who waylaid me on the first day I wore a boater to school. Pushing me into the garden of their council house, they punched a hole through its crown. My parents didn't take such a tolerant view, but Sellotape gave it what I thought was a sort of Bohemian charm.

Of course, for most London school kids, it was not a case of boaters, gymslips or pigtails. In Fulham, a young, precocious Jean Sporle was laying down a challenge at her secondary modern. She started to wear tight skirts and high heels. Her uplifted pointed bra was appreciated by the boys but not her headmistress. It was the heavy make-up and particularly the painted nails that flew in the face of school rules. At morning assembly Jean was marched to the front and on to the raised rostrum. There, in front of the whole school, her nails were cut to the quick by the needlework mistress, causing them to bleed. Once again, Jean complaining to her parents proved pointless; they thoroughly approved of the school's action. Keeping young teenagers from less-privileged backgrounds under control presented an ongoing problem. Most could not wait to leave school and to start earning. There were plenty of jobs to be had, but at fifteen and with no formal qualifications many of these youngsters faced a very restricted future.

By the mid-fifties there was a growing unease at the fairness of the eleven plus. The chance of obtaining a grammar-school place was a lottery, depending on where you lived. The places available varied from twenty per cent to forty-five per cent of those taking the examination. A reaction to so many children being academically abandoned so early in their lives led to the first LCC comprehensive school being opened at Kidbrooke in 1954. It catered for 1,700 girls and was staffed by ninety teachers. The *News Chronicle* hailed it as an educational breakthrough, calling it 'the first palace of learning'. Typically, the *Evening Standard* took a different stance, calling the school 'a sausage machine'. A new educational debate raged that still continues today.

Of course, school was not solely about work. Hours were devoted to impromptu games of football and cricket and ancient playground games remained popular. Many young girls developed skipping to an art form. Hopscotch and Blind Man's Buff also connected screaming children to the past. The collecting of cigarette cards (most of which dated back to before the war) was a must. Most popular were pictures of sports and film stars. Collections were built up by swapping and playing 'flickers', which became a craze. Flicking cards against a wall, you tried to cover your opponent's with your own. It was a real gamble as to whether you increased your collection or had it decimated, watched by a crowd of noisy bystanders. Another favourite was bouncing a ball on a coin laid on the ground in an attempt to turn it over. Arm wrestling, which dated back to antiquity, remained a favourite of the older boys. It required a combination of strength and timing. During the autumn, playing conkers became an obsession. Here, huge efforts were made in an attempt to produce a gnarly champion. Conkers were soaked in vinegar or brine and patiently baked in the oven. I had one old, bald conker that was so successful that no one would take it on. Eventually, I had to break it by smashing it against a wall. It still took a dozen or so hearty smacks before it finally disintegrated. Old playground songs also survived, including 'Oranges and Lemons', 'London's Burning' and 'Ten Green Bottles'. Children grew up with the link to the past remaining secure in the 1950s playground.

Away from school the weather influenced lives far more than today. It was quite normal in the depths of winter to wake up to find the inside of the bedroom window completely frozen. The cold gripped and gnawed away at you once you left the relative warmth of the kitchen or living room. Chilblains itched annoyingly and many wore balaclavas to protect their ears. Even after the Great Smog, the morning walk or bus ride to school was likely to be masked in a murky blanket. For much of the year life was conducted against a background of monotone gloom. The summer brought other problems. With few owning fridges, milk curdled and butter melted. A real treat for me was to go to a neighbour who did have a freezer and to suck on an ice cube. Summer holidays seemed to go on for ever. For the first few weeks children enjoyed their freedom. Cars were still a rarity in the back streets, so cricket, football and roller-skating could go on with very little interruption (except from irate neighbours). Soon boredom crept in. Longs days had to be filled and even if there was a television in the house there was little to watch in the daytime. Rainy days were worst – no cycling off to see friends, and trapped in the house with a mother who started to nag. Many (boys as well as girls) had to help around the house – hoovering, cleaning cutlery, dusting. It was almost worse than school. Gradually, indoor hobbies were developed. The technically minded immersed themselves in the intricacies of Meccano. Stamp collecting was a worthwhile interest for others. I was particularly drawn to the Nazi stamps with their sinister Swastikas, but also stamps from exotic places like Borneo and Tanganyika. Girls often used rainy days to dress up in their mothers' clothes and totter around in high-heeled shoes several sizes too big for them. Monopoly had the advantage of taking hours to finish, but often ended in family rows. Draughts and board games were also popular but, when left on your own, reading widened horizons. Lending libraries formed an important part of many youngsters' lives. If you had an imaginative mind it was possible to lose yourself and be transported far away by a well-written tale. It was a time when Enid Blyton was read by most children. Although she was ridiculed by critics and educationalists, many of us cut our teeth on the *Famous Five*.

Comics also were incredibly popular, with staggering circulation figures. Young boys often favoured the *Beano* and *Dandy*, while many girls opted for *Bunty* or *Valentine*. *Hotspur*, *Rover* and *Wizard* offered full-length stories of adventures and derring-do, often written by well-known writers like Dennis Wheatley. In the evenings when the family gathered, board and card games were very popular. By the time I was five I played a very canny game of progressive Rummy, taught by my grandmother who was a regular but charming cheat. Battleships was a favourite board game, but we often resorted to Noughts and Crosses. A regular treat was to attend Beetle Drives, a game that seems to have disappeared today. So it was a time of simple pleasures. Listening to the wireless, reading and playing board games would hardly rate against today's computer games, but the fifties generation embraced them and continue to look back on those times with affection.

The great fear for 1950s parents was the thought of their children contracting poliomyelitis. It was an insidious disease that could be fatal, but more normally caused paralysis. Its initial symptoms were not unlike many of the less-serious children's illnesses, raising further fears. I remember a boy at our school with a totally withered arm. It was not unusual to see youngsters struggling along wearing leg callipers. Winter tended to herald the arrival of the more common childhood illnesses. Whole days were but a woozy memory as we struggled with mumps, measles and whooping cough. Temperatures soared, throats were raw, skin itched. Chicken pox was particularly feared by teenage girls. Gloves were worn in an attempt to resist the perpetual desire to scratch, with the possibility of ruining a once perfect complexion. The doctors' advice for all those ailments barely seemed to change; an aspirin or two and plenty of liquids was the order of the day. Most doctors ran their practices from their own homes. You arrived and waited your turn. There was no receptionist, although the doctor's wife came in from time to time presumably to tell her husband how many more patients still needed to be seen. You had to be really poorly to call the doctor out to your house.

For a whole generation a visit to the dentist was one of fear and dreaded anticipation. Dentists at that time were either overzealous or unscrupulous. Acres of young teeth were drilled and filled unnecessarily, and all without painkilling injections. The white-clad figure loomed over you, the drill seemingly seeking out the most exposed nerve. At least when it was finished you felt fine, even elated, but extractions presented the real nightmare. For days before the appointment the prospect hung over you like a huge cloud. The dentist's chair assumed the proportions of a torture chamber. The sinister black rubber mask and the sound of hissing gas was frightening, but waking up was worse. You were drowsy, with a mouth full of blood and a wretched feeling of nausea. Then it was out into the cold to wait for the bus to take you home as you vomited into the gutter. Looking back, it all seems positively barbaric compared to today's treatments.

By comparison, the visit of the 'nit nurse' to a school held few fears for youngsters. This was not true of their parents, who were covered in shame if their child was sent home with cropped hair and tell-tale streaks of iodine painted on their scalp. While some children cringed at the indignity, others wore it as a badge of honour.

Childhood memories vary wildly, depending on experience. Golden summer days or deep unhappiness come flooding back, but for most a fifties childhood in London is framed by the drama of the streets. Weed-strewn bomb sites formed a backdrop of never-ending activity. There were daily deliveries by the milkman, whose horse was soon to be replaced by a motorised cart. It was the black-faced coalman who was the last to rely on his huge horse to make deliveries. This era represented the death throes of the sound of hooves that had dominated London's streets for centuries, with only the occasional rag-and-bone man to keep the coalman company. Bakers, greengrocers and fishmongers continued to sell door to door, while in the summer the ice-cream vendor would appear, peddling his three-wheeled van. With window cleaners, rat catchers and knife grinders, even side streets were rarely deserted. For most children Sunday was the worst day of the week. Only the newsagents were open for a couple of hours in the morning and everything was so quiet and boring. Many kids were packed off to church or Sunday school, but at least the Sunday roast was something of a treat. The worst day of the year was Good Friday. Even the wireless offered no relief, with a diet of religious programmes and gloomy classical music.

I seem to remember I received about a shilling a week pocket money at the beginning of the decade, which would have been about average. Many youngsters supplemented their income by doing a paper round before setting off to school. Despite its wage of eight shillings a week, the job lost much of its attraction when winter set in. Papers had to be sorted as well as delivered, and balancing a weighty sack on a bike while negotiating icy roads was no joke. Pocket money was mostly spent on comics and sweets, but generally most children were encouraged to save. In 1956 Premium Bonds were introduced and with them came dreams of a huge jackpot win. Woolworths was a favourite store for many children to spend their pocket money in. Each branch had a wonderful sweet counter, but the whole shop with its open displays seemed so exciting as you slowly walked round with your friends. The giant weighing machine was a great favourite and the trick was for each kid to climb on to the platform before their friend jumped off. This allowed a whole group of children to weigh themselves for just a penny. That is, if they were not chased off by the manager.

A great day in every child's calendar was Guy Fawkes' Night. Bomb sites were often used and for weeks before, wood and garden cuttings were collected as a huge bonfire began to take shape. Most children had only a vague idea about the Gunpowder Plot that had happened way back in the seventeenth century. Although adults were always in attendance, the bonfire parties were not regulated and supervised as they are today. The 'guy' was made as lifelike as possible. The effigy was stuffed with rags and newspapers. Often he was dressed in old clothes before being hoisted to the top of the pyre. In the days leading up to 5 November the guy was wheeled round in a pram or positioned outside a tube station, while his makers pleaded plaintively for 'a penny for the guy'. Hopefully the pennies added up to enough for the business-like children to buy some fireworks. Penny bangers were the most affordable, but the most prized were the rockets and Catherine wheels.

Bonfire Night tended to be rather chaotic and potentially dangerous. I remember trying to aim a rocket at a neighbour's chimney only for it to crack one of their bedroom windows. Running away didn't do any good as I was spotted. For several weeks I had my pocket money docked so that I could pay for the broken window. Bonfire Nights bring back memories of baked potatoes and parents and neighbours red-faced from drink and the heat as they huddled round the fire.

Christmas was, of course, a time of great excitement for children. Although there was the traditional giving of presents, Christmas in the 1950s was far less commercial than today, particularly at the beginning of the decade when there was still a shortage of consumer goods. Presents tended to be either second-hand or home-made. This never affected either the excitement or expectation. To receive any gift, no matter how small, was a treat.

The build-up started with the school carol concert and nativity play. Then came the ritual of putting up of the Christmas decorations at home. The streamers and paper bells mostly dated back to before the war, with few decorations available in the shops. Who cared if the tinsel was tarnished and the coloured balls for the tree chipped? In pride of place at the top of our tree was a figure of Father Christmas sitting in an ancient bi-plane. Children, who normally had to be chased out of bed each morning, were awake by daybreak, diving into sacks and pillowcases left by their parents. There was usually one major present and then lots of smaller gifts from uncles and aunts. Books and annuals were popular and most stockings contained an orange or some dates. Once the initial excitement had subsided, many children found the day itself something of an anticlimax. Families gathered and often tensions rose. Today Christmas is apparently a time when many marriage break-ups occur. At our house it was the tension between two grandmothers that often surfaced.

My paternal grandmother was teetotal. All four feet eleven of her. She sat, a Victorian figure dressed in black, managing to create a general impression of disapproval. It was the only day of the year that I can remember the kitchen door being locked. Eventually my mother would appear with her mother, both red in the face and giggly. The Booth's Gin bottle was left on the side half empty. After lunch, across London, families played Charades, had a sing-song round the piano or just slept off the excess of the day. The early days of the fifties were the last before television dominated the celebrations.

Viewed from a modern perspective, it may appear that the youngsters of the fifties had a tough upbringing. Certainly, they lacked the choice of entertainment, clothes and diet enjoyed by children today. They were also subjected to strict discipline, much of which would now be viewed with outright horror by modern society, but they survived. Most seem to look back on their childhood with a degree of nostalgia (however misplaced). Strangely, it was a time of innocence, which should perhaps be encouraged today. We all know that childhood is far too short before the harsh reality of adult life intrudes.

8
A Woman's Work Is Never Done

Much has been written about the woman's lot in the 1950s. She is generally portrayed as having a life of endless household drudgery and normally being taken for granted by her husband and children. True? Well, maybe. Rachel Cooke, in her book *Ten Extraordinary Women of the Fifties*, pictures the polar opposite, but then how many had the verve and ambition of film maker Betty Box or the skill of bestselling food writer Patience Gray? The journalist and broadcaster Nancy Spain was another who defied convention by being open about her sexuality in an age when lesbianism was scarcely even acknowledged. She was a woman of Catholic taste who enjoyed the varied delights of Windmill theatre owner Sheila Van Damm, editor Joan Laurie and, to cap it all, the alluring Marlene Dietrich. Surely somewhere between these extremes were women who led normal and rewarding lives?

Certainly the image of women tied to the kitchen sink does prompt memories. My own mother was the first to rise in the morning. The next hour was hectic as breakfast was cooked and packed lunches prepared, before she sent the children and my father on their way. Then perhaps a short break with a cup of tea and a piece of toast before the round of chores was started to a background of *Housewives'*

Choice. Beds had to be made and clothes tidied away. Apart from Mondays, which were devoted to washing, laundry and a bubbling copper, her routine rarely altered. Her day consisted of clearing grates in the winter, dusting, hoovering and cleaning silver, punctuated by a short coffee break always spent reading a book, preferably about faraway places – a temporary escape. After lunch it was off to the shops, the nearest of which was about a mile away. Although groceries were delivered to the house, a trip to the shops was seldom missed. Maybe this gave her a chance to chat to neighbours she met on the way, otherwise, it was a fairly isolated existence. Then it was time to cook the evening meal, make sure that the kids were doing their homework and await my father's return from work. The evening was usually spent reading or listening to the radio until later, when television brought a change to people's lives. Other than an occasional trip to the cinema and an annual visit to the West End for a supper at The Boulogne in Gerrard Street and a visit to the Whitehall Theatre, that was it. Boring and repetitive certainly, but did she and her contemporaries feel hard done by or unhappy? Sometimes, yes, but life for these middle-class mums had a rhythm and certainty about it that rarely exists today. Many talents were doubtless sacrificed on the altar of convention and ambitions frustrated. Of course many women chose or had to go out to work. Certainly the daughters of the middle class were not allowed to be idle once they left school. Very few went on to university and the type of work for young, well-educated girls was extremely restricted in a male-dominated world.

Many girls were guided by their parents into secretarial work or nursing, both of which were considered to be safe and respectable. Ann Baker, having completed secretarial college, managed to get a job at a leading insurance company in Moorgate. Although part of a forty-strong typing pool in the overseas accident department, her mother boasted that she was already a manager's secretary. She did take the occasional dictation from some lowly clerk, but for the most part she was confined to the clatter of typewriters and the distinctive smell of carbon paper. The company was very hierarchical, with the top floor devoted to directors and senior managers (all male). Unusually for those times, the woman in charge of the typing pool was an Indian, sari and all. She was the mother hen, protecting her girls from bad-tempered clerks and managers demanding letters to be redone even if there was only a small mistake. Mrs Patel also protected the girls from unwanted sexual advances, which occurred almost daily. She was tolerant of unnecessary visits to the typing pool from love-sick young men, but was on hand to deflect the persistent pinchers and gropers, most of whom were married. A trip to the basement to locate some urgently required policy was, for a young girl, to run the gauntlet of unwanted innuendo or outright harassment. It appeared, in this organisation at least, that it was open season on any attractive, unmarried girl, culminating with the Christmas party often ending in scandal and humiliation.

Working conditions were good, with an excellent subsidised canteen and a social club deep in the suburbs with playing fields and a club house where dances were held each Saturday night. Every morning in Moorgate, the clerical staff and typists had to sign in. A uniformed porter used to draw the line way down on his ledger page to allow latecomers to appear to have arrived on time, until one day fog led to many staff not making it into work and his ruse was discovered. To the consternation of the staff, a clock-in system was threatened. It seems difficult now to remember that overseas business had to be conducted by letter, with

queries frequently taking weeks to be answered from the
other side of the world. Ann remembers one manager who
prided himself on the brevity of his letters. They were likely
to read simply 'yes' or 'no', or if he was in an eloquent mood,
'sorry I don't agree'. Each night thousands of clerical staff, all
stiff collars and shiny suits, and their secretarial equivalents
would fight their way on to crowded tube trains, travelling
out to the suburbs. Rather than play with iPhones or listen
to music, they would strap-hang while reading the latest
bestseller or one of three London evening papers. Squashed
together, people rarely spoke and avoided eye contact at all
costs.

In the 1950s, nursing was among the most respected of
all professions. Nurses were able to walk alone, unmolested,
in areas of London where police had to go in pairs. Nursing
was considered to be a vocation and as such was revered and
thought to be a suitable occupation for 'nice' middle-class
girls. Shirley Balmer fitted the bill perfectly. Bright, bubbly
and attractive, she sailed through her interview at Guy's and
in December 1954 she arrived from Beverley to commence
her training as a student nurse. This was initially undertaken
in New Cross and Shirley was one of an intake of eight. It
was a four-year course; although qualification was achieved
after three years, they were not acknowledged as being fully
trained until the fourth year was completed. The work was
hard and the hours long before they returned to the digs they
had been allocated. Here they were overseen by a midwife,
who kept an eye on them. Discipline was strict and they lived
in fear of getting on the wrong side of Matron. Although they
only earned £8 a month, their food and accommodation were
paid for. Even so, with the return fare to Beverley costing £4,
trips home were rare unless paid for by her parents. There
was so much to learn but a pride in being a part of Guy's

was instilled into them. The hospital had been built in 1726 and its motto, 'better to give than receive', underlined the famous hospital's ethos. Despite the relentless pressure of assimilating knowledge and practical expertise, there were moments of relaxation. Visits to Lyons Corner House in Tottenham Court Road are remembered for the wonderful lemon meringue pie. With money so short, Shirley would sit for hours with friends over a cup of coffee. The high regard in which nurses were held was reflected in free theatre tickets being given to Matron at Guy's for her to allocate as she saw fit. Shirley remembers going to the Theatre Royal to see *South Pacific*, starring Sean Connery and Mary Martin. When the fabulous evening was over there was a dash back before lights out.

In those days one of the nurses' added duties was to cook breakfast for the patients on the ward. The ward sister slept on the ward, to be on hand for any emergency. The whole set-up at Guy's was extremely hierarchical, with consultants acting like gods. A look from Matron could cause sleepless nights, and reprimands from a ward sister caused deep shame, warranted or not. Despite the almost military discipline and hardships endured during training, there was a deep sense of pride on qualifying. Pride to be walking through the streets of London to silent acclaim. The mob cap secured by strings under the chin, the dashing blue cape with its red lining and the white uniform peeking out below and the whole effect completed by those oh-so-sensible flat shoes. After four years of hard slog, Nurse Shirley could only afford to live in a grotty flat in Bermondsey, but she had pride in her achievements and really did believe '*dare quam accipere*' – 'to give is to receive'.

In the fifties, lavish praise was rarely given to the young. If you were academically gifted you were likely to be told there

were plenty more of your contemporaries that were a good
deal brighter. Even if it was obvious you were a budding
sports star you tended to get only grudging praise. It was
important to keep youngsters' feet on the ground. Nobody
admired bragging – modesty was considered more becoming.
Good looks are a matter of genetics or luck, so beauty in a
girl was normally ignored by her parents to stop her getting
big-headed. Many were surprised when they started getting
attention and compliments from the opposite sex. It was a
very British thing to wear good looks uncomfortably, which
somehow magnified the attraction. Jean Sporle left school
thinking she was a 'plain Jane'. She took a typing course and
travelled up to her office in the West End each day from her
parents' house in Hammersmith. On holiday in Clacton with
friends, she was persuaded to enter a beauty contest. Wearing
only a swimming costume, she found it uncomfortable being
ogled by a crowd of admiring men, many old enough to be
her father. She was genuinely surprised to win the contest
and it made her realise that the typing pool was not for her.
She fancied a career in films, but modelling was a more
realistic option. She was too curvaceous to tread the catwalk
but she did pose for a few glamour shots in *Spick and Span*.
Like many before her she was drawn to Soho, which was
close to her office. She started taking her lunch at a coffee bar
in Gerrard Street, a haunt of resting actors, film extras and
line shooters. Soho was strange and exciting, almost like a
different country. People sauntered and stood around talking
on street corners. The smell of coffee and exotic herbs hung
in the air as a background to a gabble of foreign languages
from passers-by.

At the tacky, scruffiest end of Gerrard Street, Jean had
noticed a photographic studio. The entrance was decorated
with models wearing the tiniest bikinis. Nervously, she

entered, to be met by a beautiful blonde who introduced herself as Pamela Green, the wife of the photographer. George Harrison Marks also made her feel at ease. He offered a rate of £2 an hour for Jean to pose topless. Considering she was only earning just over £3 a week typing, she hardly hesitated. Despite Jean having last-minute nerves and being almost paralysed with fear, the session went well. The fact that Jean could type led to her getting a full-time job at the studio. She couldn't have realised it at the time, but Jean was becoming part of a small team that was redefining what was acceptable to an outwardly prudish British public. Pamela Green is remembered fondly by thousands of young men growing up in the 1950s as the magazine produced by Harrison Marks became ever more explicit. Despite her curvaceous good looks, Jean only posed a few more times. Instead, she ran the office and served in the shop, attending to the lines of nervous men anxious to purchase the latest edition of *Kamera*, the magazine which was making Marks and his wife extremely wealthy. Jean worked happily with them for a couple of years, appearing with Pam in the film *The Artist's Model*. With Marks' output now verging on the pornographic, Jean left to pursue a career in promotional work and beauty consultancy. Still outstandingly attractive today, Jean feels comfortable with her small contribution to the glamour industry. Unfortunately, the lure of big money led Marks to a squalid extension of what had been a relatively innocent industry. The permissive society had arrived.

The spring of 1955 found the fabulously named Winkie Winkfield resting. Like Jean Sporle, as a young girl Winkie yearned for a life of glamour and stardom. After six years treading the boards, she was a truly professional singer and dancer, but endless travelling and horrible theatrical digs had brought her down to earth. Success and stardom required 'a huge dollop of luck' rather than, or as well as, talent. With little prospect of work, she trawled the advertisements in *The Stage*. There were regular inserts from the Windmill Theatre, which she had always ignored in the past. In the outwardly prudish society of 1950s Britain, nudity was still viewed with grave suspicion and a stigma was attached to those who were prepared to strip off. Winkie, a cute and lively young lady, hated being idle and decided to go to the theatre for an audition. Dressed to the nines and ignoring the wolf whistles from groups of musicians gathered in Archer Street hoping to be signed for a gig, she made her way to the stage door. Directed to the audition room on the top floor, she sat on a battered settee, the only furniture in a vast empty space, except for a stand-up piano. After some twenty minutes no one had appeared and she was beginning to have second thoughts. Eventually, a rather formidable middle-aged woman loomed over her and asked her abruptly what she was waiting for. Anne Mitelle was the casting director and assistant to the owner/manager Vivian Van Damm. Her manner was aggressive and dismissive. She had not been informed of any audition. It was as if she had taken an instant, irrational dislike to poor Winkie. As she stomped off she informed Winkie 'anyway, you are too old' and with a slamming of the door she was gone. Disappointed and angry, Winkie was picking up her vanity case containing her leotard and dancing shoes when she became aware of another woman perched on the arm of the settee. A younger woman, although her figure indicated she was not part of the dance company. Winkie was queried about her background and experience. She chatted away explaining her position and was asked to wait. Without knowing it, Winkie had been interviewed by Sheila Van Damm. Enter an extremely grumpy Anne Mitelle, who told Winkie through gritted teeth that she had the job. No audition, just Sheila Van Damm backing her instinct, and she was right. Winkie enjoyed three hectic, exhausting years at the Windmill, but not through any help from Anne Mitelle, who continued to bear a grudge. Not used to her decisions being questioned, she obviously felt humiliated by Van Damm overruling her. Determined to have the last say, she had insisted that Winkie Winkfield was an absurd name and for Windmill purposes her new name was to be plain Jean Mara.

Life at the Windmill was a constant blur of performing and rehearsing for the next production. There were two companies, with each performing on alternate days. The shows were run with military precision, with dress rehearsals always performed on a Sunday. The work was so demanding that there was little time for a social life. After work it was a sprint to get the last tube train home. Little wonder, as the girls had to perform in five shows a day. Staleness was avoided by the girls alternating their routines. A roster posted each day required diverse performances: either singing, dancing or standing motionless under a spotlight in the nude. The company included comedians looking for their big break. Winkie worked with Bruce Forsyth and Harry Secombe, both of whom went onto stardom. Romances within the company were not encouraged, but Winkie fell in love with fellow dancer Alan Wren and they married in 1958. By this time Winkie's earnings had jumped from £10 to £16 a week, but Anne Mitelle's vendetta continued. Winkie's work schedule was constantly increased. She was exhausted, although Sheila Van Damm appeared not to notice that her costume changes were being shortened and her stage appearances increased. It was time to leave. Overwhelmingly, Winkie had happy memories of a family atmosphere developed against a background of frantic activity and the lingering smell of sweat and greasepaint. By 1958 the Windmill was already something of an anachronism, left stranded by new attitudes and a profusion of strip clubs. Despite her vitality and talent, Winkie never found stardom on the stage, like most who sought it. Now, some sixty years later, she has emerged as a respected and successful artist whose work is reproduced all round the world. You can't keep a good girl down!

It is doubtful whether any woman in the 1950s willingly walked the streets and sold her body to make a living. Many, of course, did and continue to do so. Today drug addiction is often blamed, but why or how did it happen in the buttoned-up fifties? Perhaps because society was so repressed. Certainly the Victorians with their double standards have a lot to answer for, as the West End was awash with street walkers, including children, during Victoria's reign. I learnt of one sad story when I was researching for my novel *The Vice Captain*. I got talking to an old lady in a rather downmarket café. I was anxious to learn what I could about Soho in the 1950s. By the time I had bought her a second drink she was in full flight. It became obvious to me that she had once 'been on the game'. An initial denial was followed by a torrent of background information, which I used in the book. 'Vera', as I shall call her, had been reduced to washing dishes at a well-known restaurant and, worried that she would be identified, I didn't tell her personal story. As over five years have elapsed it is unlikely she is still alive, and it is a sad but fascinating tale.

Vera, like Jean and Winkie, had aspirations about going on the stage. She was a talented dancer and, being a good mimic, able to give a passable impersonation of Vera Lynn. Her parents and neighbours were killed in the autumn of 1944 by a Buzz-Bomb and the young woman went off to live with her grandparents in rural Essex. She hated being away from London and having to work on a local farm. With the impetuosity of youth, after a few months she left with the little money she had saved, leaving a note for her grandmother, whom she was convinced was pleased to see the back of her. It didn't take long for Vera to find trouble. Standing in the busy concourse of Victoria station, trying to work out which tube line she needed to get to Bethnal Green, she was approached by a good-looking man in his early thirties. He took her for a coffee and told her he knew of a room she could rent in Paddington. Despite her better judgement she went with him and, sure enough, the room was warm with a bed, dressing table and an easy chair. It also had a carpet – luxury indeed. The man, who called himself Joe, was attentive and charming. She was flattered and thoughts of seeking out old friends in the East End were put on hold. Joe took her to the pictures and out dancing. He hinted at marriage. This was a whirlwind romance and she imagined she was in love. They became lovers. She wasn't a virgin, having already slept with a couple of farmhands in Essex. Well, there was nothing much else to do!

Within days the atmosphere changed. The warm flat was now often freezing, with Joe claiming he had run out of money for the meter. He disappeared for most of the day, leaving her stranded, hungry and with no money in a bleak 1947 Paddington. When he first suggested that she went out to meet men off the train at Paddington station and show them a good time in one of the darkened alleyways for money, she was appalled. It was then that she should have walked away, but she was penniless. Just this once, then. Ten bob for a knee trembler up against a wall at the back of Praed Street. That done, Joe launched another charm offensive. She was far too beautiful for that. Why not take them back to the flat and charge a couple of quid? Before long she would be independent and able to pursue her ambition as a dancer. Now Joe was attentive again, always hanging around and 'borrowing' the money she had earned.

She felt trapped, but when Joe suggested a day in the West End her mood lightened. Rather than a trip to the stores on Oxford Street, she was taken to a grubby basement club in Dean Street. She was introduced to a sallow-skinned man in his fifties who was referred to simply as 'boss'. He looked her up and down, much as the Essex farmers had at the beasts they were planning to buy at market. There was a muffled conversation with Joe who left without even offering her a glance. 'You work for me now, you understand?' Although she saw the 'boss' many times over the years, she never spoke to him again. She was left to a succession of minders and heavies who oversaw her activities. She was able to keep up to £20 a week, but was never allowed out without her maid. She was abused and occasionally beaten by her minders. Fear of violence was always lurking as over the years she became resigned and numbed by entertaining over a dozen punters a day. She was sold on to new 'bosses' over the years and even fell in love with one when she was in her forties. He promised they would make a new life for themselves, but again she was thwarted when he was sent to jail for a lengthy stretch. As she grew older her looks faded. She went solo, ending a forty-year career lurking in darkened doorways in Lisle Street. She had started drinking heavily but her earnings were not enough to sustain her.

The next fifteen years were the happiest of her life, with not a single man featuring. She had met Gloria, an attractive young prostitute, who reminded her of herself when she was in her twenties. Gloria was looking for a reliable maid, and who better than someone like Vera. Gloria was self-employed and specialised in the bizarre. Not for her was trawling the streets. Her clients contacted her by phone and she restricted her punters to three a day. At what she charged she could afford to. Vera was allowed to live in the Bayswater Road flat while Gloria took the last tube out to Kingsbury and her neat, three-bedroomed semi. The two existed like mother and daughter until Gloria retired to suburban respectability in 2000. Four years later Vera was back living in Soho as her sad life drew to a close. It is likely that some of what she told me was fabricated, but I am sure that there was an underlying authenticity to her tale. One city, millions of different stories – luckily few as sad as Vera's.

Of course, not all working-class girls took to the streets or, indeed, longed for a stage career. Vast numbers took jobs in factories. London was still a major hub of manufacturing, although this was already in decline. In my early twenties, I was a trainee manager for a handbag and leather goods manufacturer with factories in Hackney and Islington. For some weeks during my training I was the only young man working on a floor of about a hundred women assembling and packing expensive leather bags. Initially, it was quite intimidating as they set me up for various embarrassing situations. I grew up very quickly during those weeks in an atmosphere of what today would be categorised as sexual harassment. It was great fun. London humour has to be among the quickest in the world. As my confidence grew I remember saying to one girl, 'Janet, your slip is showing'. Without a moment's hesitation she replied, 'So what, mate, it's clean and paid for.' It was here that I could understand the warmth and spirit of wartime London. I thought these women were all great, irreverent, outrageous and street-wise. An apt description for London itself in those far-off days.

Based on what happened to Vera when she arrived in London, it is just as well that Anne Prowse was met at Paddington station by a universal aunt whose job it was to chaperone her across London to Waterloo. Anne remembers the hustle and bustle of the station, with its snorting steam engines and the scurrying porters with luggage stacked high on barrows. She rather liked the hectic pace, having been brought up in India. Arriving in England in 1946, she went to school in the tranquil seaside setting of Little Common, just outside Bexhill. Leaving school in 1952, like Shirley Balmer she had set her heart on a career in nursing. She had already attended interviews at St Bart's and the Middlesex hospital before settling on the latter. Having achieved more than the five required O Levels including maths and English, she was ready to take on her six-week preliminary training, during which time she was paid £1 a month. It was now down to serious training and, as at Guy's, the hours were long, the work arduous and discipline really strict. Despite this, life was fun. The nurses' home in Foley Street had a wonderful dining room and an underground swimming pool. On £7 a month when in full training, window shopping was a favourite way of spending time off. She remembers attending fashion shows with friends at Heals and falling in love with a coat that cost a full month's wages (luckily, paid for by her parents). In those days the nursing profession was generally revered and the student nurses at Middlesex also received free theatre tickets for all the top shows, including *Guys and Dolls, Oklahoma* and *Salad Days*. She also went to see Yehudi Menuhin perform at the Albert Hall with Stéphane Grappelli.

Although colour prejudice was taking hold in London, Anne remembers two wonderful Jamaican nurses who were popular with both staff and patients. During a spell in the gynaecological department, Anne had to walk each night to the nurses' home in Soho Square. An attractive young woman walking in Soho in a nurse's uniform obviously prompted a spate of outlandish offers. By 1959 Anne had qualified and she became a ward sister. She could now afford a flat in Swiss Cottage, which she shared with four other girls. Their three-bedroomed accommodation, which had a small sitting room, was rented for £40 a month. On Sundays she had to cycle to the hospital as the tube didn't start early enough. The intensity of training these young women had to undergo is vividly illustrated in Nina Sheeran's book *Tea Leaves under the Bed*. This was a golden age for nursing as career opportunities for girls were still so restricted. Nursing sixty years ago attracted a highly talented calibre of young women who today would probably find a more glamorous and better-paid occupation, but then they possibly wouldn't have ended up marrying doctors, which both Shirley and Anne did.

A love of music was the glue that joined all women from whatever background. Dance music, standards and rock 'n' roll crossed the class boundaries. For Beryl Hart who lived in Battersea, it was 'serious' or classical music that fascinated her from a young age. She attended the Royal School of Music, where she studied the organ and violin. Later, having married, she auditioned and was accepted into the Royal Choral Society. By 1957, although pregnant, she appeared at the Proms performing under Sir Malcolm Sargent in *Gerontious*.

Sixty years ago, these housewives, nurses, secretaries, factory workers, models, showgirls and prostitutes formed a 1950s sisterhood in the years before a real equality of opportunity. They represented an era which was generally tough for women, where they were in turn taken for granted or exploited, but they were a tough bunch. They endured and mostly prospered. They worked hard, whatever their calling and can surely be excused if they occasionally shake their collective heads at the accelerating changes in today's world.

9
Radio Fun

Before that rainy day in June 1953 when the nation fell in love with a flickering screen in their living rooms, the wireless held sway. For most families the radio was a constant companion, particularly for the millions of housewives whose whole lives revolved around the home. It was a background noise at breakfast before their husbands and children were packed off for the day. *Housewives Choice* offered a cheery menu of popular music to accompany bed making and general tidying. For a time the radio was blocked out as the Hoover went to work. Elevenses would be taken while listening to *Music while you work* and later in the morning *Workers' playtime* usually featured a well-known comedian. And so the day progressed with the radio still left on even when there was no one in the house. It was a constant friend to welcome you home when heavily laden from the shops.

On a winter's evening after the children had been put to bed, it was companionable to sit in front of a blazing fire with your husband, listening to *Dick Barton* or *Paul Temple*. Radio had developed since its early amateurish days to offer a diverse menu of programmes catering for a wide range of tastes. It still retained much of its Reithian ethos to 'inform, educate and entertain'. To facilitate this the BBC now broadcast on the *Home Service*, the *Light Programme* and the minority interest *Third Programme*. Between them they covered features, drama, comedy, music and outside broadcasts where the emphasis was on sport. There were also special programmes aimed at children. Before the intrusion of television, audiences regularly exceeded ten million, although the poor old *Third Programme*'s output was so highbrow that their listening figures were sometimes too small to be assessed.

During the 1950s the radio continued to be a regular companion. Its development reflected life in Britain at that time as it peeled away a couple of layers of traditional output and offered a slight nod towards the modern attitudes of the sixties. Astonishingly, there are still a few programmes that live on today. *Any Questions*, first broadcast in 1948, was an offshoot of the *Brains Trust,* which had started life seven years previously. It retains its Friday-night slot discussing world and local events of the day. It now seems rather neutered, being largely a platform for politicians to bicker. Previously, the panellists enjoyed the country wisdom of regulars like Ralph Wightman and Ted Moult. Freddie Grisewood chaired the programme for almost twenty years until 1967. Fitting perfectly into the paternal, restrained influence so admired by the BBC, he presided over heated discussions and arguments with a soothing, middle-class charm.

Desert Island Discs was created by Roy Plomley way back in 1942 and offered a rare chance to hear music on the *Home Service*. Like so many simple ideas, it has endured as thousands of the rich, famous and good have treated us to their choice of records while cast away on an imaginary desert island. The selection of guests remained pretty mainstream during the 1950s, featuring largely actors, sports personalities and serious musicians. Despite the emerging pop scene, Alma Cogan was one of the few pop stars to appear on the programme until Eve Boswell became one of Plomley's last castaways of the decade in December 1959. Like the programme itself, her selection of music was safe and uncontroversial, mixing Glenn Miller with Tchaikovsky and Ethel Merman with Rachmaninov.

'Celebrities' as such didn't really exist in the 1950s, but someone who was near to this sainted status was Wilfred Pickles. In a world dominated by perfect English, he stood out as a BBC newsreader due to his broad Yorkshire accent. For over twenty years, starting in 1942, he presented a travelling quiz show which captured a massive audience of some twenty million. The show was transmitted live and visited every corner of the country. The quiz was secondary to the interviews with the contestants, and Pickles had an ability to extract stories that charmed and amused his devoted followers.

With typical BBC patronising logic, it was presumed that after lunch the busy British housewife should be allowed an hour to herself away from domestic chores. Based on this assumption, *Woman's Hour* was launched in 1946. During the fifties, the programme generally steered clear of controversy, and the openness of some of today's topics would have had listeners colouring up with embarrassment. No matter, *Woman's Hour*, with its regular serial reading, became a friend and comfort to a generation of women who were largely confined to a life of household chores. Just before *Woman's Hour*, over a million tuned into *Listen with Mother*. This was a fifteen-minute programme of songs and nursery rhymes for children under five. Its popularity came even before its catchphrases became an obsession; 'Are you sitting comfortably? Then I'll begin' is an early memory for many.

Long-running programmes that became almost institutions followed no set pattern and yet were embraced by the public and have endured. When Alistair Cooke was asked by the BBC to give a weekly talk from America, nobody foresaw a long run. Starting at a time when almost all Britons knew about the States was gleaned by watching Hollywood films, Cooke's seemingly random chats about American life struck a chord. Despite the fact he had grown up in England, his mid-Atlantic accent became a regular favourite on the *Home Service* and his *Letter from America* ran for almost half a century.

What is it that makes panel games such a popular staple of the BBC's radio output? While not being demanding, they provide an opportunity for the listener to relax and be amused. The most popular of these shows during the fifties was *Twenty Questions*. Again, it was a simple idea, to identify an item that was either animal, vegetable or mineral within an allowed twenty attempts to find the answer. The show, broadcast in front of a studio audience, featured a panel that variously included Richard Dimbleby, Jack Train, Anona Winn and grumpy old Gilbert Harding.

Back in the fifties, the BBC liked clear boundaries in the classification of their programmes. 'Auntie' decided women were likely to be their most dedicated listeners, and programmes such as *Woman's Hour* and *Housewives' Choice* targeted them at key times during the day. Children were catered for, as were sports fans with programmes like *Sports Report*. *Workers' playtime* and *Music while you work* were assumed in a paternalistic way to be the sort of entertainment enjoyed by those 'factory types'. Despite this assumption that the 'Beeb' knew what was best for the public, all these shows continued for the entire decade. *Housewives' Choice* first appeared on the *Light Programme* in 1946. One of the most popular record request programmes, it ran until 1967. During its life it was introduced at various times by Sam Costa, Eamonn Andrews and the irascible Gilbert Harding. It was a Scottish bandleader, George Elrick, who was most associated with the show. His singing, along with the programme's theme tune, told everyone it was nine o'clock and it became something of a national symbol. Bright, breezy and undemanding, the show was the starting gun for the commencement of the day's housework.

Music in all its various forms was an important part of radio's output. *Music while you work* had been introduced in 1940 to help morale and productivity in Britain's factories. Carrying on into the fifties, it provided non-stop light music twice a day, performed by a different band for each show. There was a huge schedule to fill, so music was constantly blaring out from Bakelite sets across the land. The dreaded theatre organ of Sandy MacPherson is an early memory for those growing up in the 1950s. He also introduced a popular programme of religious music called *Chapel in the valley*. As the decade progressed, musical tastes were changing. Sunday lunchtimes were enlivened by the dulcet tones of Billy Cotton shouting out 'Wakey, wakey' to introduce his band show. This was the BBC putting its toe into the popular music pool. Popular maybe with older listeners, but it was generally derided by the young, who had now been introduced to real pop music and, importantly, Radio Luxembourg.

Two-O-Eight, your station of the stars provided a vehicle for teenagers to listen to their type of music. The station started the top twenty charts back in 1948. By the mid-fifties, youngsters turned their transistors to full volume as Elvis, Cliff and the Everly Brothers were just a few of the stars striving for the coveted number one spot. Pete Murray, David Jacobs and the now reviled Jimmy Savile learnt their trade at the station. Strangely, it is a West Country football tipster who became most associated with those days on Radio

Luxembourg. His slow Bristol accent encouraged listeners to invest in his 'infra-draw method'. Each week he gave his address as 'Horace Batchelor, Department One, Keynsham, spelt K-E-Y-N-S-H-A-M!' Somehow this has stuck in the minds of all of those who were around at the time. It seems unlikely that his 'infra-draw' method made many fortunes. His estate was valued at just over £100,000 when he died in the seventies, so it was Horace who was the ultimate winner.

The threat of Radio Luxembourg prompted the BBC to target a teenage audience, so *Pick of the Pops* was first broadcast in 1955. It was a faltering step, with Franklin Englemann being the first presenter. No way in touch with the emerging youth culture, he was quickly replaced by the knowledgeable, but hardly trendy, Alan Dell. By 1958 David Jacobs was at the helm and the show's potential acknowledged by transferring the programme from mid-week to a prime Saturday night slot. *Saturday Club*, introduced by Brian Matthew, also catered for the teenage audience. For two hours from 10 a.m. the *Light Programme* offered the best in today's 'pop' entertainment. Since 1990 Matthew has introduced *Sounds of the 60s* for a generation of geriatric 'pop pickers'.

Classical music also remained an important (if less popular) output, centring on the Promenade concerts. The 1950s was notable for the inclusion for the first time of orchestras drawn from outside London, including the Halle and the Liverpool Philharmonic. By 1959, William Glock, the BBC Controller of Music, started to alter the generally staid repertoire. Works totally new to the Proms were introduced, but it was to be the mid-sixties before foreign orchestras were invited to perform.

Since its inception, comedy had formed an important part of the BBC's output. It was important, but carefully monitored, or (perhaps more accurately), censored; no smut,

vulgarity and as little innuendo as possible. Having a dig
at foreigners with funny accents was fine, as were mother-
in-law jokes, but sex, religion and royalty were no-go areas.
Despite these restrictions, the fifties was a golden age for
radio comedy. There were exceptions, of course. Did anyone
really find *The Clitheroe Kid* funny? Also, how was it possible
to broadcast a show featuring a ventriloquist who couldn't
keep his mouth shut? Television exposed Peter Brough's lack
of technique, which saw his popularity tumble. Never mind,
for years *Educating Archie* (Brough's dummy) was a firm
favourite on the *Light Programme*. It was also a vehicle for
introducing the talents of Max Bygraves and Tony Hancock
to the listening public. Before *Hancock's Half Hour* started
in 1954, it was left to old timers like Al Read and Ted Ray
to keep the country laughing. Northern comics had always
been popular and Al Read achieved stardom in the early
fifties with his *Pictures from life* and his catchphrase 'Right
Monkey'. Ted Ray was a Liverpudlian and he starred with
Kitty Bluett, who played his wife in a wise-cracking show,
Ray's a laugh. Although Ted Ray was a product of the old
music hall tradition, here was a stepping stone towards a
new type of radio show that relied on situation comedy
rather than one-line gags.

Tony Hancock was a unique talent. For a time he was
resident comedian at the Windmill Theatre, surely the
most demanding of venues. Progressing through his radio
appearances on *Educating Archie*, he teamed up with two
of the most talented comic scriptwriters. It was Ray Galton
and Alan Simpson who made the bullets for Hancock to
fire, and Hancock did so brilliantly. He was joined by Syd
James and Kenneth Williams to create an iconic series of
radio comedy. So popular was *Hancock's Half Hour* that it
transferred to television in 1956 and for a time they ran

concurrently. Although successful, the television series never quite matched the original. The attraction of radio remained, being able to conjure up pictures in your own mind.

The biggest breakthrough in radio and British comedy came with the introduction in 1952 of the *Goon Show*. Love it or hate it, the whole concept was groundbreaking. The show began life the year before as *Crazy People* and boy, this small group was crazy. Peter Sellers, Harry Secombe and Michael Bentine had, like Tony Hancock, served their apprenticeships at the Windmill. The seemingly unstructured *Goon Show* ran for over 200 episodes, although Michael Bentine left after a few months. Together with Spike Milligan, Sellers and Secombe assembled a cult show. While Milligan created most of the bizarre characters, they were interpreted with manic enthusiasm by his talented colleagues. The BBC was extremely nervous about the content of the show and Peter Sellers was banned from his impersonations of an ageing Winston Churchill. Eventually, the three went their separate ways to varying degrees of stardom. Milligan always reckoned that the show caused him so much stress that it affected his mental health. It appears many comedians are tortured souls. The 'Goons' are important in that they broke down previously accepted barriers. The future of British comedy was also being developed by *Beyond our Ken*. With scripts written by Barry Took and Eric Merriman, the show was fronted by Kenneth Horne. He really acted as the straight man, while Hugh Paddick and Kenneth Williams (another tortured soul) got the laughs. It is one of the few comedy shows from the 1950s that remains funny today with its outrageously risqué humour. While the BBC was lowering its moral guard slightly, a live broadcast by comedian Max Miller threw them into panic. Known as *The Cheeky Chappie*, Max veered right off-piste when finishing his act with this little gem:

When roses are red
They're ready for plucking
When a girl is sixteen ...

There was then a pause as the audience drew in its collective breath. Miller concluded with a cheery 'Goodnight, ladies and gentlemen' just before the programme was taken off air. It was five years before Max Miller appeared on the BBC again.

Despite this rare lapse in perceived good taste, the BBC generally steered along a path of respectability. Controversy was to be avoided, and yet in 1951 there was an eruption of anger when it was decided to drop the exciting *Dick Barton – Special Agent* series and replace it with a boring series about the life of country folk. Since 1946 *The Devil's Gallop* had introduced the adventures of Captain Richard Barton and his two sidekicks, Cockney Snowy White and Scot Jock Anderson. They were former NCOs, thus preserving the social pecking order preferred by the BBC. It will come as no surprise to learn that most of the crooks and dangerous adversaries were foreign. No matter, an audience of fifteen million, particularly the young, loved the show and were horrified at its removal. Who would have guessed that its replacement, *The Archers*, would still be running over sixty years later? Even today the citizens of Ambridge are defined by their accents. The posh get posher and country folk are represented by actors who appear to be aping the late Bernard Miles.

The BBC was determined to show good overcoming evil in its drama productions. *PC 49* ran until 1953. Here again our hero is an ex-public schoolboy, albeit working his way through the ranks, after a stint at Hendon Police College. We were in an era where heroes had to be drawn from the establishment, loyally supported by working-class helpers, and the villains were frequently nasty foreigners. Brian Reece played the lead role and the show ran for over 100 episodes. The programme was so popular that it spawned films and books as Archie Berkeley-Willoughby, our super constable, felt the collars of spivs, louts and crooks throughout Q Division.

Another upper-crust detective also enjoyed huge popularity during the 1950s. Created by Francis Durbridge, the first series of *Paul Temple* was broadcast in 1938. Like *Dick Barton*, our hero was a gentleman, the son of Lieutenant General Ian Temple. Paul wrote fictitious detective stories and with this experience was apparently far better at solving crimes than dear old PC Plod. By 1950 he was being played by Kim Peacock with Marjorie Westbury as his wife Steve. The signature tune of Vivian Ellis's *Coronation Scot* became synonymous with the show and heightened the public's anticipation. Here was the archetypal British hero who solved the most heinous crimes, while hardly seeming to break sweat. By 1954, Peter Coke took over the role of *Paul Temple*. His wife was still played by Marjorie Westbury until they solved their last case together in 1968. Again, many of the villains tended to be shady foreigners. Even when he was in huge danger, the nearest our hero ever got to showing fear or deep emotion was to utter, 'By Timothy'. Gentlemen don't panic or swear. Not English gentlemen, anyway!

Just as class was a dominant factor in everyday life during the 1950s, so it was with the BBC's drama output, albeit preserved in a rather ham-fisted way. *Mrs Dale's Diary* was a long-running soap opera set in a south London suburb. The Dales, doctor Jim and his wife Mary, were solidly middle class. They spoke 'proper' while their daily help, Mrs Maggs, was a parody of good, honest, working-class London stock. The series followed the lives of the Dales family, including their children Gwen and Bob. Some relief was offered by Mary's rather racy sister Sally. Mary Dale was played by

1. Crowds waiting to enter the Dome of Discovery at the South Bank Festival of Britain.

2. Queues waiting to gain entrance to Battersea Fun Fair.

3. The Dance Pavilion at Battersea Pleasure Gardens.

Above left: 4. 'Square' men's clothes were gradually sidelined.

Above right: 5. A flower seller in Piccadilly – a reminder of vanishing London.

Below: 6. A drab London street in the early fifties.

7. The royal mourning coach at the funeral of King George VI.

8. Smog masks gave little protection.

9. A 1952 view of Oxford Street taken from the roof of the John Lewis store.

10. Oxford Street viewing platform for the coronation.

WHAT YOU DO

Each Souvenir is offered FREE for labels from four pounds of Bournville Cocoa. You can save four 1lb. labels, eight ½lb. labels, or sixteen ¼lb. packet tops (the part printed with the name Cadbury's) or you can mix all three, provided that your labels and tops are taken from a total of four pounds of Bournville Cocoa. You must send the complete label from the tin.

When you have the right number of labels and/or tops, write in block letters on a sheet of paper the Souvenir you prefer, your name and full address (including county) and particulars of the labels you send (see example below).

CORONATION MUG
Mrs. A. SMITH
12 HIGH STREET, SHEPSTON, KENT
3 — 1lb. labels
8 — ½lb. tops

Enclose this with the labels in a strong envelope and post (2½d. stamp) to Cadburys, Department C5, Bournville, Birmingham.

WHEN YOU DO IT

Send in your labels as soon as possible. The sooner you send, the better your chance of securing the Souvenir you choose. There is a limited quantity of Coronation Mugs. Cadburys will deal in strict rotation with all applications. You can be sure, however, that one of the Coronation Souvenirs will be despatched to you—even if your first choice is not available. Cadburys cannot begin despatch before January, 1953, but start saving now and send in your labels AS SOON AS POSSIBLE.

THERE'S A TIME LIMIT

This offer closes on May 1st, 1953, and labels cannot be accepted after that date. This offer applies ONLY TO BOURNVILLE COCOA and is valid in Great Britain and Northern Ireland only.

CADBURY'S
CORONATION SOUVENIRS
FREE
FOR LABELS FROM
BOURNVILLE COCOA
Offer closes MAY 1st 1953

CORONATION MUG

You will be delighted with the style and quality of this Coronation Mug. It was made specially for Cadburys by leading pottery craftsmen. The Souvenir design shows a charming portrait in decorative setting of Her Majesty Queen Elizabeth II.

11. Coronation souvenirs were carefully regulated.

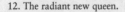

12. The radiant new queen.

13. Evening wear for coronation year.

Above: 14. Invitation to a coronation ball held at the Savoy.

Below: 15. Guests at a coronation ball.

16. A bedroom at the Savoy in the 1950s.

17. The American Bar at the Savoy. The moneyed class were elbowing their way into London's establishment watering holes.

18. The Dorchester, decorated to celebrate the coronation.

19. 'Debs Delight' at Queen Charlotte's Ball.

Above left: 20. Clothes for the smarter man in the year of the coronation.

Above right: 21. Teddy Boys were to be seen on every street corner with their foppish suits and greased-back hair. Some found them irritating.

22. The Strand Palace offered a veneer of luxury for the middle classes, but was avoided by the establishment.

23–6. The Messina brothers, kings of London's vice trade.

27. The Harrow & Wealdstone train disaster.

28. Business tycoons were beginning to be seen in luxury cars like this Daimler, previously the preserve of 'old money'.

29. West Indians arriving in London were met with hostility and were placed firmly at the bottom of the social pecking order.

30. Londoners were horrified by the redevelopment scheme for Piccadilly Circus, proposed by property tycoon Jack Cotton.

31. A horrendous 'cutting-edge' kitchen design from the early fifties.

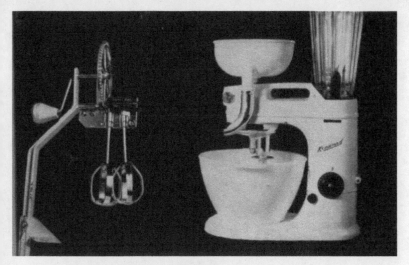

32. Modern kitchen gadgets were all the rage.

33. By the early fifties, even men were being encouraged to take an interest in the kitchen.

34. Regent Street in 1953.

35. Piccadilly Circus. London was slowly casting off the shadow of war and beginning to regain its old swagger.

36. The City of London was central to hopes of the country's financial future.

Right: 37. Princess Margaret, complete with the type of shoes condemned by Nancy Mitford as 'common'.

Below: 38. A busy street in Woolwich. It wasn't just the West End stores that attracted crowds.

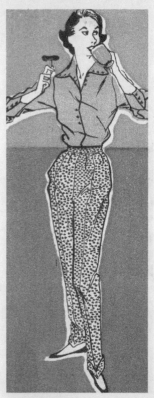

Left: 39. 1954 daytime chic.

Below: 40. Suburbia retained its air of calm respectability.

Washable, durably-pleated
cotton, in black with
rose print design.
Skirt **£6.19.6**;
strapless top **£2.12.6**;
stole **19.11**;
shirt top *(not illustrated)* **£3.9.6**

BY APPOINTMENT
SUPPLIERS OF FURNISHINGS
TO THE
LATE KING GEORGE VI.

Peter Jones

Sloane Square, S.W.1 | SLOane 3434

A BRANCH OF THE JOHN LEWIS PARTNERSHIP

41. A 1957 advertisement for Peter Jones.

Left: 42. The small, flickering screen dominated most living rooms.

Below: 43. It was television that revolutionised everyday living during the 1950s.

Above left: 44. Nurse Shirley.

Above right: 45. Meet the midwife.

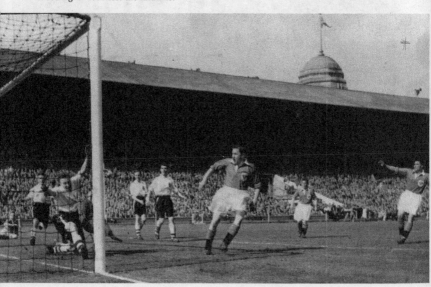

46. The 1953 Cup Final was dramatic, but soon the English game was to be exposed by Hungary.

47. With sweets off ration, children were able to indulge themselves.

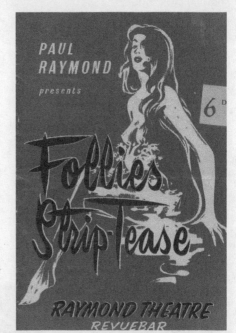

Right: 48. Paul Raymond's Revue Bar challenged Britain's previously puritanical attitude to nudity.

Below: 49. Carnaby Street became the Mecca for the fashion-conscious young.

Top left: 50. A typical early 1950s salad.

Top right: 51. By the mid-fifties, dieting was on the menu for many women.

Bottom left: 52. Fabulous 'glamour puss' model Jean Sporle.

Bottom right: 53. The floodgates to outright pornography were breached by photographer Harrison Marks, seen here with Pamela Green.

What a Good Idea!

Stirling Moss with his Idea

WE ARE STARTING an exciting new series in WOMAN this week! It's called "What a Good Idea." In it, famous people like Stirling Moss the racing motorist, Beryl Grey the ballet star and Vivian Blaine from "Guys and Dolls," and others, have agreed to share their favourite ideas with you. *In each case it's something extremely useful—an idea which you can copy*, and we show you how to do it in colour. Stirling starts the series and you can see him, with *his* idea, on the left.

The picture at the top, incidentally, comes from one of WOMAN'S complete stories—"The Wedding and the Wonder"—it's a romantic story about that fortunate couple who have obviously been lucky with the weather on their holiday. Another complete story is by Mary Sergeant, and there's a further instalment of our serial "The Dark Avenue."

Also in this week's WOMAN are highlights from the life story of Prince Philip . . . patterns for a blouse and a jumper . . . some really delicious recipes from Jersey . . . and a bright new make-up plan to keep you ready for most emergencies.

It's plain from all these good things why WOMAN is the most amazingly successful magazine in history—read by over six million women every week.

54. Women's magazines enjoyed huge circulations.

	Carafe	Half-Carafe			Carafe	Half-Carafe
BOURGOGNE ROSE	12/6	7/-	BORDEAUX ROUGE ·		10/6	6/-
BORDEAUX BLANC	10/6	6/-	HOCK · · ·		15/6	8/6
		CHATEAU YQUEM *by the glass* -		7/6		

DINER FIXE AU CHOIX 40/-

THREE COURSES

LES HORS D'ŒUVRES

Le Melon Rafraîchi   Le Saumon Fumé d'Ecosse

La Coupe de Grapefruit Cerisette

LES POTAGES

La Crème Agnès Sorel

Ox-tail Soup

LE POISSON

La Goujonnade de Sole Murat

L'ENTREE

Le Poulet du Surrey Albuféra
Roast Surrey Chicken with Rice, Foie Gras, Cream Sauce, Quenelles and Mushrooms

LES LEGUMES

Les Pommes Amandines   Les Petits Pois à l'Anglaise

Le Cœur de Laitue Princesse

L'ENTREMET

Le Parfait Glacé Napolitain   Les Douceurs de Dames

SAVOY RESTAURANT   *WEDNESDAY 23rd MAY 1956*

55. An Aux Choix menu offered at the Savoy.

56. The early fifties, depicted here by caddish-looking men and demure young ladies, had all but vanished by the end of the decade.

57. The coffee bar revolution started in Soho with popular outlets like Heaven and Hell.

Left: 58. Cute Windmill girl Winkie Winkfield.

Below: 59. Picadilly Circus by night.

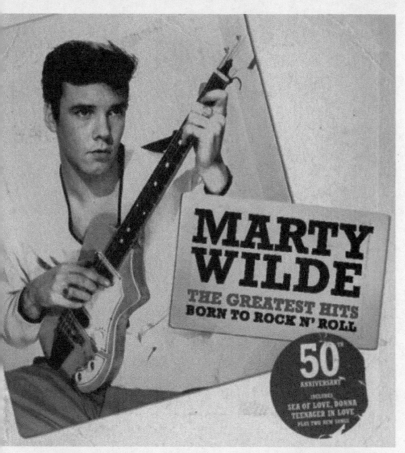

60. With the coffee bars came a string of home-grown pop stars, including Marty Wilde.

61. Somerset Maugham, along with his contemporaries, found the new wave of 'kitchen sink' writers difficult to stomach.

62. The sleek but ill-fated Comet gave Britain an initial advantage in jet-powered travel.

63. Despite all the modernisation going on, London clung to its love of ancient street markets.

64. The days of the old-fashioned grocer were numbered.

65. Grosvenor House, Park Lane entrance.

Ellis Powell until 1963. The role was then taken on by Jessie Matthews, whose real life dramas and scandals would have had the fictional Mrs Dale grasping the smelling salts.

Sitcoms were already a popular form of entertainment in the 1950s. It provided an undemanding type of entertainment, typified with the very popular series of *Life with the Lyons*. Ben Lyon and his wife Bebe Daniels arrived in London before the war. They marketed themselves as 'Hollywood's happiest married couple'. Maybe they could have claimed 'Hollywood's only happily married couple'! Whatever, their weekly show included their children Barbara and Richard, and Molly Weir who played their housekeeper. It was pretty banal stuff, but the American voice carried all before it in those innocent times. Audience figures always jumped when *In Town Tonight*, broadcast on Saturday nights, included interviews with the likes of Errol Flynn, Jane Russell or some other American mega-star.

A favourite sitcom featured a young George Cole playing the goofy David Alexander Bliss in *A Life of Bliss*. Petula Clark joined the cast in 1957 to play his girlfriend. Percy Edwards, whose animal impersonations made him something of a star, portrayed Bliss's irritating dog. Unfortunately, listening to recordings of the show today, the overall impression is also one of irritation. Like so much of the 1950s' output, it hasn't aged well. Tastes change, perceptions and accents also. A programme that became an institution and is fondly remembered by those growing up in the 1950s was *Children's Hour*. Here was a unique mix of plays, serials and features on subjects ranging from history and science to wildlife. It was introduced by Derek McCulloch, known to all as 'Uncle Mac'. He really was a kindly uncle to a whole generation, who still remember him with affection as they enter old age. The programme was particularly important to those who had lost parents in the war. In a tough and changing world, it offered a sense of familiarity and stability. A real friend. *Children's Hour* again projected what was essentially a middle-class, middle-brow view of how children should develop. It was an attempt by the BBC to guide their young listeners to be polite and caring but also inquisitive. Despite this undoubted manipulation, millions of children tuned in each weekday afternoon at five o'clock with a sense of anticipation. All ages were catered for with favourites like *Toytown*, starring grumpy old Mr Grouser, the grocer. *Winnie the Pooh* was also popular, featuring well-known actors like Norman Shelley, Jon Pertwee and Violet Carson who made regular appearances. 'Uncle Mac' finished each programme with the words, 'Goodnight children' and after a pause and with great emphasis, 'Everywhere'. This still evokes a certain emotion and was a source of well-being for many youngsters from difficult backgrounds.

One of the most popular programmes with children was *Just William*; written by Richmal Crompton and starring Charles Hawtrey and a young Patricia Hayes, it featured the horrible, lisping Violet Elizabeth Bott, who constantly threatened to scream and scream until she was sick if she was thwarted in any way. *Just William* was naughty, scruffy and reckless, and was forever annoying adults. A perfect role model for a young boy in the 1950s.

By 1954 'Uncle Mac' was introducing the first children's record request programme. *Children's Favourites* initially featured old regulars like *The Laughing Policeman* and *Tubby the Tuba*, but tastes were changing. Poor old 'Uncle Mac' was out of his comfort zone playing the likes of Elvis and Adam Faith. Space was still found for *Nellie the elephant* and *I'm a pink toothbrush*, but a gap was developing. Teenagers had left all that sort of stuff behind. Now they wanted songs of teenage angst and rock 'n' roll. They couldn't wait for ten o'clock and Brian Matthew to play some real music.

Top of the Form brought youngsters back under control. Here was a quiz show featured weekly on the *Light Programme*. Two teams from rival schools were questioned on their general knowledge. The BBC was in its element. A rather patronising tone was adopted by the question master as the youngsters either struggled with or dismissively answered the questions put to them. The teams were drawn from different age groups, ranging from under thirteen to under eighteen. It was a programme probably enjoyed more by parents than youngsters; the latter, given the chance, would creep upstairs to their bedrooms and play the latest hits on their new record player.

Signature tunes become embedded in our minds and are synonymous with certain long-running programmes. Each Saturday night during the football season Herbert Bath's 'Out of the blue' was played introducing *Sports Report*. The reading of the football results and reports of matches played all over the country continues to attract millions of loyal listeners. Possibly the best known presenter of the programme was Eamonn Andrews. The lilt of an Irish accent is very suited to radio. It has a warmth that quickly grows into familiarity. Later it was a factor in the huge popularity enjoyed by Terry Wogan. Andrews, a Dubliner, had previously been known for his boxing commentaries, but he proved an adept link man and helped develop *Sports Report* into a slick, fast-moving show. Later his career blossomed on television, and he achieved celebrity status long before his death in 1987.

The very first *Sports Report* had been introduced by Raymond Glendenning, a Welsh chartered accountant sporting a handlebar moustache. He was an excitable

commentator on a wide range of sports. He was famously
capable of speaking up to 300 words a minute, and his
commentaries were breathless and not always accurate. He
had real difficulty in remembering the colours of jockeys'
silks, occasionally announcing the wrong winner. 'Auntie'
BBC didn't really approve of gambling so no odds were
given, which rather neutered coverage of big races like the
Derby and Grand National. Glendenning was more at home
covering boxing, where he only had a couple of names to
remember. He remained the BBC's main sports commentator
until 1963, by which time experts on specific sports were
favoured.

Cricket probably had an even greater following sixty years
ago than today. It was a source of constant irritation that
broadcasts were often terminated at peak points in a game.
In 1956 it was decided that a ball-by-ball commentary would
be broadcast and *Test Match Special* was born. Allocated to
the *Third Programme*, it soon acquired a devoted audience,
many of whom had not been previously interested in the
sport. Over the years it developed into an amusing talking
shop, in which at times cricket appeared to be of secondary
interest only. Early stalwarts included Rex Alston and John
Arlott, an ex-policeman from Hampshire. His wonderfully
soft burr came to represent to many the English summer. A
man of varied interests, he would often go off on tangents
while managing to keep his audience under his spell. It was
said that he tried to imagine he was talking to a blind person
and his descriptions were so vivid that it was reckoned you
could 'smell the grass' when he was talking. By contrast, E.
W. (Jim) Swanton was very much the establishment figure.
His voice, described as 'fruity', belonged to a previous era,
but he was a knowledgeable sports journalist, who continued
appearing on *Test Match Special* into the seventies. It was

this rich mix of personalities that has helped the programme obtain its cult status.

It is strange to note how many programmes have survived and developed over the years. The *Today* programme is now moving towards its sixtieth birthday. It was launched in September 1957 on the *Home Service*. It is now considered to be the most important and influential of current affairs programmes, with politicians scrapping to appear on the key slot after the eight o'clock news. Initially the programme was presented by Alan Skempton, but in 1958 one of the great radio personalities took over. Jack de Manio was relaxed, avuncular and accident-prone, which added to his attraction. His career at the BBC was suspended in 1956 when as a continuity announcer he made the mistake of introducing a feature *The Land of the Niger* as 'The Land of the Nigger'. Public outrage led to his suspension, but within two years he was back in favour and let loose to entertain and inform the British public. In the early days the programme was less concerned with world events and politics and his easygoing interviewing style helped increase the programme's audience, as did his famously inaccurate time checks.

The decade had been extremely challenging for radio with the growth of television but, contrary to the views of many, audiences didn't collapse for long. There was obviously room for both mediums. Car radios were now being widely fitted, which provided a new and growing audience. Radio was still able to react far quicker to world events than TV. Its appeal remained unique and its future was assured.

10

The Effects of Television

Although it was the coronation in 1953 that had the public rushing to buy or rent a television set, transmissions had been made since 1935. Alexandra Palace in North London was known as the birthplace of television and London remained central to its development as its power and appeal changed a nation's way of life. By the mid-fifties, much of the BBC's output had been transferred to Lime Green Studios in Shepherds Bush, while Alexandra Palace became the headquarters for news coverage.

With a monopoly, the BBC developed their output in a responsible, measured way. While many of the programmes viewed today seem trite and amateurish, great strides were being made. Generally the mantra of 'inform, educate and entertain' was still being upheld, but any complacency encouraged by the monopoly was about to be shattered. The hypnotic effect that television had on the public was heightened with the advent of commercial TV.

Its arrival was made possible by the 1954 Television Act. The Independent Television Authority (ITA) was formed to regulate the new service. A key decision was that commercial breaks must be distinguishable from core programmes. A major problem was that new sets were required to receive the commercial programmes. No matter, the anticipation was huge prior to the gala opening on 22 September 1955. Stories of desertions by key BBC performers and producers filled the gossip columns. Despite a champagne reception at the Mayfair hotel and the filming of state trumpeters at the Guildhall, the most remembered feature on the first evening must go to Gibbs SR toothpaste. At 7.27 p.m., twelve minutes after the start of the programme, it was the first advertisement that caused the most stir. Tingling fresh it may have been, but only an estimated 200,000 homes had sets that were capable of receiving this great news. What was worse for ITA came in the form of a 'spoiler' from dear old 'steam radio'. At the very time that commercial television was launched, nine million listeners mourned as poor Grace Archer was burnt to death in Ambridge. The BBC were obviously up for the fight.

Not everyone was about to be seduced by the box in the corner of their living room. The headmaster of Manchester Grammar School declared 'over my dead body' would a TV set despoil his home. Thirty years previously, the headmaster of Rugby School had made similar claims about the wireless. A *Sunday Times* survey reckoned that only one in six were abstainers or deniers. It was mainly these same people who decreed that watching TV was having an alarming and destructive effect on our way of life. TV was blamed for divorce, a decline in the written word and causing nightmares among the young. Doctors warned of TV neck and even buck teeth were said to stem from youngsters viewing from the floor with their chins cupped in their hands. A creepily named Doctor Belsen was altogether more forgiving. He concluded television 'gave a form to the evening'. He added it 'created a feeling of togetherness'.

As more people acquired the new thirteen-channel sets capable of picking up the ITA transmitters and others had their old sets converted, a new but predictable theme emerged. Class was not about to be sidelined by television. Rather, the population's viewing habits endorsed it. While the 'U's and high-income groups remained loyal to the BBC, those lower down the social scale embraced the newcomer. ITV was less stodgy. Their announcers and newsreaders were cheerful and welcoming. The mood was upbeat and for a time the adverts seemed as entertaining as the programmes. Advertising slogans became catchphrases. 'Murray Mints, the too-good-to-hurry mints' remains firmly etched in the memory. Commercial television was classless and just a touch vulgar, but was welcomed by most.

A year after the launch of commercial television, of those who could tune into both channels, a majority were choosing ITV. By 1957 the figures were alarming for the BBC, with seventy-two per cent opting for ITV. For years the BBC had paid their presenters and contributors to their programmes civil service rates. It was a new game now and they had to compete, not only in appearance fees but programme content too. At last they took up the challenge, trading blow for blow. ITV were bringing in popular American productions like the western series *Wyatt Earp*, so the BBC countered with *Wells Fargo*, starring Dale Robertson. Lucille Ball was an instant hit for ITV with *I Love Lucy*, so the BBC offered *I married Joan*. Startled from its complacency, the BBC was now slugging it out for audience share. Their audience research department had been transformed from a comforting support unit to a hectoring critic demanding higher viewing figures. It was claimed that Americanisation was taking over our television.

A counter to this charge came in the mid-fifties with the BBC's news and newsreel service. Technology was advancing strongly and reporting reflected this with an exciting sense of immediacy. *Panorama* was attracting a weekly audience approaching ten million. It offered 'a window on the world'. Millions of people whose knowledge previously hadn't extended much beyond the sports pages or beauty tips in the national press were now exposed to what was happening in strange faraway places. It slowly dawned that events abroad were capable of affecting their lives. Khrushchev ranting in Moscow, Eisenhower on the steps of the White House, it appeared there was nothing that couldn't be beamed into their living room. The documentary was a strength for the BBC, bringing stories and opinions from people across the country. The power of television was persuasive. Archaeology took a bow when Sir Mortimer Wheeler and Dr Glyn Daniel discussed some ancient artefact revolving on a table in front of them. The attraction of animals and wildlife was given expression by Peter Scott in his *Look* series. Here was an area that really lent itself to television, particularly as cameras managed to get close to animals normally only seen in the confines of a zoo or at the circus. Armand Denis was a Belgian film maker who, together with his glamorous wife Michaela, took the viewing public right into the heart of the jungle. They made hugely successful series for both BBC and ITV. *Filming in Africa* appeared in 1955 to be followed by *On Safari* and *On Safari to Asia*, attracting massive audiences. In 1954 David Attenborough introduced *Zoo Quest*, the first of many popular natural history programmes which continue unabated today. Three years later, he formed the Travel and Exploration Unit at the BBC which allowed him to produce his *Travellers' Tales and Adventure* series. Television had unearthed a genre of programmes whose fascination and popularity remain sixty years later. With declining wildlife worldwide, their appeal and importance is probably even greater now.

So not all was being surrendered to a wave of

Americanisation. Viewers turned on to watch the rather dry Sir Kenneth Clark conduct them round leading art galleries. Active participation in painting was encouraged by Mervyn Levy giving lessons live on screen and the likes of Stanley Spencer and L. S. Lowry were filmed talking about their canvasses as they painted. Sales of artist materials soared. Levy took his series abroad to Provence, Brittany and Venice. It appeared the public liked an occasional dose of culture. Despite this we were already developing into a nation of passive viewers. A 1957 survey indicated that only about two per cent of viewers were stimulated enough to undertake further reading or active participation in the subject they had watched. We were witnessing the birth of the couch potato. In 1958 the cost of buying a new TV set was over £70, about five times the average wage. A massive rental business was developing with costs of about 10s a week, making it within most people's budget. It was estimated that over ten million sets were regularly being viewed.

Children, despite their parents' reservations, were among the most devoted viewers. By 1955 the BBC was reporting that eighty-five per cent of five to seven year olds were watching TV daily. It seems unlikely that today's sophisticated young would have been drawn towards *Muffin the Mule*, a rather crude puppet operated by Annette Mills. When she died in 1955 the series was transferred to ITV. The fight to acquire popular programmes continued. A department dedicated to children's programmes was formed by the BBC in 1951. The output was a touch condescending, but well intentioned. Huw Wheldon was an important influence and it was he who introduced a juvenile talent show in *All Your Own*. Directed by Cliff Michelmore, much of its output verged on the embarrassing, but the show did unearth a young Jimmy Page and the King Brothers. Children also enjoyed their own variety programmes, including Harry Corbett and his puppet Sooty. *Bill and Ben, The Flowerpot Men* were also part of this puppet 'army' which obviously was thought to appeal to youngsters as ordained by adult producers at the BBC. Soon tastes were to change, but even today these early icons are remembered fondly.

Quiz shows are another enduring category from early TV. They were cheap to produce, somewhat addictive and could command huge audiences. In the fifties, commercial stations were in danger of overestimating their appeal. At one stage they were running a give-away quiz show every day of the week, with two on Saturdays. Among the most popular was *Take Your Pick*, hosted by Michael Miles. In 1955 *Double Your Money* was transferred from Radio Luxembourg to become a flagship for ITV. Hosted by the gushing Hughie Green, it was the forerunner of other shows that offered contestants the opportunity of winning huge amounts of money. Based on the 64,000-dollar question, the contestant doubled their money with every correct answer given. If the contestant managed to reach the magic £1,000 they were asked to enter a sound-proofed booth. Once inside, the temperature was raised. The nation could watch and sweat along with the contestant. The show was ridiculed as mindless nonsense, but the public didn't agree, with *Double Your Money* surviving well into the sixties.

We were seeing the beginning of the TV 'celebrity'. The oily charm of Hughie Green was also seen to effect when he hosted the talent show *Opportunity Knocks*. Another concept pinched from BBC Radio, it was first shown on ITV in 1956. An early-day *X Factor*, it discovered or helped a number of contestants on to stardom, including Les Dawson, Max Boyce and Pam Ayres. So, although tastes change, popular basic formats for successful TV remain. Long-running serials

which have become known as soaps were already staking a
claim sixty years ago. One, of course, famously continues
today. Tony Warren was a young writer employed in 1950 by
Granada TV. His pilot script for Florizel Street was greeted
with apathy by Granada's board, but given the benefit of the
doubt it was produced as *Coronation Street* and a legend was
launched. Conceived in 1959, it finally made it to the screen
the following year.

Realism and the lives of ordinary people were migrating
from films, but the BBC clung to the past with *Dixon of Dock
Green*. From 1955 to 1976 an increasingly infirm Jack Warner
fought crime in Dock Green, seemingly single-handedly.
The crooks and villains were a pastiche of the real thing
and the programme followed the moralising tradition long
established in BBC programming.

Television now had the power to project previously little-
known personalities to star status. This was certainly true
of *What's My Line*, a panel game originating from the
States. The panellists simply had to question contestants
to establish their occupation. The make-up of the panel
was vital to the show's success. First shown in 1951, regular
panellists included the bubbly Barbara Kelly, the rather
aloof Lady Isobel Barnett and the grumpy, irascible Gilbert
Harding. He was regularly rude to the contestants, which
kept people watching, whether they were incensed or simply
amused. The show was chaired by the amiable Eamonn
Andrews and variously included Katie Boyle (posh), Jerry
Desmonde (diffidently charming), Cyril Fletcher (funny) and
Marghanita Laski (toothy, clever and acerbic).

While panel games, soaps, quizzes and programmes
featuring antiques and wildlife have endured over the
decades, variety shows have not. Yet back in the fifties
Sunday Night at the London Palladium was one of the most

popular programmes on television. Produced by ATV for the ITV network, it was a very British follow-up to traditional music hall, which was ironically in its death throes. Because it was staged at the iconic Palladium, it drew in stars from around the world, all of whom wanted to boast that they had appeared at the world-famous venue. Initially, it was hosted by Cockney comedian Tommy Trinder. The first show featured Gracie Fields, lured from her luxury home on Capri, and American singing star Guy Mitchell. This formed a template for what was to follow over the twelve years that the show ran. Huge stars were to top the bill to be preceded by dance routines carried out by the Tiller Girls and acts featuring acrobats and magicians. It's strange that this old- fashioned format remained so appealing to a modern audience. The show reached the height of its popularity when compèred by Bruce Forsyth between 1958 and 1960. Evening services in churches were brought forward to enable the congregation to get home in time for the show, which now had an audience of fourteen million.

It is perhaps surprising to learn that the BBC was the first to appreciate the potential for pop music shows. Traditionally, there had been a programme shut down between 6.00 p.m. and 7.00 p.m. to allow small children to be put to bed. After lobbying from ITV, the government agreed that programmes could continue without a break. During weekdays the BBC filled the slot with *Today*, a topical news magazine, but on Saturdays they introduced *Six-Five Special*, presented by Pete Murray. It featured many of the new British stars emerging from the coffee bars and clubs. Planned only to run for six weeks, it was soon attracting an audience of over twelve million. Stunned ITV snaffled *Six-Five* producer Jack Good and launched a head-on assault with their own show *Oh Boy*. The first edition featured Cliff Richard and Marty Wilde.

Despite Cliff's make-up being compared to that of blonde bombshell Jayne Mansfield, pop music was another staple that television producers would rely on over the coming years.

By the end of the decade the public and the BBC had become used to the addition of the commercial stations. There is no doubt that for the most part competition had raised the standards of programming. ITA had 'generally maintained a proper balance of good taste and decency and a high general standard of quality'. The commercial breaks were 'recognisably separate and conforming to the highest standards of advertising conduct'. The high cost of making television programmes allowed commercial TV to be largely financed by a huge influx of advertising revenue. Between 1956 and 1959 television advertising quadrupled. Astonishingly, this exceeded the amount spent on all national and London newspaper advertising put together. There was now a multi-million captive audience stranded on their sofas. Other than going out to make a cup of tea there was no escape. Brain-washing democratic style was in full swing. By 1958 mass-selling products were allocating up to half of their budgets to television advertising.

Elsewhere, television was beginning to discuss previously barred subjects. Abortion, prostitution and homosexuality could be handled sensitively and in a balanced way so that both sides of arguments were aired. Could television really be witnessing the growth of an educated, well-informed democracy? Maybe, but Britain's first decade of TV didn't impress one influential American commentator. He lamented that 'the British had decided to paint this gaudy thing a sombre grey to blend with the general fog'. Few would have agreed with him. Television may have ruined conversation, and led to snatched meals on trays while staring transfixed at the screen, but for most it had revolutionised their lives and generally for the better.

The effect of television was also far reaching for other industries. Pubs were often deserted, theatres played to half-empty houses and cinema queues were a thing of the past. Posed with the threat of the wireless back in the twenties, newspapers boycotted BBC programmes and barred it from collecting news. Having learnt their lesson the press now embraced television. Acres of space were devoted to TV gossip. Serious critiques of programmes were offered daily and celebrities signed up to add their views. The magazine sector was more vulnerable to the TV onslaught. There was genuine sadness when in 1957 *Picture Post* was forced to close. This marked the end of an era of magnificent photographic journalism. News now travelled fast and was reported upon instantly. *Picture Post* found itself marooned. Other illustrated magazines followed. Not long before, this section of the market had enjoyed circulations running into the millions. Now they were gone, swallowed up by new technology, a theme that was going to accelerate over the coming years.

The newspaper industry, which had enjoyed a boom in circulation since the end of the war, now needed to pause and take stock. Provincial newspapers were badly hit, with several, including the *Birmingham Gazette*, closing. Some nationals were also tottering, although it was 1960 before the *News Chronicle* finally folded. Fleet Street needed to reposition itself to meet the new challenge to its all-important advertising revenue. In November 1958 Cecil King, the formidable chairman of the Mirror Group, made a bid for The Amalgamated Press, which had previously been owned by his uncle. The offer was accepted and the following year its name was changed to Fleetway Press. Shortly afterwards the massive Odhams Group absorbed Hulton Press, creating the largest magazine organisation in the world. King now acted again to rationalise what he saw as an overcrowded market by making a bid for Odhams, a deal that was not finalised until 1961. The rationalisation left King's Mirror Group in possession of the bulk of popular magazines in the UK. The *Daily Herald* and *The People* were also added to his stable. Sentiment had no place in the emerging world. The era of the 'number cruncher' had arrived.

Before the war the circulation of *Woman* magazine had been 75,000. This had mushroomed to over two million by 1952. It continued to grow and its success led to a proliferation of titles appealing to the middle-class housewife. By the mid-fifties over twelve million women were reading at least two magazines a week, from a choice of fifty titles, with new ones still being launched. It couldn't last. King was right, there had to be a cull. Feminists were appalled at the content of most magazines. They tended to offer banal advice on dress or how to entertain. There were endless knitting patterns and tips on how to make curtains or cook a roast to please hubby. The statutory love story was fuelled according to the editor of *Woman* by 'a unanimous acceptance that to be loved and loving is better than to be brainy'. Surely it was time for a change of emphasis on and perception of a woman's role in life? By the end of the decade it was possible to detect the first faltering steps towards Women's Lib. Sex, formerly a taboo subject, had an occasional outing. Not much equality here though, with articles and tips of how to keep your husband or boyfriend on the straight and narrow. Over five million women were contacting *Woman* each year. The 'agony aunt' was central now to a magazine's success. Further criticism was being made of women's magazines regarding their blatant materialism. It was true that the women's magazine sector virtually ignored any serious coverage of what was happening in the world. The publishers obviously felt that women's only interests revolved around their home, family, knitting and, of course, the latest fad in dieting.

Meanwhile, men were being encouraged by a constant stream of advertising to tackle do-it-yourself rather than spending Saturday afternoons watching football. Trips to the pub were not so frequent as sales of draught beer dropped. Between 1954 and 1959 cinema admissions slumped, leading to over 800 closures. Giant Wurlitzers were ripped out and sold off as junk. Nothing, it appeared, lasted forever. Television's influence grew like Japanese Knotweed. Some organisations were killed quickly by its arrival, while others endured a lingering death. Those more nimble learnt to live and thrive alongside this phenomenon, which had done more to change the lives of ordinary people than any other invention, except the train and car, for centuries past. Sixty years later, television is still central to our lives, albeit available now through a whole variety of clever gizmos and gadgets.

Television in the 1950s also produced the first of a new breed which today flaunts and propounds like latter-day prophets on our screens. They are the new gurus, the television chefs. With his pointy beard and striped butcher's apron, Philip Harben was the first 'television cook'. He couldn't have realised that some of his successors would become superstars. Not just famous, but fabulously wealthy too. He must be looking down and cursing his luck for being born just a few years too early. He was not alone, being just one of that early group of personalities which helped British television become the force it is today.

11
Sporting London

Every Saturday afternoon during the 1950s, buses and tube stations across London were choked with hordes of football fans. From Highbury to Craven Cottage, an army of cloth-capped Londoners flocked to support their local team. Even amateur clubs drew crowds that would be the envy of many lesser professional clubs today. Soccer was as much the working man's sport as beer was his choice of drink. Huge banks of scarf-clad supporters, clutching rattles, cheered from the terraces. Youngsters were passed and lifted to the front so they could get a better view. It was tribal and raucous. The noise heard from outside a full stadium was reminiscent of a dictator's rally. It was a game of universal appeal and one that reflected London's abrasive nature. Phil Woosnam, who played for West Ham in the late fifties, gave a great description of the game at the time as: 'The rules of soccer are very simple. Basically it is – if it moves, kick it; if it doesn't, kick it until it does.' This was no game for over-paid, diving prima donnas. It was all about physical contact, crushing tackles, elbows and shoulder-charging goalkeepers. Although there were supremely talented players in Britain our presumed world dominance was shortly to be exposed as a sham.

Boxing was the sport that offered an escape for young men

from deprived backgrounds. Cigar-smoking toffs would watch from the safety of their ringside seats at the National Sporting Club as the fighters sought to knock each other out. Sport, as in life, was dominated by class. Sometimes the well-to-do would watch as spectators, but rarely would the classes meet in direct competition. Depressingly, boxers who did hit the big time were frequently tricked out of their hard-earned money by their managers or dishonest promoters. Those who did make money tended to self-destruct on a tide of high living and booze.

Strangely, it was cricket where the different classes mixed and played alongside each other. This, presumably, dated right back to the origins of the game. The squires and landowners didn't really fancy the arduous job of bowling and, therefore, co-opted staff to hurl balls down at them so they could develop their batting skills. Despite the gradual integration, the annual Gentlemen versus Players match held at Lord's was a reminder that people were still expected to know their place in society.

London was a haven of sporting activity. Most was undertaken as purely recreational activity. Professional sport was still rather frowned upon and, apart from championship boxers, not particularly well paid. The amateur ethos was embedded in the British psyche and extended to not appearing to try too hard in order to achieve success.

Two football matches that took place in 1953 were to have a profound effect on British sport, for different reasons. In May, a month before the coronation, the BBC heralded the emerging importance of outside television broadcasts by covering the FA Cup Final. Millions had purchased a television to view the coronation and the Cup Final offered a good opportunity for the BBC to develop their outside broadcasting expertise. Many cup finals turn out to be

drab affairs, but the match between Bolton Wanderers and
Blackpool has become part of football's abiding folklore.
Although both sides featured several international players,
it was left to a thirty-nine-year-old winger to turn the match
on its head. With twenty minutes to go, Blackpool were 3-1
down. With a Bolton player injured and a passenger on the
wing, Blackpool channelled their attacks down the right
wing. Stanley Matthews was the master of dribbling. He
would glide past opponents as if the ball was tied to his boot
laces. He made the goal to bring Blackpool back into the
game, scored by Stan Mortenson. A soaring free kick brought
the teams level. Then, with just a minute to go, Matthews
shimmied past defenders before squaring the ball for Bill
Perry to score the winner. Pandemonium. Matthews was a
hero but, more importantly, a nation had been transfixed.
Sport on television was live drama with mass appeal. The
seeds were sown that day for all the multi-million TV deals
that were to promote sport as a global business.

Six months later, on a misty November afternoon,
Wembley Stadium was again packed to capacity. Matthews
and Mortenson were part of an England side that had never
been beaten at Wembley by a side from outside Great Britain.
Although Hungary were Olympic champions, they were
given little chance by the British Press. The sports editor of
the *Daily Telegraph* reckoned that any English championship
club side would simply 'run through the Hungarians'. It soon
became obvious how wrong he was. Here was a completely
new brand of football based on movement and ball control.
While England hoofed long balls and played with their
usual physical commitment, the Hungarians weaved magic
patterns and finished with a sharpness that left the crowd
stunned in admiration. The 6-3 defeat didn't really illustrate
the light years between the sides. English football looked as

old fashioned as the bulky shin pads, toe-capped boots and baggy shorts they wore. For those who kidded themselves that the result was a fluke, worse was to come. In a return match held in Budapest the following year, the Hungarians inflicted an embarrassing 7-1 defeat. English football had to change, but it was not the only sport where we had been forced to realise that our attitude and methods were outmoded.

England's cricketers had also been humiliated by Australia's vintage side, captained by Don Bradman in 1948. This in no way dampened spectator enthusiasm and county matches were often played in front of capacity crowds. London featured two iconic grounds – Lord's was the home of cricket, while The Oval traditionally hosted the final test match of a touring sides series. Rather like football, cricket was not a game for the timid in the 1950s. There was little protection from a leather ball being hurled at you at speeds in excess of eighty miles per hour. There was no protective helmet or body padding. Maverick batsmen like Dennis Compton didn't even wear a traditional cap, which gave at least some minimal protection. The England side managed to win back The Ashes in 1952, but it was four years later at The Oval that history was made. Here, Jim Laker, a Yorkshireman playing for Surrey, tortured the Australian batsmen with his slow, off-spin bowling. Suspicions remain that the wicket had been 'doctored' to help the home side. Maybe, but Laker went on to be the first player to take all ten wickets in a test match innings, bagging an amazing match total of nineteen. In what was at the time a typical British reaction to sporting triumph, he allowed himself no show of emotion. Victory and defeat were expected to be treated with the same stoicism. A New Zealand cricketer had been booed by a crowd in Yorkshire for diving at a ball in order to stop a boundary. It was left to successive visiting West Indian sides to open up a glorious, new, uninhibited attitude to the game. Carefree batsmen and frighteningly fast bowlers combined with athletic fielding to produce real excitement in what had been a generally sedate game. Their supporters, thousands of whom were now living in London, brought a new carnival atmosphere. MCC members spluttered into their pink gins, but cricket in England was changed forever.

Boxing was the third most popular professional sport. It was not just Randolph Turpin who achieved fame and (temporary) fortune. Fights between huge physical specimens always attracted massive interest and capacity crowds. During the decade Britain produced a clutch of heavyweights who fleetingly offered hopes of becoming the world champion. Most of the major fights were staged in London at Wembley, White City, Earls Court or Haringey. Jack Gardner, an ex-guardsman, was once ranked above Rocky Marciano, but he lost in a European championship to the German Hein Ten Hoff. He subsequently lost his British title to Johnny Williams in a savage contest, after which he very sensibly retired. Joe Erskine was a very skilful boxer, but ultimately too small to succeed at the very top level. Fellow Welshman Dick Richardson was also hailed as a new 'white hope' but was usually found wanting at the very top level of competition. It was left to Brian London who did eventually fight for the world title against Floyd Patterson in 1959, and particularly Henry Cooper to keep British hopes alive.

Cooper, the archetypal Londoner, went on to be the acceptable face of British boxing. He was small compared to modern heavyweights, but had a devastating left hook. Unfortunately, he was prone to terrible cuts around his eyes, which hampered his career. By the end of the 1950s, he was British and Commonwealth Champion and he also recorded a victory over the highly rated American Zora Folley. It was, of course, to be another four years until his first fight with (the then) Cassius Clay, which went on to define his career.

For most Londoners, sport formed a large part of their social and recreational interest. Tennis is among the most social of games and across the capital and in its suburbs tennis clubs flourished. Here was a convivial venue for young couples to meet. White flannels remained popular with the older men while ladies still wore discreet pleated skirts. Young bucks lounged against the railings of the wooden pavilion shouting 'oh good shot' to the girl who had attracted their attention on court. This was English tennis, where the teas and the evening dance was more important than the game itself. For most, tennis was little more than pat-a-cake over the net, particularly in mixed doubles. It was considered to be extremely rude for a man to serve too hard to a lady. While many romances blossomed from meetings at tennis clubs, they tended to be socially exclusive. It was a place where middle-class parents were happy for their daughters to meet 'the right sort of chap'.

Wimbledon fortnight was one of the great social events of the year. The grass courts, strawberries and the sound of ball on racquet to a background of enthusiastic applause symbolised the English summer. The men's game was dominated by the Americans and, increasingly, the Australians. Only Jaroslav Drobný, a left-handed eastern European based in Egypt, broke the stranglehold they had on the men's singles championship. No Briton had won since Fred Perry in 1936 and the current crop of British players struggled to get through the opening rounds.

The British women did little better, although Angela Buxton did reach the final in 1956, being beaten 6-3, 6-1 by the American Shirley Fry. It was the Americans that dominated the women's game, spearheaded by 'Little Mo' (Maureen Connolly) when, like her compatriot Louise Brough back in the forties, she won the title for three years in succession. 1957 saw the first black winner when Althea Gibson claimed the title, as she did the following year. American dominance was dented by the arrival of the elegant Maria Bueno of Argentina who triumphed for the first time in 1959.

If lawn tennis was the preserve of the middle classes in England, real tennis offered the ultimate in elitism. Dating back centuries to continental Europe, it is thought initially to have been played with the palm of the hand and later with a glove. The popularity of the game was restricted by the large, expensive indoor courts required. As such, participation was confined to a privileged few. The prestigious venues in London underlined this. The Royal Tennis Court at Hampton Court is the oldest surviving venue in England, but it was also possible to play at Lord's or Queen's Club if, of course, you had the right connections. As ever, sport and class were as divided as society itself.

Golf had become increasingly popular during the early twentieth century. Most leafy suburbs boasted a course and only a few miles from London's centre flourishing courses thrived in Hampstead and at Highgate. Here was a game offering both social and sporting opportunities. Social pretension created its own elitism. The golf club was an important bastion for the well-to-do middle class. An ability to play well was less important than your connections. A. A. Milne was correct in saying 'Golf is popular simply because it is the best game in the world at which to be bad.'

The golf course had become a place where useful contacts could be made and business discreetly discussed. So it was important to be proposed and seconded for membership, before being interviewed to see if you passed muster. There was little chance if you were Jewish. Although rarely admitted outwardly, anti-Semitism was rife. Many of London's golf courses continued to bar Jews. Perhaps this was just an extension of the general suspicion of foreigners, but it led to the opening of several Jewish clubs. Class, religious and racial prejudice constantly lurked just below the surface.

For those who did gain entry to a club, the game offered important advantages. Unlike many active sports, you didn't have to be young for golf, neither did you have to be particularly fit. For married couples it was a game they could play together. The club was also a place where you could enjoy a convivial drink after a difficult round. Then, perhaps, a relaxing game of billiards while the ladies played a few hands of bridge. You were made to feel important at your club. The professional and steward were deferential and you were able to mix with people you felt comfortable with. The club secretary tended to be a dependable ex-military type, who saw to the upholding of standards at the club. Blazers and club ties underscored the necessity for a strict dress code in the club house. There was not a single tradesman's van to be seen in the car park!

Being appointed club captain was considered to be a great honour, although an expensive one. The captain was expected to provide competition prizes, pay for trips to other clubs and host dinners. There were speeches to be made and jokes to be told. Only the wealthy could contemplate taking on the responsibilities. The golf club was a refuge from what many saw as a threatening change in society. A questioning of long-established standards and tradition was both tiresome and worrying, but, for a few hours at least, the golf club held these concerns in check.

Many of those who joined golf clubs in later life would have played rugby in their youth (or at least claimed to have done). The game was known by most who played it as 'rugger'. Here again was a sport divided by class, widely described as 'a game for gentlemen, played by hooligans'. It was a wholly amateur sport, which was played at most public schools, and it was old boys' teams that formed the backbone of London's active participation. Many old boys' clubs would field seven or eight teams on a Saturday afternoon. At the elite level, teams that are still around in today's professional game were still dominant. The Wasps, Harlequins and Saracens all have long histories, and it was from such clubs that the international players were selected. London also supported three 'exile' teams – London Irish, London Welsh and London Scottish provided opportunities for the huge numbers of people from the Celtic fringes living in London to get together at the weekend. Rugby offered the great advantage of appealing to young men of all shapes and sizes. The 'fatties' could shove at the scrum, while behind them the 'beanpoles' caught the ball at the line-outs. At the back the 'pretty boys' zipped about, generally scoring the tries. It was an era when Twickenham witnessed some of the greatest Welsh players gracing its turf, but it was the awesome All Blacks from New Zealand that set the gold standard.

Along with Wimbledon, one of London's great social events was the annual Royal Regatta at Henley. Even if your rowing experience was only the occasional spin on the Serpentine, you simply had to be seen sporting a striped blazer and boater. However, it was the other great sporting event held on the Thames that really captured London's attention. The Varsity Boat Race from Putney to Mortlake saw the towpath and bridges packed with raucous spectators sporting rosettes of light or dark blue. Here, to this most elitist of events, came supporters from across the social divide. For a day Cockneys qualified for Oxbridge. Allegiances were even split between families and the enthusiasm for the event dwarfed that of today. The Thames, the life-blood of the capital, drew its citizens in their thousands, shouting, cheering and boozing. Here was a glimpse of old London, noisy, irreverent and intent on enjoyment.

As buildings and concrete ate up most of London's green spaces, horse riding was largely the preserve of a moneyed few. Rotten Row was originally built in the seventeenth century to provide a broad thoroughfare through Hyde Park to St James's Palace. Increasingly, it became a place for the well-to-do to be seen. By the 1950s money rather than noble birth dictated who trotted down the most famous of bridle paths. Bankers, businessmen, film stars and popular singers paraded. The arrival of the black entertainer Hutch dressed in Savile Row finery caused a communal intake of breath. Hand-made boots and a silk top hat were all very well, but ...

Of course the sport of kings appealed to the working man just as much as the aristocracy. One of its attractions was the heady mix of spectators attending. Londoners loved their racing. They had easy access to Sandown, Kempton and Hurst Park, as well as the quirky Alexandra Palace track. Ascot and Epsom provided some of the finest racing in the country. Derby Day still drew massive crowds and endless traffic jams as Londoners converged on the Downs for their special day out. There were double-decker buses, charabancs, together with family cars and luxury limousines. There were gypsies with skin-like leather peering into crystal balls. There were dodgy-looking characters selling tips and claiming to be in the know. Many were attracted to the feathered head-dress of Prince Monolulu, who shouted out, 'I got an 'orse!'

Little seemed to have changed since William Powell Frith had captured the chaos of the Derby Day in his 1858 painting. Race track gangs still operated, extorting money from bookies. With the collusion of the police they were able to offer 'protection'. Those bookies who tried to ignore the threats were effectively sidelined by fights organised outside their pitches and continual disruption of their business. If that didn't work, then the razor normally did.

To this background of violence and lusty excitement, some of the turf's greatest races were run. While the Derby was a day for all Londoners, Royal Ascot was perhaps the pinnacle of the social scene. Each day the royal coach procession arrived on the course from Windsor. There were outriders dressed in vivid scarlet and gold uniforms, postillions sporting grey wigs and jockey caps. The gentlemen raised their top hats while the ladies in their expensive finery curtsied.

At the other end of the spectrum, greyhound racing, introduced into Britain from the States in 1925, unleashed a wave of interest from the working man which was still alive in the fifties. London was well served with tracks across the capital, many of which have subsequently closed, including White City, Walthamstow and Hendon. Racing also used to be staged regularly at Stamford Bridge, home to Chelsea football club. Greyhound racing, perhaps unfairly, acquired a reputation for attracting criminals and layabouts, prompting the expression of 'going to the dogs'. With no betting shops it was still a time of bookies' runners and there was a general feeling that having a flutter should be confined to doing the football pools. It was possible to have a credit account with a bookie, but this was not normally a facility extended to the working man, hence bets were left in pubs and cafés for the bookies' runner to pick up. Enterprising milkmen and delivery men also collected money for bookies. It was to be years before betting lost its rather grubby image.

Speedway shared many venues with greyhound racing. It

drew great crowds who were attracted by the powerful 500 cc bikes, the noise and dramatic spills on the cinder track. The acrid smell of exhaust from rasping engines hit a nerve with Londoners, who had always enjoyed dangerous live theatre. Teams were formed and the races pitched two from each side against each other, leaning over so that their knees almost scraped the ground as they tore round the track on bikes with no brakes. Leading riders became household names as the sport enjoyed a period of unprecedented popularity during the early years of the 1950s. Split Waterman attracted a world record transfer fee of £3,000 when he signed for Haringey Racers in 1950. Although he only ever became runner-up in the world championship, it is his name that remains synonymous with the heyday of the sport. To increase revenues it was necessary for stadiums to maximise their usage. Perhaps the most successful was the White City Stadium. Built in 1908 to help stage the London Olympics of that year, it offered Speedway, greyhound racing, boxing and major athletic meetings. With Roger Bannister being the first to break the four-minute mile in 1954, interest in athletics soared. Here was the last generation of truly amateur athletes (both in their training methods and outlook), who managed to take on the best in the world. Chris Chataway was known to like a pint and a fag, yet he was able to have a number of epic encounters with Vladimir Kuts, the 'Iron Man' of Soviet middle-distance running. There were other stars like Gordon Pirie, a lanky middle-distance runner who during his career broke five world records. In 1955 he beat the legendary Emil Zátopek and became the BBC sports personality of the year, underlining athletics' popularity.

It was television that launched another sport. It seemed the whole country would sit round their television sets whenever show jumping was transmitted from Wembley or the White City. Colonel Harry Llewellyn and his horse Foxhunter became household names. A unique attraction of this sport was that women were able to compete with the men on equal terms. Pat Smythe won every title available to her, both in Britain and America. Her horses Prince Hal Flanagan and Tosca were also taken to the collective national heart. The sport was perfect for a television audience, with mounting tension as the competition progressed.

Sport continued to reflect life in 1950s Britain, with its perceived and real social barriers – but not for long. The potential for sport through the power of television as mass entertainment was only now beginning to be understood. National, international and finally global coverage would follow in the decades to come. Fortunes would be made, millionaires a-plenty. Those footballers playing in the 1953 Cup Final still reckoned fifteen quid a week wasn't a bad wage.

12
Food for Thought

It is difficult for those who were not around at the time to appreciate the direness of British food in the 1950s. Generally, meals served at home were an extension of school dinners, and worse still at many hotels and restaurants. It was as if a whole generation of British housewives had lost either the skill or the will to cook a decent meal. The nation was being fed a diet of overdone meat and soggy vegetables that had been boiled to death. In those days it was a case of be thankful for what you've got! Of course, a decade of constant shortages was partly to blame for a cuisine which simply set out to fill empty stomachs with a diet of stodge.

I remember my mother being particularly sniffy about the cooking of an attractive French neighbour. I was constantly drawn to her kitchen by the delicious smells being created on her ancient gas cooker. Given tastes on a huge wooden spoon, I would return home later with tales of these wonderful, exotic morsels I had tried, tales which didn't go down too well. A salad at home consisted of tinned sardines or pilchards, a tomato cut into quarters, a few lettuce leaves and the whole concoction smothered in salad cream. Using similar ingredients, Suzanne tossed everything in a bowl and then poured a dressing made up of olive oil, vinegar, mustard and sugar. The difference was extraordinary. As my visits increased during the summer holidays, my mother learnt that Suzanne was sunbathing topless and I was banned. French cooking and bare breasts were a heady brew for a young teenager, but within months Suzanne was gone. Her husband, a talented illustrator, took her away to America, where he worked for the Disney Corporation.

Like other areas of British life, the appreciation of good food developed and evolved during the decade. By the early fifties supplies of food available were becoming more plentiful. Consumption of butter, cheese, eggs and milk, along with vegetables, was increasing. Sales of bread declined to be replaced by a surge in the purchase of biscuits. By 1955 a new food revolution emerged in the shape of the deep freeze. Even corner shops invested in a cabinet and the sale of frozen foods doubled as canned and tinned food went into decline. Tinned salmon and pineapple took a back seat in favour of frozen chicken, fish fingers, frozen chips and peas. The problem that remained was how to make these new additions into acceptable dishes.

So how did British perceptions relating to food change? Why were stodgy suet puddings and dishes fried in lard gradually sidelined? Although the process was slow, it was spearheaded by two unlikely characters. They were in many ways total opposites, but they highlighted the dreadful food being endured in Britain. Their mission was to improve standards and to educate the public on what could be achieved. Raymond Postgate was a left-wing, conscientious objector who had gone on the run during the First World War. He was a journalist, novelist and biographer who acted as editor of the *Encyclopaedia Britannica* for a time during the 1930s. Appalled by the standard of food on offer after the war, Postgate formed the *Good Food Club*. Volunteers were asked to submit reports on restaurants around the country.

This in turn led to the publication in 1951 of the first pocket-sized *Good Food Guide*. It declared its purpose was to improve British cooking and service in hotels and restaurants. It was proud to announce that the guide had no funds, premises or meeting place; it relied on reports from members of the club informing the guide of exceptional food and service. It was decided that London establishments should be judged more harshly than their country cousins, due to the number and variety of restaurants in the capital. Postgate stated he was out to eliminate dullness and incompetence.

At about the same time as the publication of the *Good Food Guide*, another influential player entered the fray. Stand by for a glamorous lady with an exotic past. Elizabeth David, the daughter of a Tory MP, grew up in some style in her parents' manor house near Folkestone. As a teenager, she attended the Sorbonne in France. Returning to England, she tried her hand at painting and acting, while turning her back on being a debutante. France and its cuisine influenced her decision to return to mainland Europe. No doubt her new lover Charles Gibson-Cowan was an added attraction. They bought a small boat and decided to sail to Greece. Arriving in France, en route, in the midst of impending war was not her brightest decision, but when you are young and in love, why not? The couple lived for a couple of years in France, moving ever southwards, during which time Elizabeth started collecting regional recipes. She may have been strong on cuisine but seemingly totally oblivious to the war engulfing Europe. Eventually the couple arrived in Sicily in their boat to be met by the Germans and interned. After some months they made their escape to Yugoslavia before finally making it to Greece in July 1940. Once again the Germans were on their heels and they moved on to Alexandria in Egypt. Here their love cooled and Elizabeth, a competent linguist, was given a job in the British naval cipher department. All the time she had continued collecting recipes. Now on the cusp of thirty, she had moved to Cairo and decided it was time to get married. After a succession of lovers, she settled on Lieutenant-Colonel Tony David. She accompanied him when he was posted to India, but she found being a service wife intolerable and returned to England alone in 1945.

After her absence of seven years, the bleakness of post-war London came as a ghastly shock. She started writing articles on cookery for *Harper's Bazaar* in 1949. These were well received and encouraged her to collate many of her recipes to form a book. The result – *A Book of Mediterranean Food* – was promptly rejected by a number of leading publishers. Taking advice, she then linked the recipes with short, punchy prose, quoting extracts from famous authors like Compton Mackenzie and Lawrence Durell. This, with a cover designed by John Minton, did the trick and the book was published in the spring of 1950. Despite the fact that many of the ingredients she listed were unobtainable in Britain, the book opened up a new world for many. Reading the book became a form of escapism.

Even in London, outside of Soho you would have struggled to find aubergines, langoustines or even olive oil. The book found favour with the middle classes, particularly those who had served abroad during the war. *The Observer* enthused that the book 'deserves to become the familiar companion of all who seek uninhibited excitement in the kitchen'. *French Provincial Cooking* provided a follow up success in September 1951 for lovers of *Tartelettes à la Provençale*, *Crevettes sautées à la crème* or simply *Omelette à la tomate*. Regional favourites were listed from Paris, Provence, Alsace, Burgundy and the south west, including Languedoc. In 1954 David honed in on *Italian Cooking* and the following year with

Summer Cooking, but in retrospect it is her first two offerings which are considered to have been the most influential in convincing British housewives to be more adventurous. Her books were reported to have encouraged a number of French bistros to appear across London. Many think that Elizabeth David's influence has been exaggerated. Certainly, other writers achieved higher sales. David's titles were essentially aimed at the middle class and generally ignored the slowly emerging mass market. She was fortunate that gradually the ingredients required for the recipes became more readily available. Or did they surface because of her influence? Whichever, along with the arrival of the *Good Food Guide*, at last there was an acknowledgement that foul food should not be tolerated.

Lauded by today's celebrity chefs, she also found favour with Evelyn Waugh's son Auberon, who insisted 'her books and articles persuaded her readers that food was one of life's great pleasures and cooking should not be a drudgery but an exciting and creative act'. In doing so, she inspired a whole generation not only to cook but to think about food in an entirely different way. Others feel her influence has been over-hyped, helped by her subsequent cookware range developed years later which helped introduce her to a new generation of consumers.

Certainly, other cookery books far outsold David's in the 1950s. Published in 1957, *Plats du Jour* was written by Patience Gray and co-author Primrose Boyd, and was aimed at the mass market. Although largely forgotten today, it sold over 50,000 copies within a year. The authors stated 'this is not intended as an armchair cookery book. It is designed for action in the kitchen. The underlying theme is a concentration of excellence in one main dish, rather than dissipating thought and care on several, and it contains a collection of recipes, mainly French and Italian, for dishes which can be served with no further sequel than salad cheese and fruit.' Here was a simple cook book introducing a new readership to French and continental cuisine. There followed a rash of books highlighting not only French, Spanish, Portuguese and Yugoslav, but even Vietnamese recipes. Pizza made an appearance in milk bars and suddenly scampi was everyone's favourite. Traditional cafés serving fry-ups, along with huge hunks of bread and margarine washed down with a mug of sweet tea, were not about to disappear. In fact there were still many of these working men's cafés to be found in the West End. The battle for the British diner was in full flow, but still not won. Early intrepid holidaymakers to Majorca returned with harrowing tales of 'Spanish Tummy'. Foreign food was unhealthy muck. What was wrong with a roast and two veg or good old fish and chips?

Elsewhere in the food jungle there were more problems. After people had survived the privations of war, there was now talk of obesity, caused by overindulgence after years of enforced fasting. The women's magazines were quick to spot an opportunity. A new slimming diet fad was taking shape. Diets sold extra copies and made money. The never-ending dieting roller coaster was underway. Suddenly, women were unhappy with their shape, their extra few pounds here and unwanted rolls there. The all-protein-and-fat diet, they were assured, would see their weight falling away. My mother opted for the banana-and-milk diet and we had to suffer her mood swings as she struggled with it. If that didn't work, it's because she should have tried the Swedish milk diet. When did you ever see a fat Swede? Come to think of it, when did you ever see a Swede in those days, except those blonde beauties endorsing the diet? Obviously, the solution was to opt for the Gay-lord Hauser Diet. Developed by American nutritionist Benjamin Hauser, it promoted 'natural eating'. The diet encouraged consumption of food rich in vitamin B and excluded sugar and white flour. His 1951 book *Look Younger, Live Longer* was banned for a time in the States, but subsequently Hauser has been hailed as the founder of the natural food movement. Women started counting calories and the 1950s saw the birth of that killer of conversation, 'the weight bore'.

There were two huge catering organisations that dominated London's culinary scene. There was scarcely a high street that didn't feature a Lyons Tea Room. They were often rather scruffy, with many tables left with dirty cups and saucers still to be cleared when you took your seat. Service was undertaken by waitresses known as 'nippies', but by the 1950s these uniformed goddesses had slowed to a sullen crawl. More fondly remembered are the Lyons Corner Houses. These had been introduced before the war and were giant, gilded palaces with marble halls that brought a splash of opulence. They offered a different type of themed restaurant on each floor, some with their own resident band. The ground floor was given over to a delicatessen department and counters selling cakes and sweets. There was also a florist's department and a hairdressing salon. Branches occupied prime sites in Coventry Street, Shaftesbury Avenue, Marble Arch and the Strand. Although not known officially as a corner house, there was another branch at the Angel, Islington. This never received the same level of investment as the West End outlets and was looking distinctly tatty before its closure in 1959. As a concept, these huge palaces were still popular, but the call now was for a brasher, more modern, environment. Seen eventually as a symbol of a bygone age, the Corner Houses finally closed in the seventies.

While the bosses of Joe Lyons didn't seek a high public

profile, by contrast Charles Forte soon became a well-known figure. Born in Italy but raised in Scotland, he opened his first milk bar in Regent Street in 1935. He went on to become the most successful caterer in the land, with his empire stretching across Britain and beyond. He initially established a position midway between the downmarket tea shops of Joe Lyons and the ABC chain, but without the pretensions of the garish Corner Houses. It was impossible to avoid his restaurants in the West End. A walk around Piccadilly Circus would reveal milk bars, mock brasseries, steakhouses, fish and quasi-Italian restaurants. The food served was invariably mediocre, but convenient and well priced. In 1954 Forte bought the iconic Café Royal in Regent Street. For decades the haunt of leading writers, artists and politicians, its regular clientele were horrified. Members who regularly attended the National Sporting Club to watch boxing bouts choked on their Havanas. Their worst fears about the downgrading of British life and the lowering of standards generally were confirmed as they retreated to their gentlemen's clubs, where nothing changed in a hurry. Charles Forte was in full flow. The opening of his first motorway service restaurants in 1960 saw thousands of Londoners charge up the M1 to Newport Pagnell. The novelty soon wore off, but with no speed restrictions motorway driving was a major attraction. For a time the police were constantly having to clear lay-bys of picnicking motorists. The feeling that the Forte set-up was just too huge for adequate standards to be upheld was confirmed when the company acquired the catering concession at London's Heathrow airport. It didn't take long for complaints to be voiced about the quality of the food and the dreadful service. It was described in the press as a national disgrace.

The closing down of London restaurants popular in

Edwardian times pointed towards the restless desire for change. Oddenino's, Frascati's and the Holborn Restaurant all disappeared. Now, democratic Britain demanded fast food American style, and it arrived in the anglicised form of the Wimpy Bar. Grilled hamburgers appealed to the young, washed down with sickly milkshakes and followed by knickerbocker glories. The combination tested even the strongest digestive system. The burger was usually covered in ketchup squelched from a plastic bottle representing a tomato. Strangely, it was the Joe Lyons organisation who became aware of the potential for fast food and acquired the licence. The first Wimpy opened within the giant Corner House in Coventry Street in 1954. The restaurants multiplied until being acquired by United Biscuits in 1977.

New eating trends were also affecting our liquid intake. Coffee consumption was three times greater than before the war. Steak was now considered the ultimate luxury. Although the Berni steakhouses didn't arrive in central London until 1962, they were already popularising eating out in the West County. The classic British meal of prawn cocktail, steak and chips followed by Black Forest gateau was upon us. Washed down of course with a bottle of plonk or a schooner of sherry. Wine was no longer the preserve of the elite. The mystique was removed by names like Blue Nun, which was easy to remember and could be ordered with confidence. Wine stores started appearing on the high street and sales boomed, as did consumption of lager-type beers. If it was foreign, or at least sounded foreign, the British public snapped it up.

Dry sherry was still very popular with the middle classes as a pre-supper tipple, but Berni promoted the rather cloying Bristol Cream. Sherry was still extensively advertised in the early fifties. Costing about £1 a bottle, Gonzalez Byass, Dry Fly and Dry Sack all featured prominently. Royal Decree upped the exclusivity stakes by claiming a royal decree from Queen Isabella. Spirit sales were also staging something of a comeback after wartime shortages. Names like Vat 69 and 'Don't be vague, ask for Haig' were popular whiskies. Gordon's Gin was available at 33s 9d a bottle, but traditionally Londoners preferred Booths. That lovely, yellowish tinge ensured that the contents hadn't been watered down.

Where there was a drink, be it tea, coffee or alcohol, it was normally accompanied by a cigarette. The link with lung cancer was already known, but the tobacco industry was very powerful and for years successfully created their own pro-smoking propaganda. Virtually everyone in 1950s London smoked. You were considered weird if you didn't. Men carried leather cigarette cases. Having a slick Dunhill lighter indicated a certain social standing, as to a lesser extent did a Ronson. Some ladies affected a more glamorous image by using a long cigarette holder. The nation was united in its dependence and enjoyment of a gasper, ciggy or plain old fag. Every high street was dotted with specialist tobacconists. Their shelves heaved, not only with popular brands, but obscure ones for people with more exclusive tastes. Rows of pipes were also on show and pipe tobacco could be mixed from giant jars to your own recipe. Shops specialising in hand-made cigarettes and expensive cigars flourished in and around Jermyn Street. Top cigarette sellers were Players and Senior Service, while the working man either rolled his own or stuck with Weights or Woodbines. The choices were endless: Capstan Full Strength (for the serious smoker), Passing Cloud, favoured by ladies and luvvies. A random selection gives us State Express 555, Kensitas, Craven A and Craven Plain. Want something really cheap? How about Turf? Du Maurier had a certain cache as did Balkan Sobranie. Then, of course, you were 'never alone with a Strand', which was launched with an atmospheric television advert in 1959. Filmed on a dark and deserted London street, it featured a character played by Terence Brook with the moody music of *The Lonely Man* theme! A great advertisement visually. Unfortunately, it prompted an unwanted reaction from its target audience who didn't want to be lonely. Sales bombed and the brand was withdrawn within a year of its launch.

So it was against this background of smoke-ridden mass catering that Raymond Postgate set down his marker for improving British food in his search for excellence. In the first edition he mourned the revamping of the Café Royal, informing readers that the 'Garrick hotel in Charing Cross Road was the last great red plush restaurant in London where the ghosts of the nineties reside!' Most of the establishments listed in the guide were in the West End, particularly around Soho where a variety of appetites (not all to do with food), were catered for. One of those further afield was Blue Cocktail in Cheyne Walk, which was 'just the thing for visitors hankering after a touch of Bohemia. The sixteenth century house was lit by candles.' It was quoted as being very cheap, but not licensed.

A feature of the restaurants listed was that most were foreign, and that in a time when London's population was overwhelmingly, if not local, then certainly British. Across London on the Edgware Road was The Czech restaurant, boasting the best selection of Viennese and Czech dishes in the capital. Just down the road in Nugent Terrace, Maida Vale, The Chef's Kitchen served great risottos and omelettes, with dinner available at 3s. The new Burma Orient restaurant in St Giles High Street served delicious curries. 'Even those with no knowledge of Eastern food will find the menu attractive', enthused the guide, who advised it was best to go to the restaurant in a group and to order a selection of dishes, each costing 2*s* 6*d*. One of the few British entries in the guide was awarded to the famous Wapping pub, The Prospect of Whitby, a must for visiting tourists, with views over the Thames. Fish was particularly liked, although the service was slow. If you fancied a 1912 Dow Port, it was available at a hefty 45*s* a bottle.

Moving into the West End, '96' Piccadilly was lavishly decorated in pink. The cooking was 'ambitious and very good'. Table d'hôte was 10*s* 6*d*, with specialities ranging from 6*s* 10*d* to a stratospheric 21*s*. Over in Fitzrovia, Au Savarin was reckoned to be an 'excellent little restaurant', offering good grills ranging from 2*s* 6*d* to 4*s* 6*d*. The guide noted, 'the cooking is better than the price suggests.' Further down the road in Charlotte Street you would find L'Etoille. Here they 'make attempts to keep the standards up to a really good Parisian restaurant'. They always offered a dozen starters and a good selection of fish dishes. Wines were hefty, ranging from 26*s* to 40*s*. The finest French restaurant in London before the war was A L'Ecu de France in Jermyn Street. Its reputation had slumped during the war, but the guide was happy to report that a recovery was underway. Even lunch cost 12*s* 6*d* and the price of dinner was listed as 'very high'. Maybe you were better off at The Haywain restaurant in Haymarket, which was 'a quiet restaurant in the noisiest part of London with food up to Soho standards'.

So it was that visitors to London were drawn to this rather grubby square mile which offers pleasure, temptation and danger in that order. Pleasure from its hundreds of restaurants, its jazz clubs and theatres. Temptation in the coded voices coming from the shadows asking any man from his teens to his eighties if he's 'looking for a good time'. And the danger for some of those accepting these offers, of being 'rolled' or having their wallet taken when otherwise engaged.

Soho is a village within a city. A foreign village of exotic smells and erotic distractions. A place where people sidle and stand idle, talking in seldom-heard languages. So much squeezed into such a small area. Street markets, delicatessens, dirty book shops, sinister-looking men in trilbies, shifty-looking men in bowlers, and women, lines of them. Older ones standing in darkened doorways, young girls leaning against lamp posts, and all this to a rhythmic beat of music rising from a nearby cellar.

This, then, is the home of many of London's finest eating places. An area that has attracted foreign migrants for hundreds of years, who brought with them many of their traditions and customs, but also importantly their varied cuisines. It was really not until the 1970s that China Town, as we know it today, developed around Gerrard Street. In the fifties, Choy's in Frith Street was considered to be the best Chinese place in town. The guide urged readers to try noodle soup, Pekinese chicken and sweet-and-sour pork. This would be considered rather old hat now, but was new and exciting sixty years ago. As wine was expensive the guide suggested that green tea was a better match. Pierre Auguste, who ran his restaurant in Gerrard Street, was a well-known character who had served with the Free French during the war and had been awarded the Croix de Guerre. It was reckoned he knew all of London's celebrities. Their weaknesses and indiscretions were safe with him as he ushered in their mistresses one week and their wives the next, without a hint of surprise. He offered a high standard of French food and a carafe of wine was available for just 10s.

A Soho landmark is the York Minster in Dean Street, often known as the 'French pub'. Two days after the French government collapsed in June 1940, Charles de Gaulle made a famous speech from a small room above the bar calling on the Free French to fight on against the Germans and the Vichy Government. The pub was run by Belgian Victor Berlemont and it attracted a Bohemian crowd of regulars, including Dylan Thomas and the young Jeffrey Bernard. The guide warned readers they would be greeted by rows of Pernod, Suz Cap Corse and Belgian beers. Upstairs the restaurant served 'cuisine bourgeoise', making you feel as if you were in Paris. Wine was on offer by the glass from 2s, while a good Côtes du Rhône set you back 15s. For cheap Soho food you headed to the Blue Windmill in Windmill Street. Nominally a Greek restaurant, it served escalopes of veal or steak and chips for 3s 6d. If you wanted a drink they fetched it in without charge. The guide praised the food for being rich and substantial.

Two restaurants I remember from that time that didn't warrant inclusion in the guide were Schmidt's and the Omelette Bar. Schmidt's in Charlotte Street was the haunt of the young, particularly students. The food, Germanic and stodgy, was cheap and we were all attracted by swaying waiters carrying loaded trays and dressed in long, white aprons. The Omelette Bar in Lisle Street was all gingham tablecloths and bring your own wine. Here, a chef cooked whatever type of omelette you fancied on a little stove. There was salad available and a wonderful apple pie for pudding, and all this for about 5s. Hardly fine dining, but memorable, particularly when accompanied by a pretty girlfriend.

The 1950s had seen a gradual change in the British attitude towards food, a shift from cremated meat and soggy vegetables to an acceptance of the merits of some foreign influences. A myth that Chinese restaurants were serving cats and dogs still led to the more conservative diners eating in them insisting on ordering steak and chips. No matter, even my father was becoming more adventurous, although

I did wish that on his visits to Del Monico on Old Compton Street he would stop selecting wines whose only advantage was to have the most attractive label. Our tastes in food and drink were in transition and so was London.

13

Changing Attitudes

During any decade public attitudes and perceptions invariably shift and none more so than in the 1950s. As always there were those seeking to maintain the status quo and others pushing for change. This tussle was conducted on a broad front and one of the most contentious controversies related to capital punishment. Few grieved when serial killer John Christie was hanged at Pentonville in July 1953, but two other cases accelerated a public debate that eventually led to the abolition of the death sentence for murder in 1963.

Back in 1930 a parliamentary select committee had recommended abolishing the death penalty for a trial period of five years. This ignored the fact that the majority of the population remained firmly in favour. They took the moral high ground in demanding retribution against the killer. While the number of executions was small and declining, they had a symbolic value which was ingrained in the public's mind. The House of Commons finally passed an abolition amendment in 1949 only to see it defeated in the Lords. They were supported by the judges and the Lords also rejected a compromise 'degrees' of murder bill. The government then appointed another royal commission to explore different, supposedly more humane, methods of despatch. The merits of the hypodermic needle, electric chair and even the guillotine were earnestly discussed before the whole matter was thrown back into the government's court.

Real public unease about capital punishment was finally prompted by a seemingly trivial event in the winter of 1952. A young girl preparing for bed at her home in Croydon saw two figures climbing into a warehouse across the street. She alerted her father, who promptly rang 999 and within minutes the police arrived. The two figures could be seen on the warehouse roof and the police climbed up to apprehend them. A single shot rang out and a struggle could be seen. There was shouting and two more shots. A small crowd that had gathered below saw the gunman run to the corner of the roof. Standing on the edge he hesitated before pitching into the dark. His fall was broken and the ground was soft after heavy rain. He survived. He was a sixteen-year-old called Christopher Craig.

Within minutes his accomplice was brought down by the police. He was nineteen-year-old Derek Bentley. Today he would be described as having 'learning difficulties'. In fact he was extremely backward, having only the mental ability of a child. A second person was carried down the stairs. A dead policeman shot between the eyes. The case lit the fuse for an impassioned public debate. Juvenile delinquency was rampant, surely reflecting a general moral decline. What was to be done? Knife-wielding Teddy Boys on street corners and gun-carrying teenagers brought fear to the honest, law-abiding majority. It was truly alarming. Worse, it transpired that Craig was not the product of a problem, criminal family. He came from a respectable neighbourhood and his father worked in a bank. His action was greeted with general bewilderment and not a little soul searching. Being under eighteen, Craig escaped the death penalty, but what of the none-too-bright Derek Bentley? At the time of his arrest, Bentley was carrying a knife and a knuckleduster. Not only was he not in possession of a gun but he was held and restrained by the police before a shot was fired. No matter, he was heard to shout 'Give it to them, Chris'. That was enough. During a lengthy trial these few words proved fatal for Bentley. In strict accordance with the law he was found guilty and sentenced to death.

A national campaign for clemency was soon underway. 'Should Bentley hang?' dominated conversation in every bar, club and home. Telegrams of protest from all over the country poured in. A letter signed by over 200 MPs urging clemency was ignored by the Home Secretary, Sir David Maxwell-Fyfe. He had been a judge at Nuremberg and the prospect of one more hanging was not about to change his hard-line attitude. On the night before the execution, emotions ran high in the House of Commons when the Speaker refused to allow an emergency debate on the matter. There was a last-minute all-party deputation to Maxwell-Fyfe, but he was unmoved. During the night hundreds of demonstrators gathered outside his chambers in The Temple. They were wasting their breath. The morning papers headlined 'Bentley will hang today'. Overall the nation was horrified. How was it possible to execute a young man who not only didn't lay a finger on anyone but was also mentally challenged? The morning press pictured his distraught family making their last emotional visit to the prison. Several hundred onlookers gathered outside Wandsworth jail on that cold morning of 28 January 1953, while inside Albert Pierrepoint went about his work. After a constant and tireless campaign by his family, Derek Bentley was finally granted a royal pardon on 30 July 1998. Even after sixty years his execution still prompts anger and anguish, but it was fundamental in a change towards not only capital punishment but also mental health issues. Timothy Evans was also mentally retarded and yet he had been hanged for the murder of his daughter in 1950. Evans had lived in the same house as John Christie and three years later Christie confessed to the murder of Evans' wife just prior to his own execution. There had always been doubts about the soundness of the Evans conviction and this was confirmed when an official enquiry in 1966 led to a posthumous pardon. Despite these miscarriages, the debate relating to capital punishment continued unabated.

In 1955 a new motion to suspend hanging, proposed by cross-party members in the House of Commons, was defeated by thirty-one votes. Opinion polls continued to show a sizeable majority in favour of retaining the gallows. In the same year the execution of Ruth Ellis was responsible for a significant shift in sentiment. Ellis proved to be something of an enigma. A peroxide-blonde, good-time girl, she acted with a calmness, grace and bravery during her trial and the lead up to her execution. On arriving in London, she had worked in a variety of dodgy clubs and had a number of short-lived relationships leading to unwanted pregnancies and subsequent abortions. By 1953 she was managing a rather sleazy club and it was during this time that she met David Blakely. He was a rather dashing racing car driver three years her junior. It didn't take long for him to become her lover. A slight snag was that he was already engaged to another woman. Being no angel herself, Ellis started seeing Desmond Cussen, and when she was sacked by the club she set up house with him. During this period, although they lived apart, she kept up her relationship with the more glamorous Blakely. He was becoming increasingly violent towards her, but thinking she was in love with him, she continued their affair. She had attracted violent men previously and sadly seemed prepared to accept this as normal behaviour. She subsequently had a miscarriage after being punched in the stomach by the boy racer. Finally she snapped. Jealousy and fury at her treatment led to her killing David Blakely on Easter Sunday 1955. Knowing that he was drinking in the Magdala pub in Hampstead, she waited for him to appear. As he stepped onto the pavement she called out his name, but he ignored her. As he went to open his car she took a revolver from her handbag and shot him. The first bullet missed and, alarmed, he started running away. She followed him and the second shot grounded him. Standing over him she then pumped three more bullets into him. Eye witnesses said she acted as if in a trance. On her arrest she said, 'I am guilty. I'm a little confused.'

Having undergone a variety of tests and having been examined by the principal medical officer in Holloway jail, she was declared sane and fit to stand trial. A day and a half was all the time needed to convict her. The evidence against her was conclusive. The prosecuting counsel, Mr Humphreys, only asked Ruth one question, 'Mrs Ellis, when you fired that revolver at close range into the body of David Blakely, what did you intend to do?' Dismissively, she replied, 'It is obvious that when I shot him I intended to kill him.' The jury took less than half an hour to reach their guilty verdict. She responded with a wan smile, simply mouthing a barely audible 'thanks'. After Mr Justice Havers passed sentence, she cut a frail figure as she clattered down the steps to the cells below in her high heels.

It was only hours before her execution that Ruth Ellis admitted that she had acquired the gun she used from her other lover, Desmond Cussen. The Home Secretary recorded that 'our law takes no account of the so-called *"crime passionnel"*'. He went on to state, 'If a reprieve were to be granted in this case I think we should have seriously to consider whether capital punishment should be retained as a penalty.' Despite a petition containing 50,000 signatures and the support of many influential figures, nothing was going to save this tragic, frail and vulnerable blonde. She was the last British woman to be executed and there is no doubt that her death created the climate for change. Many were outraged at what seemed a quite barbaric sentence. A new Homicide Act created an unsatisfactory compromise. It provided 'diminished responsibility' to be used for a reduction of a murder charge to manslaughter. In doing so it opened the way for discretion to be used in sentencing.

A large crowd gathered outside Holloway prison on the morning of the execution, including the veteran abolitionist Violet van der Elst. Was it possible that the emotion surrounding this execution led to Albert Pierrepoint's retirement the following year?

The public debate about capital punishment was just one factor in the angst being expressed about the overall moral climate in Britain. The decline of the family was thought to be accelerating, but each generation feels its problems are unique. In fact, this had been the subject for earnest discussion since the beginning of the twentieth century. Divorce had increased fourfold since the end of the First World War and organised religion was in decline.

By the early 1950s London had become a Mecca for commercialised sex. Foreigners were shocked by the women lining the streets of Bayswater, Paddington and Soho. Even the fashionable avenues of Mayfair were not immune. London was quoted as being 'the worst city in Europe'. Perhaps this was a hangover from an outwardly puritanical upbringing passed down from our Victorian ancestors. There was obviously a huge market for the services of these ladies and predatory pimps were always on hand to control them.

One Maltese family took this control to new levels with
a mixture of oily charm and subsequent violence. The
Messina brothers had been brought up in Egypt where their
parents ran a chain of successful brothels. Well versed in the
niceties of their trade, they had, by the early 1950s, refined
their methods of control, employing some borrowed from
legitimate businesses. Time and motion was introduced
to the sex industry. Targets were set, which if not met
were punished by violent retribution. The ten-minute rule
governed the time allowed before the girl was expected to
be back on the street. Many of these women were initially
inveigled into this way of life by promises of marriage
from one of the brothers. Soon they were trapped, not even
allowed to go shopping without being escorted by their
maid. No freelancers or any other non-Messina girls were
allowed near their territory. To do so risked a visit to hospital
nursing razor-slash wounds. The Messinas even organised a
dress exchange scheme for clothes. The girls were allowed
to keep about £30 a week, which was a great deal more
than they could have earned in a shop or a factory, but their
productivity targets required them to entertain up to a dozen
clients a session.

Enter a weird character who was to lead to the Messina
gang's undoing. Duncan Webb was a crime reporter on the
Sunday newspaper *The People*. In September 1950 a headline
in the paper demanded the arrest of these 'kings of vice in
the heart of London'. In the most sanctimonious tone Webb
went on to expose 'these sordid men who operate and profit
from their shameful trade'. The public were hooked on the
exposé and the paper's circulation soared. Webb revealed
further juicy facts for his readers.

'Why do these women submit themselves to such a tawdry
life? A comfortable flat is provided together with first class

meals served in their own room.' Together with their clothes exchange it was beginning to sound more like a recruitment campaign than a condemnation. For three weeks the articles continued. Squeaky-clean Webb announced, 'I have made it my duty to check on the prices charged. I found two pounds was the absolute minimum. Later investigations revealed that certain women indulged in the most ghastly perversions. These practices encouraged clients to pay up to twenty-five pounds for a half hour session.' The Messinas were obviously flexible about time when it came to their à la carte clients.

Despite the fact that Duncan Webb had connections with the London underworld and he was himself a convicted criminal, his articles had the Messina boys rushing for cover. Eugene and Carmello jumped into their Rolls Royces and headed for France, soon to be followed by Salvatore and Attilio. Alfredo stayed put and was sentenced to two years following his trial at the Old Bailey. A battle was lost but not the war. The Messinas' influence continued, albeit weakened, with Martha Watts, who was controlled by Eugene, organising increasing numbers of girls recruited on the Continent.

Duncan Webb, always something of a fantasist, now claimed to be a devout Roman Catholic. He placed an advertisement in *The Times* offering thanks to St Jude as patron saint to hopeless cases. He next cropped up as the ghost writer for the gangster Billy Hill, with his biography *Boss of Britain's Underworld*. Something of a weirdo to the end, he took it upon himself to marry the wife of murderer Donald Hulme. Cynthia was a widow within a fortnight when poor old Duncan died aged just forty-one.

Time for streetwalking, if not prostitution, was limited. The Sexual Offences Act of 1959 outlawed soliciting and suddenly the landscape of central London streets was changed. For centuries whispered invitations had come from darkened doorways. As always, opinion was divided. Some missed the girls under the lamp post twirling a set of keys. The outrageous, the seemingly demure, the beautiful, the ugly, all were now forced to advertise their services in telephone kiosks or corner-shop windows. The moralists' victory was instead submerged by a tide of brash strip clubs and grubby book shops.

For twenty-five years the Windmill theatre was the only place where men could legally gawp at a nude woman on stage. Despite a few illegal clubs trying to run the gauntlet, the Lord Chamberlain's diktat relating to nudity had gone largely unchallenged. Trust a lawyer to find a way round the law. A bespectacled Bengali barrister, Dhurjati Chaudhuri, was an unlikely owner of London's first non-stop strip club. He took advantage of a loophole that had previously been used by theatre clubs which allowed them to stage plays that had previously been banned by the Lord Chamberlain. With money haemorrhaging from his Asian Institute of Art and Theatre in Irving Street, just off Leicester Square, Chaudhuri decided to take the plunge. The lawyer's initial optimism was challenged by the existing laws that required a forty-eight-hour waiting period from the time a prospective member signed the application form. In addition, a public music and dancing licence was required, which the London County Council refused to issue. His pragmatic solution was to pay the regular £100 fines and cost it into the fixed overheads. The summer of 1957 saw lines of men snaking their way down Irving Street, anxious to pay their 25s for membership. The Irving theatre had a certain ring to it and Chaudhuri tried to retain a surface air of seedy respectability. In a nod to the Windmill, the shows were produced along conventional lines with comedians and singers alternating with the girls, who looked wholesome rather than sexy. The shows were dreadfully amateurish, but the punters didn't mind, compensated as they were by acres of moving flesh.

Original ideas, however poorly executed, are always copied, refined and improved. Paul Raymond, all pencilled moustache and loud suits, looked the archetypal spiv, which in a sense he was. After the war he had turned to stage management. As such he was an expert wheeler-dealer and now he used these skills to great effect. He had been monitoring the Irving theatre carefully and was convinced that here was an opportunity to make some serious money. A fortune. He was right. First he needed suitable premises. Despite warnings about criminals demanding protection money, he decided Soho was the place. It was normally crowded and rather tacky, but was an area where property was cheap. The grand-sounding Doric Ballroom was in truth a run-down building in Walkers Court, an alley connecting Brewer and Berwick streets. Only Isow's restaurant offered a glimpse of glamour among a sea of grimy, small shops. It was Jack Isow who owned the unloved Doric Ballroom. A Polish Jew, he was fat, fifty and avuncular, but shrewd. Like Raymond, he had been involved in the black market during the war. Alike in many ways, their relationship was tricky from the outset. They deserved each other. Isow must have realised that the property would be difficult to let. The two sides of the building were connected by a footbridge and how was it going to be possible to run a successful club other than at ground level? Eventually, after long negotiations, Raymond signed a twenty-one-year lease early in 1958. Isow was thrilled to have obtained a hefty rent of £5,000 a year, but he had made a vital error. Normally, few of his tenants in his Soho properties stayed in business long enough for rent reviews to apply. He had calculated Raymond's madcap scheme would fold. He was wrong; it was to cost him dearly.

Raymond had sufficient funds to completely refurbish the down-at-heel property. Isow would not be the last to underestimate Paul Raymond, who eventually became one of the richest men in Britain based on his Soho property portfolio and sex empire. With his wife, Jean, he interviewed staff for front-of-house jobs and spent long hours auditioning potential performers. A giant neon sign was erected announcing the arrival of Raymond's Revue Bar in Walkers Court. This was not going to be a 'shrinking violet' operation. It was brash, flash and proud. Dance routines choreographed by Jean were up to West End standards. News came of a competitor with the opening of the Café de Paris in Denman Street, which promised to push the boundaries of decency to new levels. Raymond really didn't need to worry, with over one thousand members signing up during the first week membership went on sale. Adjacent to the club's box office there was a grand, sweeping staircase, with a fountain and a thick crimson carpet. The venue offered a kitsch glamour not normally associated with grubby, squalid strip clubs. As the first punters entered, they passed posters of erotic nudes, heightening their anticipation. The upstairs bar was lit by glowing red bulbs. This was more Las Vegas than the Ritz, but then there were skimpily dressed girls, all fish-net stockings and six-inch heels, serving drinks and selling cigarettes on a tray set low enough to display an inviting cleavage.

The shows didn't disappoint either. Slick and professional but, more importantly, openly erotic and provocative. From the beginning, Raymond was pursued by the police, who were intent on closing the club down. Some driven by moral outrage, like Superintendent Strath, others corrupt, like the unhinged Sergeant Harry Challener. By the end of 1959 Raymond was putting on three shows a day, plus a late-night cabaret. Profits had soared to over £2,000 a week. London was being swept away by its success. Even the newspapers were endorsing 'the most fantastic evolution in British entertainment since the talkies'. Raymond, also getting carried away, was quoted as saying 'The female form is one of God's most beautiful creations.' Raymond's success was drawing in celebrities and the great and the good. He proclaimed it was a place where you could bring your wife.

Maybe he was on rocky ground there, but changing moral perceptions were also being driven by the young. They queried and challenged everything. The boundaries were being pushed back further by a photographer based in Gerrard Street. George Harrison Marks had begun his career snapping holidaymakers on the Brighton seafront. By early 1952 he was renting a first-floor flat on Gerrard Street that today is the centre of Chinatown. In the early fifties there were only a couple of Chinese restaurants and the area was run-down and scruffy. Finding it difficult to make a living doing work for local theatres, a chance meeting led to a change of direction. George had photographed Norman Wisdom when he had appeared in Brighton and it was through this contact that he obtained a commission to photograph the cast of a show being produced by Bernard Delfont. One of the chorus girls was the beautiful Pamela Green. Very soon she moved in with him. She had already done some nude poses for another photographer who packaged them in packs of five and sold them to the array of bookshops in and around Soho. These were attracting repeat orders within hours of being displayed. It was time for Pam to switch her allegiance, and the germ of a business was born.

Although outwardly the British public was uncomfortable

with nudity, this masked a huge potential market of sexually
repressed men. Initially, Harrison's shots featured only
Pamela Green with her hourglass figure of 38-24-36, but it
was obvious they had to recruit more models. They feared
this would be difficult, particularly as the girls had to be
well endowed. Gradually, applicants came forward and one
of their first new models was Lorraine Burnett, who had
previously been a Windmill girl. As their stable of girls grew,
sales boomed and the couple were already making a good
living. The potential was enormous and in 1957 they took
the plunge by producing a magazine. The competition was
limited to magazines featuring wholesome pin-ups. *Kamera*,
a thirty-two-page pocket-sized magazine, was anything but.
Launched just months before the opening of Raymond's
Revue Bar, its timing could not have been better. Marks took
an incredible risk by ordering an initial print run of 15,000.
The first edition featured sixteen different models shown
in provocative poses, which were far raunchier than those
shown in *Lilliput* or *Spick and Span*. Within days it became
obvious that they were on to a winner. Priced at 2s 6d, the
first edition sold over 100,000 copies. It was a recipe to print
money. The format was simple, a colour front cover followed
by a collection of alluring models, keeping within a whisper
of the existing law for the time being. They airbrushed out
any hint of pubic hair. A generation of schoolboys grew up
confused about the female anatomy. The models were like
mermaids with legs. Marks added new titles each edition,
tilting towards outright pornography, something he did
become involved in during the 1960s after he had split from
Pamela Green.

Marks and Paul Raymond, who knew each other socially,
were responsible for pushing the boundries of what was
considered acceptable for public consumption. From today's

perspective, they treated women like objects and just as a vehicle to making fortunes. Raymond continued to accumulate this wealth, while Harrison Marks squandered his with a life of hedonistic excess. The fortune made by Paul Raymond seemingly brought him little joy. Despite his huge houses, numbers of luxury cars and jet-set living, he died a sad man. His marriage failed as he embarked on a series of short-lived relationships, increasingly finding solace in the bottle and drugs. He was devastated by the death of his daughter, Debbie, from an overdose in 1992. He lived until 2008, spending his final years as a virtual recluse in his Mayfair penthouse.

Under the surface, attitudes to sex were already changing. The *Kinsey Report* of 1948 had caused a universal intake of breath. Could those revelations be true? Five years later saw the publication of Kinsey's second report, *Sexual Behaviour of the Human Female*. The publication date became known as 'K Day'. The report was greeted with the expected outrage. In Britain, women's sexuality had been generally thought to be subordinate to men's. Modesty was the role to be played by long-suffering wives. To be told that women had their own desires and fantasies shocked and intrigued the British public. The newspapers saw their circulations rocket as they informed their readers that over eighty per cent of women preferred to make love in the dark. That twenty-three per cent of them reached orgasm while merely petting had the *Daily Mirror* producing double-page spreads with intimate photographs illustrating in detail what was meant by petting. The *Sunday Despatch* devoted huge coverage over three weeks, whose details had maiden aunts reaching for the smelling salts. Many thought they were being given too much information, but young men who hoped that the report would open the floodgates to free love were to be disappointed. For a few years at least, the stigma of a child born out of wedlock remained. The arrival of the contraceptive pill in the early 1960s largely eliminated that danger and its effect was as profound on the behaviour of the young as it was for family planning.

Homosexuality remained an area for heated debate, which was fanned by a public scandal during the summer of 1955. One of those involved was a twenty-eight-year-old socialite, Lord Montagu of Beaulieu. At his trial the following year, he was one of three men convicted of 'consensual homosexual offences'. Thousands of men were being imprisoned following a clampdown encouraged by our old friend, Home Secretary Sir David Maxwell-Fyfe. He instigated 'a new drive against male vice that would rid England of this plague'. By 1952 the number of cases brought against 'these abominables of male perversion' had risen five-fold since before the war. The Montagu sentence led to a wave of public sympathy. In August 1954 a committee was appointed under the chairmanship of Sir John Wolfanden to examine 'the whole law and practice relating to homosexual offences and prostitution'. When the report eventually appeared three years later, it was clinical and pragmatic, although one committee member dissented from its findings. James Adair, a Scottish former Procurator General, thought that a proposed relaxation might be seen as a licence for further undermining basic moral standards. The report was in favour of making homosexual acts between consenting adults (over twenty-one) in private no longer unlawful.

The press were divided. The *Daily Mirror* stated 'It's the truth. It's the answer to life.' They were supported with varying degrees of reservation by 'the serious press'. Predictably, the *Express* and *Mail* agreed with James Adair. Opinion polls conducted at the time revealed that the public were still split right down the middle. It was to be a further ten years before gay sex was finally decriminalised in England and Wales, but the balance of opinion was now set on backing Wolfanden's recommendations.

The drift towards more permissive public attitudes was not entirely one way. March 1954 witnessed the start of an extraordinary religious crusade conducted by American evangelist preacher, Dr Billy Graham. This was two years in the planning, and his unique preaching style touched a nerve, particularly with the young. Some felt he sold God as a product in much the same way any businessman would market a new product, but the results were astonishing.

Addressing his first rally at Haringey Arena, he started his sermon, 'We've not come here to the City of London to save England. We have not come here with any great ideas that we are going to tell you how to do it. We haven't come here to reform you. We have come here at the invitation of these churches to help you in a crusade to win men to Jesus Christ and help promote the kingdom of God in Britain.'

His style of preaching had an almost hypnotic effect on the vast audiences he addressed as thousands came forward with a pledge to dedicate their lives to God. He held nightly rallies, with two or three separate gatherings on Saturdays. He addressed a huge crowd in Hyde Park and 12,000 heard him preach in Trafalgar Square. His simple message drew a response not so different from those enjoyed later by the emerging pop stars. Some reckoned he produced a mass hysteria, not dissimilar from a Hitler rally, albeit the message was very different. The crusade ended with a rally at Wembley Stadium that attracted 120,000, while almost 70,000 gathered at nearby White City Stadium.

How many stayed converted to a life honouring God and the gospel is unknown, but Graham's ability to reach into the hearts and consciousness of Londoners was unique. Almost two million attended his crusade during the three months he was in the capital. Despite all the changes that were taking place at an accelerating pace, there was obviously an underlying conflict in many people's minds. Perhaps most of us want to live a good, and even spiritual, life. Unfortunately, rather like dieting or making New Year's resolutions, we tend to fall by the wayside as temptations present themselves.

Despite Billy Graham, there was a sense that the overall change in society was generally for the best. The young continued pushing the agenda. Nothing was set in stone. Only the criminal fraternity carried on, seemingly oblivious to what was going on around them. They continued their heists and carved lumps out of each other. The alliance between Billy Hill and Jack Spot crumpled like a doomed love affair. Hill was clever, a meticulous planner, while Spot was just a thug. He hit the headlines when he was involved in a razor fight in Frith Street with Albert Dimes, a henchman of Hill's. Fearing his influence was on the wane, Spot launched himself at Dimes after a perceived insult. Both were carted off to the Middlesex hospital for running repairs, while the press warned of outright warfare on the streets of London. In truth, London in those days was perfectly safe for those not seeking trouble. The fight for control of London's underworld was ongoing, with the Kray twins waiting to take centre stage.

London was safe, but edgy. A 1950s Soho guide described its Latin quarter as 'vice-ridden, glamorous, dirty and yet romantic, where the streets are shady on both side of the road'. It was not just criminals who were drawn to London. It also acted as a magnet for writers, artists and people of creative talent who contributed to a decade of outstanding achievement.

14
The Creative World

Popular music is possibly the best barometer for defining a decade and the changes taking place in society. Throughout the arts there was a constant tension and shift as writers, artists and composers sought to break new ground. This antagonism between the emerging talents and those of the arts establishment was vividly illustrated by a broadcast speech given by Sir Alfred Munnings as President of the Royal Academy. A superb painter of horseflesh (preferably with some decorative lady aboard), he loathed modern art. Fuelled by too much booze and the encouragement of his friend Winston Churchill, he was not about to hold back. Describing Picasso's work as 'queer distortions', he continued, 'they say there is something in this so-called modern art!' He obviously disagreed; 'if you paint a tree, for God's sake try and make it look like a tree'.

By 1957 Churchill was joining the debate. A considerable artist himself, he had become infuriated by a portrait of him by Ruskin Spear which was exhibited at the Royal Academy. He confided in James Lees-Milne that it was a gross caricature. Worse, Sir Winston had neither sat for the portrait nor even been approached. Here were old men railing against change which had led to paintings they didn't understand or appreciate. It was not as if Ruskin Spear was at the cutting edge of the emerging art scene. Abstract art had been around for years, but figurative art was still loved by the general public. Artists like John Minton, Frank Auerbach and Francis Bacon were now the new pin-ups of the art world. A group known as the 'constructionists', including Kenneth Martin and Anthony Hill, sought to combine figurative theory with the practice of abstraction. Few understood what this meant. The majority rather agreed with Munnings and were accordingly dismissed by the so-called art elite.

Similar battles raged across the whole artistic landscape. Somerset Maugham at least acknowledged that there was 'a certain vigour and power of expression' in Dylan Thomas' poems, but that his 'syntax was deplorable and there was little intellectual content'. For a man weaned on Shelley and Tennyson, there was no meeting point. Like abstract painting, Maugham did not understand and neither did he want to.

Writers are among the most important and influential of all those involved in the artistic field. Stemming from their thoughts and ideas come books, plays, shows and even television dramas. It was the popularity of television that again helped accelerate the change in writing during the 1950s. Somerset Maugham, Terrence Rattigan and even Noel Coward were in danger of being swamped by aspiring, new, exciting writers and playwrights breaking down barriers of what was considered acceptable subject matter. Rattigan's *Separate Tables* opened at the St James Theatre in 1954. Although enjoying good reviews both in London and New York, to be followed four years later by a successful film version, the work vividly illustrated the gulf in taste that was developing. Repressed emotions, however well crafted by the playwright, were now considered old hat. Noel Coward, to his sorrow, was similarly condemned. His play, *The*

Ace of Clubs, received mixed reviews and the film version was savaged by the critics. Simple comedy represented by *Seagulls Over Sorrento* or brash, American musicals like *Guys and Dolls* were what was wanted by audiences, not buttoned-up, beautifully spoken actors understating their true feelings. In 1956 a new phrase, 'angry young men', entered everyday vocabulary. There was no doubting Jimmy Porter's feelings in John Osborne's play *Look Back in Anger*. Yet to the old school it was as if Osborne was writing in a foreign language. After reading *Look Back in Anger*, Noel Coward was confused: 'I wish I knew why the hero is so dreadfully cross and what about.' The play opened at the Royal Court in May 1956. Directed by Tony Richardson, it was lauded by the influential critic Kenneth Tynan. Recently he had been directing his bile at poor old Terrence Rattigan, constantly lampooning him. The great divide in appreciation extended to the critics. A story of a destructive relationship in squalid conditions between a working-class man married to an Army officer's daughter prompted this little gem: 'It is difficult to believe that a colonel's daughter brought up with some standards would have stayed in this sty for a day.'

While *Look Back in Anger* was a swipe at authority and the status quo, it also had some worrying, underlying themes. In common with *A Streetcar Named Desire*, it demeaned women with physical and mental abuse. Jimmy warns his wife that he has no public-school scruples. He declares, 'If you slap my face, my God, I'll lay you out.' Women, it appeared, were still a long way from obtaining equality. For generations many had lived in fear of male brutality. If Jimmy Porter was to be believed, their future prospects were no better.

Look Back in Anger opened the floodgates for other young, provincial, working-class writers. While rejecting that they were 'angry young men', they were bracketed together in the public's mind. Alan Sillitoe hit a chord with his *Saturday Night and Sunday Morning*, particularly when the film was released, starring Albert Finney. For those of us who were young at the time, here at last was a British film depicting real life. Real, everyday language, swearwords and all. Sitting in the darkened cinema, I was aware of a groundswell of approval. At last a generation and a class were gaining a realistic voice. Joe Lampton, in John Braine's *Room at the Top*, was another flawed hero from a humble background. He is ambitious and ruthless in his resolve to escape his working-class roots, even if it means getting the boss's daughter pregnant. Shelagh Delaney wrote *A Taste of Honey* when she was only eighteen. Planned as a novel, it was produced as a controversial play by Joan Littlewood's Theatre Workshop before transferring to the West End and ultimately being made into an award-winning film. Here was a 'kitchen sink' drama tackling subjects that only a few years before would never have seen the light of day. Illicit sex, abortion, race and homosexuality were all covered and while the young and trendy loved its honesty, much of middle England longed for Rattigan and Noel Coward.

Kingsley Amis came from a respectable, south London, middle-class background, but he too was at the forefront of changing the British literary scene. He set out to thumb his nose at and debunk British society with his first novel, *Lucky Jim*, published in 1954. Sixty years later, he is acknowledged as one of the finest writers of the late twentieth century. He also had a reputation for being a serial adulterer and an iconic consumer of alcohol. Grumpy old Somerset Maugham took up cudgels again, describing the character of 'Lucky' Jim Dixon as 'scum', but he did concede that it was a remarkable novel, possibly because it won the Somerset Maugham Award For Fiction in 1954. Depicting the exploits of a red-brick university lecturer, the leading character is outspoken and outrageous, but the book is written with the style of an educated man, not a provincial oaf. Despite this and generally glowing reviews, old-established writers found it hard to praise. They were more comfortable with an upper-crust elite with worthwhile ideals. V. S. Pritchett thought Amis 'brashly vulgar', neatly summing him up as 'a literary Teddy Boy'. Critic F. R. Leavis thought Amis to be a pornographer. Together with the kitchen-sink writers, Amis had stepped outside the comfort zone of a previous generation and engaged a younger audience. Together, they were changing the British literary landscape.

Another writer with no particular high-flown literary ambition was to become a bestselling novelist and the founder of a character who lives on today, long after the author's death. Ian Fleming was certainly not of the kitchen-sink school. The son of an influential banker, Fleming was educated at Eton and Sandhurst. Working during the war in naval intelligence helped him in the creation of James Bond, the secret agent with licence to kill. His novel *Casino Royale* was published in 1952 with a retail price of 10*s* 6*d*. It was a huge success. Fleming offered adventure and glamour in faraway places – a sure-fire recipe for success in dark austerity Britain. Escapism at the cinema or through reading provided an outlet and escape from what was for most a humdrum life. *Live and Let Die* and *Moonraker* consolidated his success. Criticism was levelled at him for voyeurism and what was interpreted as sadomasochism, but Fleming could hardly have cared less as his books leapt off the shelves and he became a household name. *Diamonds Are Forever* and *From Russia With Love* saw him at the top of his form. Kingsley Amis (not an easy man to please) loved the Bond books. They were 'far more than simple cloak-and-dagger stories with a bit of fashionable affluence thrown in'. It was in the 1960s when the first Bond films were made that brought Fleming international fame and fortune. While in no way as socially challenging as Sillitoe, Wesker, Braine or Osborne, Ian Fleming tapped into the changing cultural climate in Britain. In doing so, he created a very British hero not so different from those of John Buchan and Sapper. Still from the officer class, but not so wet. Calm and understated in a crisis, with a sense of cruelty. Across the country young men secretly imagined themselves to be just like James Bond and their girlfriends wished they were. In the long tradition of British thriller writers, many of Bond's adversaries were foreign. Some things never change.

Authors were being helped by a revolution in reading. Public libraries issued over 300 million books in 1958 and an opinion poll found that fifty-five per cent of the population were currently reading a book, when questioned. Another factor in the rapid growth in reading was the increasing popularity of the paperback. Although not new in concept, marketing and the type of subject on offer led to sales of sixty million in 1958. In addition, the four major book clubs could claim 350,000 active members. Books were being read by new groups, particularly the young, as the paperback revolution took hold. Reading was no longer just for swots and academics. Reading was fun. Popular fiction, thrillers, love stories were all on offer for just a few shillings. Away from the earthy kitchen-sink brigade, Hammond Innes and Nevil Shute fed middle England with bestselling tales set in faraway places. They offered a suburban voice without recourse to sex and squalor. British authors were as varied as the subject matter they covered.

Evelyn Waugh was already acknowledged as one of Britain's greatest writers. *Helena*, published in 1950, was followed in 1952 by one of his greatest successes. *The Sword of Honour* was a trilogy which was inspired by his own service in the Second World War. It was hailed as a satirical triumph in which he explores the futility of war against a background of seeking spiritual fulfilment, no doubt fuelled by his conversion to Roman Catholicism.

Another creative genius, Graham Greene, was also much affected by his Roman Catholic faith. Like Waugh, he was already a respected writer by the fifties. He had just enjoyed great acclaim for writing the script for the film *The Third Man* in 1949. Many of his stories were made into films or adapted for TV, including *Brighton Rock* and *The End of the Affair*. His greatest achievement during the 1950s was *Our Man in Havana*. It was made into a memorable film in 1959, starring Alec Guinness.

It is perhaps surprising that an intellectual professor of physiology at Oxford should have written a children's tale that still resonates, with the genre still copied today. J. R. R. Tolkien wrote *The Hobbit* in 1937 and *The Lord of the Rings* was completed over a twelve year period before being published in three volumes during 1954 and 1955. It has become one of the bestselling novels of all time and is a mind-bending work of extraordinary imagination.

Here was a golden age for British writers who encouraged a whole generation to bury their nose in a book. The breadth of their appeal remains and influenced subsequent generations.

Meanwhile Binkie Beaumont, sitting in his office above the Globe theatre in Shaftesbury Avenue, was a worried man. Binkie, who quietly controlled much of the West End theatre productions, had a new powerful enemy. Television was keeping people at home, leaving the theatres often playing to half-full houses. For years he had provided theatre-goers with a diet of light comedy laced with classic drama, but now it was obvious he needed a change of direction. The most successful shows in London were lavish American musicals, which began in 1950 with the staging of *Oklahoma* at the Stoll theatre. The same year saw the launching of another Rodgers and Hammerstein blockbuster, *Carousel*, at the Theatre Royal. Dreary old London was captivated by the sheer vitality and exuberance of the shows. The very English *King's Rhapsody* with music by Ivor Novello was well received, but was somehow tame and restricted set alongside the US offerings. I remember being taken to see Novello's (aptly named) *Gay's the Word*, starring an over-the-top Cicely Courtneidge and the lovely Lizbeth Webb. I enjoyed it but would have preferred Cole Porter's *Kiss Me Kate*, which was being performed at the Coliseum. In 1951 Rogers and Hammerstein were back with *South Pacific*, which again was a smash hit. Binkie imagined he had already been taking a risk in staging *Seagulls Over Sorrento* at The Apollo. Working-class characters weren't really his thing and although the show, starring Ronald Shiner, was a success it was slowly dawning on the old impresario that musicals were the way forward.

Still they came and filled theatres, these brash, noisy shows. *Paint Your Wagon* opened at Her Majesty's Theatre to be followed in coronation year by *The King and I*, whose storyline so appealed to the London audiences. Sandy Wilson's *The Boy Friend* flew the flag that year for Britain, its small budget and quaintness vividly illustrating the difference in power and financial clout between British productions and those from the States. Julian Slade followed up this success with *Salad Days*, a rather potty but likeable low-budget musical featuring goofy young men and gorgeous, dizzy blondes. My parents obviously favoured these British shows but I longed to see the real thing – an all-singing-and-dancing American show. The time was right for Binkie Beaumont to embrace the musical. By turn charming and persuasive, he could also be underhand and duplicitous. He had already gone to work.

In 1956 Binkie took Elizabeth Seal to Paris to see *Irma La Douce*, a show with music by Marguerite Monnot. He had seen Seal appear in the *Pyjama Game* and was convinced she was suited to the star role in the French musical. He duly secured the British rights. His conversion to musicals complete, he was also cunningly negotiating to stage what were to be his two greatest successes. Offering Elizabeth Seal £120 a week to star in *Irma La Douce*, he added that he expected her to dress at all times like a star and not a beatnik. Enter her agent who pointed out that if she was to look like a star she needed to be paid accordingly. £200 was agreed upon, but it is not clear whether Seal ever matched up to Binkie's required haute-couture standards together with the statutory long, white gloves. No matter, the show opened to rave reviews. Binkie ensured that the great and the good flocked to the Apollo to be photographed on the opening night. Directed by Peter Brook and also starring Keith Michell, the show subsequently enjoyed great success on Broadway.

Binkie's next production heralded a golden period for him and the London theatre. *West Side Story* opened at Her Majesty's Theatre on 12 December 1958. Although in a sense the ultimate American musical, it had its roots in England, being loosely based on Shakespeare's *Romeo and Juliet*. With music by Leonard Bernstein and lyrics by Stephen Sondheim, it had the effect of making earlier American musicals seem almost as outdated as works by Ivor Novello. This was modern, edgy and exhilarating. The upper west side of New York with its teenage gangs was a shock to staid British audiences. What were they to make of it? Well, they loved it, as did most of the critics. The musical had been taken to a new level – a sort of opera for the masses. Superb music and choreography without overweight ladies of a certain age pretending they were young and alluring. This was raw, red-meat drama. One critic referred to the 'radioactive fall-out' from *West Side Story*. Was it just the setting or the more challenging subject matter? Maybe both, but what came next even trumped the success of *West Side Story*, which did go on to run for 1,040 performances.

My Fair Lady had opened on Broadway in 1956 to fantastic reviews. The story of *Pygmalion* set to music had British producers rushing to the States in an attempt to secure the rights for a London production. Lulled by Binkie Beaumont's previous inclination not to get involved in musicals, the other leading players – Grade, Hylton, Parnell and Littler, set off full of hope. Unfortunately for them, they had wasted journeys. Binkie had outflanked them by securing the rights some eighteen months previously and keeping it a secret. Originally, Michael Redgrave had been the first choice to play Henry Higgins. The Broadway producers were thwarted as Redgrave didn't want to be tied down to play the part for the two years they were demanding. Despite lengthy discussions he would only consent to six months.

In January 1955 the American production team arrived in London to persuade Rex Harrison to take the part. There were more complications as Harrison and his wife Lilli Palmer were appearing in *Bell, Book and Candle* for Binkie at the Phoenix theatre. Worse, Harrison had started an affair with the gorgeous Kay Kendall and playing love scenes with his wife was making him tetchy. Eventually, although Harrison agreed to play Higgins in principle, he was still contracted to Binkie. Beaumont played the Americans as an expert fisherman would a salmon. Of course he would co-operate by withdrawing *Bell, Book and Candle* in the spring. Then attendances bucked up and the play was attracting full houses again. Good news for Binkie, potential disaster for the Yanks. They had already booked the theatre on Broadway and the cast had been finalised. A postponement was out of the question. With Harrison still under contract, Binkie held all the cards. They had walked straight into his trap. Harrison had been practising the songs for months. He was perfect for the part. They knew it, Harrison knew it but, more importantly, Binkie knew it. Now, ever so politely, he turned the screw. How could he help? He would release Harrison, but he would need some compensation. Surely that was reasonable? He struck a hard bargain, the best in a lifetime of deals. He required not only the British, but also the continental, rights to *My Fair Lady*. Also one and a half per cent of the gross Broadway takings and, of course, the provincial tours as well. The Americans swallowed hard but Binkie wasn't finished yet. Smiling, he also told them he needed £25,000 in cash. Herman Levin, the Broadway producer, knew a pro when he saw one. The deal was settled at the table always reserved for Binkie at Scott's. Harrison went on to star in the famed Broadway production for two years. It was in the spring of 1957 that plans were finalised for the London opening. Greedy old Binkie sought to maximise his investment by persuading the Society of Authors (who managed George Bernard Shaw's estate) to ban all productions of *Pygmalion* in Great Britain for ten years. Their decision was eased by a payment which strengthened their fragile financial position. Binkie also imposed a ban on any of the songs from the show being broadcast prior to the opening. Even he couldn't stop long playing records being imported from the States, but he could live with that.

Public interest in the show was being stoked to hysterical levels. The production was booked for months ahead and tickets were changing hands at unprecedented prices. The chances of attending the opening night for most were nil. Binkie was always careful to reserve seats for the rich and famous for any of his show openings, but this was different. International stars and celebrities were to be even found in 'the gods', alongside captains of industry and London socialites. The great and the good, the not so good and the filthy rich jostled at the bar. Outside, rows of cameramen recorded the arrivals on the red carpet. The social editor of *Tatler* was almost moved to tears. Here was everything, everybody he wanted under one roof. The blue-bloods, featured in *Debretts*, rubbed shoulder to shoulder with glamorous film stars. So many rich Americans had flown over that Martini cocktails were more popular at the bar than whisky, but still a poor second to the popping of champagne corks. The crush, the slightly hysterical babble of conversation drowned the five-minute bell, which was ignored. Binkie was getting agitated. Everything about the night was manic and different. Finally the curtain went up, fifteen minutes late. Luckily, the performance lived up to all the hype. The audience played their part. They were out to enjoy themselves. There was a buzz of expectation as the curtain went up. The extravagance of the sets and costumes and the performances of Harrison, Julie Andrews and Stanley Holloway had them cheering wildly. Many had never experienced such a reaction in a theatre. It was part carnival, part football crowd, as the show ended. The curtain calls were endless, lasting almost half an hour. The reviews were overwhelmingly positive. The show was a triumph, eventually running for over five years and to 2,200 performances.

This was to be the high point of Binkie Beaumont's career.

The years that followed witnessed a gradual weakening of his hold on West End theatreland. The success of *My Fair Lady* is, in a sense, ironic. The British theatre, having been swamped by successive American blockbuster musicals, finally reached their public with the most English of themes. One that dwelt on the class system, which was still so apparent in British society. Despite the emergence of kitchen sink, rock 'n' roll and a desire for change, there was still room for nostalgia. A hankering for more elegant times, for a Britain of leisure and good manners, an escape from the pressure of modern life, and yet now many are beginning to look back at the 1950s in the same way that our parents viewed Edwardian England.

The new demon in the shape of television also had an initial effect on cinema attendances. While there were fewer queues, a trip to the cinema remained one of the most popular forms of entertainment. While Shaftesbury Avenue had been developed during the late nineteenth century as the centre of London's theatreland, within fifty years, just round the corner in Leicester Square, glitzy cinemas dominated. There was a certain symmetry developing across the arts in the 1950s, as new talent challenged the traditional. It coincided, or possibly spawned, a new youth culture and in the cinema this was spearheaded by America. The arrival in Britain of the method school of acting merged with rock 'n' roll to give a sense of liberation to a group of youngsters who had grown up under the shadow cast by the war. Elia Kazan had worked as an actor for years before co-forming the Actors Studio in New York. He developed a gritty, realistic form of acting for the screen and introduced a number of hitherto unknown actors who leapt to stardom under his direction. Marlon Brando swept to fame in *A Streetcar Named Desire* and *Zapata*. It was his role in *On the Waterfront* that really touched a nerve with British youth. Blue denim jeans and

T-shirts were the new uniform of choice. We all effected a new moodiness in our attempts to impress the girls. That same generation of teenage girls swept all thoughts of Brando aside with the arrival of James Dean. They loved him in the film of John Steinbeck's *East of Eden*, but it was *Rebel Without A Cause* that perfectly fitted the mood of the young. Dean, like Brando, was moody and mumbled, but he was vulnerable as well, and the girls loved him. We young men wished we could be more like him. By the time his third film, *Giant*, arrived in London in 1956 he was already dead, killed in a car crash in September 1955. Over 29,000 waited outside the church in Indiana where his funeral was held. Having only appeared in three films and dying aged just twenty-four ensured his lasting iconic status. He projected the image of rebellious youth and within a year of his death he had a fan club of almost four million.

There seemed little British film makers could do to compete with the massive productions arriving from the States. Lavish musicals like *Singing in the Rain*, *White Christmas* and *The King and I* guaranteed success with British audiences. These offered pure escapism from reality. Walt Disney's *Peter Pan* and *Sleeping Beauty* provided fun for the whole family, and then came the ultimate blockbusters. Huge productions shown on wide screens, drawing the audience into the heart of the action. *The Ten Commandments* showed the enduring attraction of a religious theme, no matter how schmaltzy, as did *The Nun's Story*, starring a demure Audrey Hepburn. It was left to *Ben Hur* to scoop the pool in the lavish production stakes. Starring Charlton Heston and Stephen Boyd, its chariot race remains one of the most memorable scenes in cinematic history.

Without the financial clout of the leading Hollywood studios, Britain's film industry had to find a niche that would appeal. Comedy had always been a strength, with a string of successes from Ealing Studios. These continued in the 1950s with *The Lavender Hill Mob* in 1951 and *The Lady Killers* four years later. With the war having affected almost every family in the country, it was natural that war-themed stories still filled cinemas. *The Cruel Sea*, based on Nicholas Monsarrat's story of war in the Atlantic, set the scene for a raft of productions which had filmgoers cheering uninhibitedly from their seats. *The Dam Busters* told the story of the Rhein dams being destroyed by the 'bouncing bombs' invented by Barnes Wallace. *Reach for the Sky* continued the theme of honouring our war heroes, but it was in 1957 that David Lean directed the epic *Bridge on the River Kwai*. A story of British prisoners of war in Burma, it had a stellar cast led by Alec Guinness. It remains one of the best British films ever made. It hit home to me, as one of our neighbours had returned having survived working on that very railway. He remained gaunt and slightly haunted-looking as he resumed his life in advertising. Like so many who had gone through ghastly experiences in the war, he never talked about Burma or the Japanese.

A gentler success came with *Genevieve*, a film about a vintage motor rally from London to Brighton. Still, the film caused an outcry when Dinah Sheridan whispered 'make love to me' to John Gregson. Outrage, letters to the newspapers! Was this a last gasp as the walls of decency were even being pulled down in what was supposedly a family film? While *I'm All Right, Jack* was a comedy, it underlined the deep divisions in British society and the growing power of the unions. The kitchen-sink brigade were represented by the film version of John Braine's *Room at the Top*, but the decade ended with a film so dark and distasteful that it confirmed in many minds that 'things were going too far'. Surely the country was sliding into a moral morass? *Peeping Tom*, made in 1959, was directed by Michael Powell. Viewed today, it still has the power to shock. A serial killer murders women while recording their last moments on a portable camera. The film is now hailed as a masterpiece, but on its release it was met with a storm of protest. It is moody, claustrophobic and downright creepy, but emphasised the gap that had grown up in the country. Some of the most creative spirits reckoned there should be no subject that couldn't be explored, while middle England feared for a future with seemingly few rules or boundaries. It is an argument that continues today.

Sculptors always seem to be ahead of the curve in their pursuit of the abstract. Visitors to the Festival Gardens couldn't really understand the works of Henry Moore, but found them somehow comforting as opposed to the futuristic daubs by the new wave of painters. Perhaps it was the solidity of the base materials that they found so satisfying. In avant-garde circles Moore was already considered rather dated.

The summer exhibition at the Royal Academy had become one of the social events of the London season. It was a way for the great and the good to show that they had some understanding of the creative spirit. Better still to be seen buying work from the exhibition. Although there were abstract subjects on view in 1959, many of the leading modernists continued to ignore this last exhibition of the decade. There was nothing from Bacon, Freud or Robert Colquhoun. Peter Lanyon and Robert MacBryde didn't want to be associated with the exhibition either. It was left to the likes of Munnings with his *A Winner at Epsom* and *Warren Hill, Newmarket* not to alarm the visitors. The outrageous and attention-seeking Augustus John sent his final canvas depicting *Dorelia*. Edward Seago, who had tutored Winston

Churchill, showed a work of *The Thames at Millbank*. Not to be outdone, the former prime minister showed a fruit study and a painting of *Notre Dame De Vie above Cannes*. The public felt more comfortable with recognisable figurative works and landscapes. Even at the end of the decade the schism between artistic aims remained as huge as ever.

While the well-to-do lined their walls with paintings (hopefully of ancestors), their love of art did not always extend to artists. That arch snob James Lees-Milne, on meeting Duncan Grant, described him as being '... a roguish fellow, a kind of everlasting child whom the world protects ... very dirty and unkempt, his long, wispy, ratty hair most unattractive'. What the artist thought of Lees-Milne is not recorded.

The tensions of everyday British life were being mirrored throughout the creative world. Change, represented by fresh talent, was often resented, except by the young. A sense of grave unease that old, established values were being jettisoned to accommodate people of little talent who were just out to shock. Added to this was a developing teenage culture. Older people in all spheres of life were feeling uncomfortable. It was as if the values that they had been brought up to believe in were being eroded. The writer and broadcaster Godfrey Winn spoke for many when he stated that modern drama was dominated by 'dirt, depression and depravity'. Writing in 1959, he insisted that 'everyone concerned with the putting on of plays today seems obsessed with the same idea. Unless a play scours the depths and empties the garbage tins in front of the floodlights, it won't be a success. What nonsense. What complete, utter nonsense!' A decade had passed and the differences remained, but it was the young that were setting the agenda now.

15
The Young Ones

You couldn't avoid them. On every tube train, bus and mainline station there were men in uniforms. Some carrying kit bags, either home on leave or returning to their camps scattered throughout the British Isles. Conscription had been introduced during the war and it continued throughout the 1950s. After basic training it was a lottery as to where they would be stationed. Some were confined to the boredom of home postings or at one of the vast camps in Germany. Being assigned to the warmth of Cyprus or Kenya was usually welcomed, but was rather more dangerous. By 1951 national servicemen accounted for half of the overall services manpower. Hundreds were killed in action in Korea and at Suez. Those seeing active service were kept busy by successive governments trying forlornly to maintain Britain's influence in a fast-changing world.

Those young men crowding the stations in their khaki, light blue and bell-bottoms gave Londoners a sense of comfort. A false sense maybe, but support for the military and for National Service was widespread. Young men needed discipline and most, it appeared, benefited from their time taking orders without question for a couple of years. Support was increased by the worries about juvenile crime, in part attributed to another army that had overtaken parts of the country. These young men were civilians, but they too wore a uniform of sorts. It was a uniform of teenage revolt. These were the 'new Edwardians', the Teddy Boys. Since before the war the real earnings of teenagers had doubled. In 1938 a survey estimated a youth's earnings at 26s a week with girls at 18s 6d. Fast forward to the fifties and average teenage spending power had mushroomed to between £2 and £5 a week.

The Teddy Boy cult had begun in the 1940s in the establishment environment of Savile Row, but was taken up by fashion conscious, working-class youngsters with money to spend. A style much favoured by elitist cavalry officers migrated to the tower blocks and council estates of London. Soon, street corners were lined with groups of young men wearing semi-frocked coats, often with velvet collars. Their trousers were tight and the string tie much favoured was more Mississippi gambler than genuine Edwardian toff. Decried by parents, who were alarmed at their sons' appearances, the Teddy Boys formed a sort of tribal alliance. They fought or shouted insults at passers-by and slashed cinema seats with the arrival of Bill Haley's film *Rock Around the Clock*. From a harmless expression of individual style, within months the Teddy Boy acquired a reputation for violence and intimidation. This was largely unfair, but the slicked-back Tony Curtis hair, cutaway shirts and 'slim Jim' ties, allied to those distinctive jackets, caused untold angst among the older generations. Most reckoned the sooner these young men were called up for National Service, the better.

The girls were not about to be left behind in this newly fashion-conscious world. Out went the twin set and pearls. The 'New Look' was already a thing of the past. By 1958 the *Sunday Express* was announcing a fresh look. 'There is an entirely new kind of girl around, awkward and angular, pouting and petulant; history has seen nothing like her before.' It was a look that changed swiftly from the gamine charm of Audrey Hepburn to the waif-like appeal of Bridget Bardot. In 1957 'the sack' arrived with a nod back to the twenties. Legs were back in fashion, so were bare shoulders. Busts were accentuated, waists pulled in and acres of legs exposed. Flat chested girls were helped by padded bras, but girls with milk-bottle legs were snookered until saved by a pair of denim jeans. Just as street corner tailors benefited from the Teddy Boy fad, so ladies' hairdressers broke out like a rash across London and the suburbs. Styles changed as rapidly as the fashions. There was a new urgency about how you looked and how you were looked at by others. Today, the 'beehive' to be replaced tomorrow by the 'poodle cut'. Want to look more natural, yet sexy? The Bardot dishevelled look should do the trick. Enter the pink rinse, the silver streak. The young were setting the fashion agenda and it was the retailers who were answering their persistent call. Mums were left to their knitting, while dads mumbled their dismay about modern life to the landlord of their half-deserted local pub. The young gave little thought to the worry they were causing their parents. It was they that were creating this exciting new world with their own fashions, music and way of life.

The *Drapers Record* reflected that with half a million teenagers arriving each year 'the teenage trade cannot be treated as a sideline'. Far from it, with the average teenager was buying five pairs of shoes a year. In a bow to youth, Norvic crowned their 'Miss Norvic Teenager' at a reception launched at the Mayfair hotel.

The youthful revolution, as represented by the Teddy Boys, was a 'V' sign to authority and the establishment. It was breaking the shackles of conformity and was a sign that for once it was not only the wealthy and influential who could display arrogance. As the fifties progressed, this youthful 'revolution' faltered and faded. The young require constant change, and this was provided by blue jeans and windcheaters. Suits still appealed, but now it was the continental look. Italian chic with bum-freezer jackets, complemented by American crew-cuts or college-boy styles. Cecil Gee in Shaftesbury Avenue was, for a time, the new Mecca of male fashion, having moved from its humble surroundings in the Charing Cross Road.

Young men had finally discovered fashion. By the end of the fifties, even middle-class youngsters had chucked out their duffle coats or passed them on to their fathers. The Kangol cap was an embarrassment – if you were seen wearing one you were 'square' (the ultimate insult). The working-class youngsters, having ditched their cloth caps in favour of the Teddy Boys suits, were now seeking new inspiration to maintain their dandified status. Soon the young were joined as one as they headed for a run-down street just off Piccadilly Circus, which was soon to draw people from around the world for the next decade. Carnaby Street was a drab thoroughfare that was populated mainly by dowdy suppliers to the catering trade. Few people realised that it would soon become one of the most popular tourist attractions in London, but its emergence was a slow burner which was lit by a young Glaswegian.

John Stephen, on arriving in London, went to work in the military department of the staid outfitters *Moss Bros*. Restless, he moved on to work at *Vince*, a shop in Newburgh Street in Soho which was the centre of small workshops producing garments for tailors in Savile Row and Jermyn Street. It was run by Bill Green, whose tight black sweaters imported from Paris and garish shirts produced in primary colours were thought by many to be outlandish and shocking. Much of his stock was aimed at the relatively small underground gay market and was sold by mail order. Stephen was convinced there was a far wider market to be developed. In 1957 Stephen opened his own shop in Beak Street. He introduced hipsters and jackets using patterned fabrics. It was not only the gay and camp community that loved what he was producing. Word went round and soon the pop stars appearing on *Six-Five Special* and *Oh Boy* were beating a path to his door. His shop *His Clothes* was decorated in canary yellow and announced his arrival at 5 Carnaby Street. Pop music blared out on to the street and the first London male boutique had arrived.

The recipe for his success was simple and infectious. He offered a relaxed atmosphere, albeit with the latest hits blaring out. The clothes were slightly crazy, breaking many of the established rules that had been in place for decades. Jackets in outlandish fabrics and colours, with no lining, were unstructured and easy to wear. He concentrated on short runs. It was a case of make your mind up quickly or the item was gone and unlikely to be repeated. He employed attractive young sales staff. The whole experience was unstuffy and, to the young, somehow liberating. They felt that in a small way they were part of something new and unique. John Stephen had succeeded in making shopping enjoyable for men. Over the next decade he extended the number of his retail outlets in Carnaby Street to thirteen. His arrival complemented the developing pop scene and was the launching pad for the swinging sixties.

While their children's outlandish clothes caused arguments and concern for parents, it was a change in the young's attitude to sexual matters that created real alarm. The Archbishop of York spoke of 'our moral chaos' and declared

a new commandment of 'Thou shall not be found out.'
But doing what? Surely middle England's daughters were
not indulging in casual sexual activity, even though it was
reported by the Registrar General that in 1955 sixty per cent
of young ladies were pregnant on their wedding day. The
courts reported increases in offences by teenage youngsters
having sex with girls under sixteen. Victorian morality, still
so influential in their parents' upbringing, was being swept
aside under a tide of carnal lust. What was the cause? There
were virtually no drugs and young men would rather be seen
drinking a coke or a coffee than the traditional pint. That
Doctor Kinsey had a lot to answer for. Improved nutrition
was seeing young girls mature more quickly, seemingly
pushing them ever earlier into danger. Childhood was being
sacrificed on the altar of instant gratification. Young men
who had been cocooned in public schools were egged on
by their peers to 'break their duck'. Pressure was being put
on young girls as never before. The permissive society, as
we came to understand it, was yet to arrive, but there was a
new frankness in discussing sex by teenagers that shocked
their elders. A casual attitude that was increasingly leading
to unwanted pregnancies.

Despite a 1959 survey that recorded two-thirds of young
voters considered themselves middle class, their leisure
activities suggested otherwise. With a five-day working week
now almost universal and with money to spend, the six
million British teenagers were trailblazers for this new age
of leisure. There was a boom in playing football. Thousands
of teams played in hundreds of leagues throughout London
and the suburbs. These tended to attract young men from
the lower-income groups, while the boys from middle-class
homes played 'rugger'. Each of London's public schools ran
'old boys' teams of varying ability. After football, fishing

was the most popular working-class activity. This attracted enthusiasts of all ages who lined the river and canal banks. Even gravel pits and reservoirs were popular with the working-class anglers, leaving their richer, upper-crust fellow enthusiasts to the prized banks of the Test and salmon fishing in Scotland.

The age of leisure saw an increase in active participation. Drama societies mushroomed, as did a massive interest in photography. It was time to throw out the pre-war Brownie box camera. As the decade progressed, increasingly advanced cameras became available. They were more compact, many were fitted with flash lights. By the end of the fifties, sales of flash bulbs had soared to twenty million, ten times those recorded earlier in the decade. Holiday snaps were taken to the local chemist for developing with the results eagerly awaited. By 1959 many were investing in expensive cine-cameras. It seemed quite incredible that family and friends could be captured on screen. A source of joy for some, but misery for friends who were subjected to an evening of jerky films relayed on a folding screen of a latest holiday enjoyed on the Costa Brava. With their limited attention span, the young made a swift exit. They couldn't understand the attraction of their parents' interests. A trip to the pub, a game of darts or a visit to the dog track left them cold. The thought of pottering in the garden or growing vegetables on an allotment appalled the new generation. They wanted constant action. Boredom was an experience to be avoided. There was a fad for judo and ice skating, but the interest that was universal was, of course, music.

Wherever there was music there was dancing. Even their parents understood this attraction. They had swayed to the big bands of the thirties and bopped their way through the war. Most had learnt to waltz and foxtrot, but this was far too tame for this new generation of dancers. Rock 'n' roll had released them from learning set steps. This was the age for free expression and gymnastic ability as youngsters threw themselves into jiving routines. Across London they trekked to Palais, Meccas and Locarnos. They danced in the aisles when *Rock Around the Clock* was released in September 1956. Dance halls even opened in the afternoons, but not for the discreet tea dances of pre-war years. Even those youngsters not involved in playing sports were becoming honed like athletes as they threw themselves (quite literally) into the latest dance craze.

Popular music was central to most youngsters' lives. Much of Saturday was devoted to a visit to the local record shop. The lightweight micro-groove disc had revolutionised the market. No longer easily breakable, the long players' attraction was heightened by their colourful sleeve covers. The Hit Parade was dominated by singles throbbing out their beat from living rooms and juke boxes, but it was the LP that was becoming something of a prized collector's item. The emergence of transistor radios helped keep up the constant exposure to music. By 1958, together with tape recorders, thousands a week were being sold. Record shops became 'melody bars'. They were a meeting place for earnest youngsters to listen to and discuss the merits of the latest Elvis or Cliff. Having grown up in a period of austerity, these kids were now spoilt for choice in their search on how to spend their money.

For most youngsters, buying a car was out of the question, but a motorbike was a realistic possibility. For those seeking rather less macho power, there was another, rather more sophisticated, form of transport. How about a sleek Italian scooter? Cheap to run and maintain, the Vespa and Lambretta were very much part of the London scene.

They had the great advantage of being easy to park in the clogged streets of the capital. The Vespa was first shown at the Earls Court Motorcycle Show in 1949. By the early fifties, the Piaggio machine was being built under licence in Bristol. Unfortunately, unknown to the Italians, the Douglas company was bust and in administration. Supply to the British market was well below the Italians' expectations, until in 1955 the faltering British manufacturer was taken over by Westinghouse. Continued lack of investment meant that sales remained disappointing, which allowed Italian competitor Lambretta to enter the market, but here again distribution was patchy. Although scooters were loved by the young, much of the potential was missed with the arrival of the revolutionary and keenly prized Mini in 1959.

Despite full employment, there were fundamental changes taking place with the gradual decline in manufacturing in London. Although many thousands were still employed in factories, the work tended to be repetitive and boring. Old traditional firms were migrating to cheaper areas of the country, and already imports were eating into our increasingly uncompetitive and strongly unionised manufacturing base. While working-class youngsters were often tied to factory or warehouse work, the possibilities for the educated young seemed endless.

Noel Cash, having completed his National Service in 1954, joined Middlesex hospital as a medical student. Based on his Higher School Certificate results, he was excused the first year's training. He was given a grant of £400 a year to cover his accommodation and food. His first digs were in Clapham, within walking distance of the medical college in Cleveland Street. His room had no heating, and hot water for washing or shaving had to be carried up in a huge jug. His landlady fed him reasonably, but occasionally he treated himself to a meal at the Hurricane Café close to the hospital, run by two ex-RAF pilots. Meat pie and peas was good value for just 1s 3d. Later he had a year living in the college, which had squash courts and a billiard room. During his last six months of training, he was allowed to eat in the junior doctors' dining room. Training was long and arduous, including anatomy, with dissecting cadavers being essential. Years were then spent on clinical studies, including stitching and giving anaesthetics under supervision. There was some time for playing rugby, but as finals loomed, increasing hours had to be devoted to revision. A treat involved going for a pint at Finches (the One Tun) in Goodge Street, where an Irish doctor used to hold his surgery in the bar. Eventually, Noel passed his finals and was appointed as a junior doctor at the Middlesex on a salary of £543 a year, less £250 deducted for living expenses. The hours were horrendous; he was on call at all times of day and night, but at least there was a two-week holiday to look forward to after each six-month stint.

The film *Doctor in the House* was released in 1954. The following year another medical student was doing his best to emulate the pranks carried out by Dirk Bogarde and Donald Sinden. Mark Biggin was training at Guy's Hospital. 'Borrowing' a skeleton, he dangled it from his bedroom down to the dining room below, where his formidable landlady was eating her supper. This was a rare moment of light relief in what was again a seven-year slog of study and work. With virtually no money, Mark supplemented his meagre income by driving a taxi. His digs were on the Old Kent Road opposite Caledonian Market where, bizarrely, he remembers a stall selling suits of armour. The Old Kent Road back in the fifties was a tough neighbourhood and he used to be ribbed about having to wear a suit and tie to the hospital each day. His memories are of a really friendly atmosphere and of the quick wit and repartee of ordinary Londoners. Asking politely of a neighbour 'How are you?' the reply was invariably 'Up and down like the bridge, mate.'

Again, following the lead from *Doctor in the House*, Mark found romance when he met his future wife, who was a nurse, while putting up the Christmas decorations in the spinal ward at Guy's. These young medics had to work hours that would be deemed dangerous today, but they emerged knowledgeable, dedicated and willing to take on the world.

Apart from working and enjoying themselves, the young seemingly lacked any great social or moral cause to pursue. They were appalled by the brutality of the Soviet Union in putting down the Hungarian Uprising in 1956. The following year Kingsley Amis highlighted the problem. He lamented 'there was no Spain, no Fascism, no mass unemployment'. The young needed something to rail against. They were all becoming too satisfied with their lot. Where was the youthful dissent? Then, in December 1957 on far away Christmas Island, Britain exploded its first 'A' bomb. Now, some youngsters had found themselves a cause to support. Out came the placards 'Ban the Bomb'. Rather than join the Liberal party, which had recently welcomed hordes of young people, there was now a more radical cause to support. The Campaign for Nuclear Disarmament was formed in 1957. Although the CND appealed to so many young, the leadership of the organisation was from a much earlier generation. The white-haired philosopher Bertrand Russell was already in his eighties. He was joined by Canon John Collins, who was determined to resist what he saw as the moral evil that nuclear weapons represented. The moral debate had been set in motion from an article written by the popular novelist J. B. Priestley. Writing in the *New Statesman* in November 1957, he warned that a nuclear Britain could be 'turned into a radioactive cemetery'. Opinion was split, but emotions about the danger of nuclear war were rising.

On the coldest Easter since the war, some 4,000 protestors gathered in Trafalgar Square. It was Good Friday 1958 and it marked the first Aldermaston march. The young had a cause to support and, clutching banners bearing the organisation's distinctive logo, they set off for the Berkshire countryside and Aldermaston, home to the atomic weapon establishment. Here was a new form of protest. Not backed by any political party, it drew its support mainly from the ranks of the middle classes. The supporters were soon being categorised as sandal-wearing beardies who were accompanied by a weird army of women of all ages. Proudly wearing their distinctive CND badges, said to represent an unborn child and a dying man, they were housed during their long march in churches and village halls. The annual march became something of a fixture in the London calendar and despite the marchers' earnest beliefs, their protests had little effect on British defence policy and none at all on the great nuclear powers of America and the Soviet Union. A great cause maybe, but most Londoners were too busy, idle or ignorant to get involved. Marching in the rain held little attraction for most, whatever the cause. The young had already changed society. Maybe their devotion to music and fashion was shallow, but the effects were ongoing. Perhaps it was apt that in an era when a British prime minister boasted 'you have never had it so good', the youthful revolution was based on consumption rather than ideals.

16
Music, Music, Music

Two small, overcrowded, sweaty rooms, situated only a few hundred yards apart in central London, provided convenient bookends for British popular music during the 1950s. They reflected not only the shift in musical taste, but changes also in British society. They symbolised a gradual, grudging move towards a youth culture and a country less dominated by class and racial intolerance.

In 1950 the Humphrey Lyttelton Club at 100 Oxford Street acted as a magnet for plummy-voiced girls and their earnest boyfriends to listen and dance to Humph's brand of revivalist and traditional jazz. The tall, elegant, ex-Etonian guards officer was surrounded by an early version of 'groupies', all bulging sweaters and skirts puffed out by layers of petticoats. They gazed longingly at the maestro, their boyfriends, all beards, sloppy sweaters and sandals dismissed from their minds. These were respectable, middle-class youngsters, thinking they were living dangerously.

Ten years later, just down the road in Old Compton Street, another breathless crowd of youngsters had gathered to listen to live music. They too were sweaty and there were still a few beardies, even the odd sloppy sweater, but no sandals. This was the world of coffee bars and rock 'n' roll. Now the girls wore heavy make-up and tight jeans. The young men no longer gauche or earnest, but moving in time to the hypnotic beat. Any voices heard above the blare of the music were no longer exclusively well modulated. Life and music had moved on as if in concert, as they jived towards the future. It had been a strange, muddled journey.

A turning point in the British popular music scene occurred in 1952 with the publication of the first official chart, published by the New Musical Express. It was hardly an in-depth piece of research, with just twenty leading stores forwarding details of their bestselling discs. Prior to this, popularity had been based on the sale of sheet music. The appearance of affordable, portable record players helped the lurch towards record buying, spearheaded by the young. With full employment they had money to spend and a major industry was about to be launched. Before the formation of the chart, the airwaves had been dominated by established American stars. The first UK number one hit continued this trend with Al Martino's recording of 'Here in my heart'. British artistes hardly got a look in as US giants like Eddie Fisher, Frankie Laine and Guy Mitchell found favour with easy listening ballads. Only a banal recording of 'How much is that doggie in the window', performed by Lita Roza made any British impact during those early months of 1952.

Britain did have an established popular music industry centred on Archer Street in Soho, where musicians gathered each day in the hope of obtaining work. Big bands, like those of Joe Loss and Geraldo, were still popular, but increasingly expensive to maintain. The most popular British solo artists in the early fifties were still Vera Lynn, Ann Shelton and a pudgy Welshman, Donald Peers. The strangled tones of David Whitfield also managed to reach number one early in 1953 with 'Answer me'. So it was that lusty ballads and novelty numbers formed a background to everyday life, all of which were despised by the jazz lovers. They were a stroppy lot, even falling out among themselves. The modernist devotees of Miles Davis and Charlie Parker were viewed as zealots by the revivalists, who stuck to the authentic sounds of New Orleans.

Jazz clubs of whichever persuasion conjure up images of sweaty performers and serious head-nodding, toe-tapping audiences. Certainly, Club Eleven in Great Windmill Street conformed to the stereotype. The first jazz club to open in Soho after the war, it acquired an increasingly dubious reputation and was closed down in 1950. It featured two bands, one led by Ronnie Scott and the other by Johnny Dankworth. Scott, a superb saxophonist, teamed up with Tubby Hayes, eventually forming his own jazz club in Gerrard Street before transferring to 47 Frith Street, which today continues to be a London institution.

The grotty surroundings of Ham Yard were the venue for a club run by Cy Laurie. Opened in 1951, the entrance was approached through rows of barrows parked overnight by Berwick Street traders. The interior was even less appealing, with threadbare settees masked in a fog of cigarette smoke. Nobody ever thought to clean the toilets, but at least the music was intoxicating. The line-up at the club often included Chris Barber, Diz Dipley and George Melly, who famously didn't just rely on the music for their intoxication. Strangely, Cy Laurie, a wonderful clarinettist, didn't really fit into this hard-drinking Bohemian set. A teetotaller, he gave little thought to commercial success, and yet for many years his club became a magnet. It attracted young female students from nearby St Martin's Art School, and an army of admiring young men from the suburbs dipping their toes into Bohemian London. Despite acquiring something of a cult status, Laurie became increasingly disillusioned.

Attracted to philosophy and meditation, he beat an early path to India, studying under Maharishi Mahesh Yogi, a route to be followed later by the Beatles.

Trumpeter Ken Colyer was another major influence on the British jazz scene. Jazz enthusiasts, always judgemental, reckoned that 'Humph was for tourists, Colyer for purists and Cy for jiving and raving.' In 1953 Colyer opened Club 51 in Great Newport Street. He continued to play in the New Orleans tradition, but it was obvious that, despite heated internal disputes, a crossover in styles was underway. The divisions between traditional jazz, blues and folk were often becoming blurred. It was from this mixture that British skiffle emerged. It developed as an offshoot from Ken Colyer's revitalised New Orleans jazz band. It offered two huge advantages for a young audience. The music was catchy but, importantly, only required the most rudimentary instruments for it to be performed. Its initial success was due to one man. Lonnie Donegan was a guitarist and banjo player in Colyer's band. During intervals, while other band members took a break, Donegan started performing skiffle numbers. Suddenly, crowds were going to the club to hear Donegan rather than the resident band. It didn't take long for record producers to become aware of his popularity. He cut his first LP with Chris Barber and one track, 'Rock Island Line', hit a chord with the public and it was released as a single. It soared to number one in the charts, selling over three million copies. It also became the first British record to feature in the US billboard chart. Not only did his music influence future stars, including Bill Wyman, the Beatles and Van Morrison, it also unleashed a craze for skiffle music. Throughout the country thousands of youngsters formed skiffle groups. There was a boom in the sales of cheap guitars. Discarded tea chests became 'must have' items, while hardware stores reported a surge in the sales of broom handles. Within days, with the help of a washboard and kazoo, it was possible for a group to make a passable attempt at entertaining a crowd of enthusiastic youngsters. Skiffle groups were erupting all over London like acne on a teenager's face. Although for a time Donegan continued to achieve considerable success with numbers like *Cumberland Gap*, public taste moved on as his dated style was consumed by the hypnotic beat of rock 'n' roll.

Another Scot, Chas McDevitt, helped to secure skiffle at the forefront of British popular music, at least for a time. He teamed up with folk singer Nancy Whiskey to record *Freight Train*, which was a massive hit. In 1953 it was an everyday drink that led to a dramatic shift in popular music culture. Not an alcoholic drink, but coffee. The first coffee bar in Britain opened at 29 Frith Street in Soho. The headquarters of the Italian Gaggia Company was located round the corner in Dean Street and it was their influence that led to a migration of popular music from the dance halls to the coffee bars. While film star Gina Lollobrigida drew in the crowds for the opening of Moka, no one foresaw the astonishing popularity of the coffee bars for the years to come.

Frothy coffee produced from snarling, stainless-steel machines was a revelation. Coffee in Britain since the war had largely been confined to acrid-tasting coffee essence. It was music that was to form the cornerstone for the coffee bar success. Every coffee lounge gave pride of place to their jukebox. Youngsters sat round Formica-topped tables while the latest hits blared out. In the evenings many establishments made room for a live band and a dance floor. Within months of Moka opening, almost every street in the West End sported a coffee bar and soon, like an epidemic, they spread outwards into the suburbs. Old Compton Street became 'Espresso Valley' with outlets including Amalfi, Act One Scene One, the Pollo and Heaven and Hell. Outlets fought for attention by offering ever more outlandish settings. At Le Macabre in Meard Street you sat on wooden coffins among hanging skeletons. Pubs were now generally being ignored by youngsters. For a time they became home only to those seeking to escape the perpetual din of the jukebox. The true jazz devotees shook their heads in disbelief at this new generation.

Across London at the Royal Albert Hall and south of the river at the Royal Festival Hall, lovers of classical music attempted to maintain the capital's reputation as being a centre for culture. Each July saw the beginning of the Promenade Concert season. The brainchild of Henry Wood, it succeeded in bringing classical music to a mass audience, with the concerts being broadcast by the BBC. Since the bombing of the Queen's Hall in 1941, the concerts were transferred to the Albert Hall where they have stayed ever since. The first Prom of the 1950s took place on 19 July and contained music by Elgar, Vaughan Williams, Delibes and Hector Berlioz. The rather satanic-looking Malcolm Sargent was the principal conductor at this famous music festival from 1948 until his death in 1967. Something of a showman and a snappy dresser, he was often referred to as 'Flash Harry'. However, this could not disguise his deep knowledge and skill as a leading conductor who did much to help popularise classical music. He was expansive and connected with his audience as well as those playing under him. His conducting of Handel's *Messiah*, with its huge choruses and orchestra captured in recordings, gives an indication of the power and emotion he was able to bring.

It was an era of iconic British conductors who found worldwide fame and recognition. John Barbirolli was born in Holborn to continental parents. He became largely associated with the Hallé Orchestra based in Manchester, but who appeared regularly at the Proms. Barbirolli became best known for his interpretations of British composers, particularly Elgar, Delius and Vaughan Williams. Like Sargent, he had charisma, with his flowing hair and an ability to draw memorable performances from his players.

The third musketeer of Britain's leading conductors was Adrian Boult. He became conductor of the BBC Symphony Orchestra in 1930. Under his leadership the orchestra gained a reputation for excellence. In 1950 he was removed from the post, at which time he took on the chief conductorship of the London Philharmonic Orchestra, which had once rivalled the BBC Symphony in terms of recognition. It was under his leadership that the orchestra's reputation was revived. A shy man, it was felt that Boult was more at home in the recording studio than in the spotlight of the podium. With the help of these three maestros the 1950s was a golden decade for the Promenade Concerts, which were completed in September 1959 with the traditional finale of 'Rule, Britannia' and 'Jerusalem'.

The Royal Festival Hall provided another important venue for serious music lovers. It was not long after its inauguration concert that acoustic problems became apparent. Despite scientific principles being applied to its design and construction, performers were experiencing difficulty hearing each other on the concert platform. Sound was being deflected away from the stage. Tempers frayed and performances were compromised. Exasperated, John Barbirolli was quoted as saying, 'Everything is sharp and clear and there is no impact, no fullness on the climaxes.' This was not a problem for jazz musicians and by 1956 Chris Barber was holding popular concerts at the Thames-side venue.

By the time the Moka coffee bar opened in 1953, the hit parade still continued to be dominated by ballads. Mantovani even reached number one with the theme from the film *Moulin Rouge*. The following year, the trumpeter Eddie Calvert got in on the act with 'Oh Mein Papa'. This was hardly cutting edge or the stuff of youthful revolution. Where did it all start? Perhaps with the arrival of Johnnie Ray, an American singer whose antics on stage created hysteria from a young female audience and ridicule from their parents. He pouted, contorted and tore at his clothes while singing hits like 'Cry, Such a night' and 'Walking my baby back home'. The fuse he lit erupted into fire with the arrival of another unlikely American who sported a kiss curl. It was in Coronation year that Hayley wrote 'Rock around the clock'. He recorded it the following year and it looked like being the briefest of one-hit wonders, appearing for a single week only in the American charts. Together with his band, the Comets, he did have a huge hit with 'Shake, rattle and roll'. It sold over a million copies and was the first rock 'n' roll disc to get into the British charts. Haley was one of the earliest performers to introduce essentially African/American influenced music to a white audience. In 1955 Evan Hunter's book *Blackboard Jungle* was made into a film starring Glenn Ford. The opening credits featured 'Rock around the clock' and this time round it became an instant hit, topping the US charts for eight weeks. Almost overnight, ballads, big bands and jazz were confined to the back burner. Dickie Valentine was allowed a seven-day window for his 'Christmas Alphabet' to claim top spot, but in the first week in January 1954 Bill Haley was back and Teddy Boys were slashing cinema seats as their sign of approval for the exciting new sound which was to change so many lives. Tommy Steele reached for pop stardom with his cover version of Guy Mitchell's 'Singing the blues', but another major force was about to invade Britain, albeit only in the form of a recording. 'All shook up' was Elvis Presley's first British chart topper and nothing was ever going to be the same again. After seven weeks at number one it was followed by Paul Anka's 'Diana'. These exciting rhythms and plaintive lyrics reached out to a whole generation, who embraced them. They brought with them a sense of difference from previous generations, of liberation, almost as if at last they had been released from the constraints and restrictions of their upbringing. Convention was being cast aside. It was exciting to be young and part of what seemed like a new beginning.

At about this time, London's most famous coffee bar opened and became the iconic centre of British rock 'n' roll. The 2i's at 59 Old Compton Street was named after two Iranian brothers who leased the property to an Australian wrestler Paul Lincoln, who fought under the name of Doctor Death. With Lincoln having little business experience the venture was haemorrhaging money until on a miserable, wet afternoon in July 1956 chance led to a massive change in fortune. Wally Whyton was part of a skiffle group known as the Vipers. Taking shelter from the torrential rain on their way to the Soho fair, they started an impromptu session. Lincoln was astonished at how quickly a crowd gathered to listen. He promptly offered the group a regular opportunity to perform and in so doing stumbled on a winning formula. Other groups lined up for a chance to perform, together with crowds of teenagers who wanted to listen. He opened up the cellar that had previously been used as a storeroom. It was a tiny, dark room with a small platform at the back that acted as a stage. It was decorated by Lionel Bart, a former student at St Martin's Art School. The black ceiling drew the room in still further and the walls were decorated with spooky, painted eyes that seemed to follow you. Hundreds packed into this suffocating space each night. Sweat, cheap perfume and smoke clogged your lungs and outside on the pavement an overspill crowd waited their chance to join the throng. Like the earlier jazz clubs, the overall appearance was tacky, bordering on squalid, but nobody seemed to care. There was a grubby coffee machine, an orange juice dispenser and rows of tired, curled up sandwiches. Outside a sign proudly proclaimed 'The world famous 2i's coffee bar, home of the stars.'

Perhaps they were somewhat premature in making their bold claim, but each night would-be stars entertained the crowds and soon they were joined by musical agents. Many convinced themselves that the rock 'n' roll phenomenon would be a fad and dead within weeks. Larry Parnes, previously a fashion retailer, disagreed. With his partner John Kennedy, he sensed the excitement and feeling of liberation among the young. He felt it too, and he understood and knew there was money to be made. Through the fog of the coffee bar it was money that he smelt, not sweat and cigarette smoke. He was right. Parnes was to become the archetypal rock 'n' roll manager. He cruised all the West End venues looking for talent. He developed a sense of who would appeal to the British public. He combined this with a surface charm coupled with an ability to persuade.

It was important that Parnes' early signings should be a success. Tommy Hicks, a young lad from Bermondsey, had been seen performing at the 2i's and The Cat's Whisker, both solo and with Wally Whyton's Viper group. It was after Hicks performed at the Stork Room in Regent Street that Parnes persuaded Hicks to appoint him as his manager. With his name changed to Tommy Steele, he was marketed as Britain's somewhat unlikely answer to Elvis Presley. Although Steele was soon to establish himself outside the pop industry, initially he received blanket coverage in the British press, making it much easier to attract other performers to Parnes' growing stable of acts. George Melly observed that Steele's gyrations on stage were 'not so much a sexual courtship dance, as a suggestion that he had wet himself'.

Parnes' next major signing was again to be dubbed Britain's Elvis Presley. Unlike Tommy Steele, at least Marty Wilde looked the part. Parnes had been told by Lionel Bart that a tall, well-built teenager with raw talent was performing at the Condor Club. This was a slightly less dingy basement situated below the Sabrina Coffee Bar in Wardour Street. Parnes arrived late at the club and missed the performance. After making enquiries he tracked the young man, Reg Smith, back to his house in Essex, where he still lived with his parents. Young Reg looked every inch a pop star and had a powerful, likeable voice. The young man had been performing as Reg Patterson, which was hardly an improvement on his real name. Parnes became known for the exotic names he gave to his stars. He suggested Marty Wilde fitted the bill. It was manly with a whiff of danger. Reg really liked his Christian name and by way of compromise suggested Reg Wilde, but Parnes prevailed and Marty Wilde was launched in to the excited and excitable pop world.

Wilde was a good deal smarter than many of those who were seeking fame at any price. He had quickly dismissed the 2i's as his launching pad, reckoning that the clientele at the Condor were more likely to provide him with a breakthrough. The club attracted celebrities of the day, including racing driver Stirling Moss and glamour puss Diana Dors. He also appeared at the upmarket Blue Angel. Marty had been warned about Parnes' negotiating skills and was really rather pleased with himself when he signed a deal in which he kept sixty per cent of his earnings. It seems monstrous that his manager should retain a whopping forty per cent, but it subsequently became obvious that Marty had done much better than most. Parnes' stable of would-be stars all had much in common. They were good looking, could hold a note and, importantly, had no business experience. Many signed their rights away, with Parnes restricting their earnings to a few pounds a week. He grew immensely rich on their naivety. Eventually, he owned a penthouse in Kensington, a house in France and racehorses. It wasn't long before he was known as 'Mr Parnes, shillings and pence'.

Although Parnes' reputation has taken a battering since his death in 1989, Marty Wilde still remembers him with affection. Larry Parnes was gay, but once Marty had brushed off his manager's half-hearted sexual advances they enjoyed a mutually beneficial relationship. Parnes was astute and it wasn't long before this young Marty Wilde was appearing on *Six-Five Special* and ITV's *Oh Boy*, and his popularity soared. The two programmes were fighting for a teenage audience reckoned to be in the region of fifteen million. Marty Wilde's biggest hit was 'A Teenager in Love' and, strangely, it was his love for Vernon girl Joyce Baker that eventually led to his decline in popularity. Although their courtship was followed avidly in the national press, young pop stars were not supposed to get married. When he was no longer available, many of Wilde's young fans deserted him. Marty and Joyce's love has endured and they remain happily married, having created something of a rock dynasty with their daughters Kim and Roxanne.

For once Larry Parnes' antenna let him down. He saw the young Harry Webb perform at the 2i's but failed to sign him. Instead the future Cliff Richard appointed Harry Greatorex to be his manager. Although many of the stars who made their debuts at the 2i's were Londoners, now hopefuls from all over the country were heading for Soho. They included two Geordie lads who supplemented their earnings working the coffee machine at the 2i's when they were not strumming their guitars to an increasingly adoring audience. Bruce Welch and Hank Marvin were aggrieved to find out that the 2i's manager, Tom Littlewood, was taking a ten per cent commission of their meagre earnings. Larry Parnes' influence was obviously spreading. Welch and Marvin eventually teamed up with two other wannabes, Jet Harris and Tony Meehan. One afternoon they were taken round to a tailor in Dean Street to meet Cliff Richard. This too was to prove a happy marriage, which led Cliff and the soon-to-be-formed Shadows to head out on the road to international fame.

Larry Parnes continued to build a stable of home-grown stars, most of whom were discovered singing in West End coffee bars. He gave them crazy names and groomed them to appeal to the emerging, affluent, teenage market. Parnes had built up good connections with the major record companies and he introduced a rash of new performers with attention-grabbing names. Dickie Pride, Johnny Gentle, Rory Storm and Lance Fortune met with varying success. Joe Brown stood alone in refusing to change his name, but he had talent and an easy charm that was bound to lead to success. The less savvy of these performers earned little more than pocket money for their efforts, having signed away most of their rights in carefully drafted contracts. One of his performers could not really sing in a conventional sense and yet even the gravel-voiced Tommy Bruce was to have his moment of fame.

Ron Wycherley met Parnes almost by default in Birkenhead. He was seeking out Marty Wilde, who was heading up a touring show. Ron had written some songs that he thought would suit Marty Wilde. Entering the stage door the young man bumped into Parnes in the corridor who took him to Marty's dressing room. Nervously, he performed a couple of numbers, which Wilde loved. To his credit, Wilde suggested the young man could perform the numbers himself. Despatched to London, Ron Wycherley was given a new hairstyle, a couple of sharp suits and a new name. A record deal was signed with Decca and Billy Fury was launched to the delight of an array of adoring fans. So the Svengali of British rock 'n' roll had made his greatest signing, but his instinct was not infallible. Alongside Cliff Richard he also failed to recognise the potential of the Beatles, and it was their eventual flowering that led to the gradual decline of his power and influence.

He appeared to have picked another superstar with the emergence of Terry Dean, whose early recordings, including 'A White Sports Coat' and 'Stairway to Heaven', soared up the charts. Although Dean had a good recording voice he took it upon himself to set new standards of outrageous and loutish behaviour, so often associated with pop stars. He was arrested for smashing a shop window and telephone kiosk while drunk. Pretty tame stuff compared with what was to follow, but middle Britain was appalled. He was dubbed the 'bad boy' of British rock. The press labelled Dean as representing everything that was wrong with British youth. He played right into their hands by trying to avoid National Service.

Still they came, these legions of young men seeking fame and fortune. Rick Hardy, Vince Taylor and Wee Willie Harris. Mickie Most was more astute and after a stint as a singing waiter emerged as one of Britain's most successful record producers. Terry Nelhams was performing with The Worried Men who had become the resident band at the 2i's. Enter another major figure in the record industry. Jack Good saw the potential in this slightly built young man with blond hair. He changed his name to Adam Faith. The young man had a style that set him apart from the current crop of singers. His first record failed to make the charts but regular appearances on television kept him on the public's radar. In 1959 it was his association with John Barry that led to his distinctive recording of 'What Do You Want'. His pronunciation of 'baby' as 'bay-bee' was enough to do the trick. It proved to be the first number one hit for the Parlophone label before the arrival of the Beatles. Of all those emerging from the chaotic British pop scene of the late 1950s, it is surely John Barry who was the most enduringly talented. From the faltering beginning with the forming of the John Barry Seven in 1957, he went on to compose some of the most memorable film themes, including some for James Bond films, 'Born Free', 'Dance with Wolves' and 'Out of Africa'.

So a decade that had started with Humph and a subsequent dominance in popular music from across the Atlantic ended with local talent making a stand. Many have now been forgotten, but these young men caught and bottled an enduring nostalgia with their music which no other medium can capture so vividly.

17

End of an Era

As a new decade beckons, the focus tends to be on the future, but it's natural also to look back and take stock. In October 1959 the Tories won their third consecutive general election. Their slogan was 'Life is better under the Conservatives.' Some might have disagreed, but all would have acknowledged that life in London had changed significantly over that ten-year period.

In 1950, London still bore the visible wounds of war. Vast areas were still given over to weed-strewn rubble. Regency squares and Victorian avenues alike saw ugly gaps in their symmetry, an ongoing reminder of the grief and misery the bombs had brought. It was hoped that there would be a grand plan to rejuvenate sad, battered, old London. The 'County of London Plan' was devised by Sir Patrick Abercrombie, but despite best intentions only the tower blocks of Churchill Gardens in Pimlico resulted. They housed about 6,000 people where cramped Victorian terraces had stood before. It hardly represented a great vision for the future. A lack of money and an acute housing shortage guaranteed no inspirational plan. After the war architects were constrained by the Labour government licensing regime. Almost half of the building taking place across London was being constructed for public authorities. Schools, tower blocks and housing estates were usually practical, but soulless and ugly. Ancient and well-designed modern buildings can often complement each other, but the offerings of early 1950s architecture made no concession to the past. They were like plastic flip-flops being worn with a classic Dior gown.

By the middle of the decade, the fixers, wheeler-dealers and speculators had moved in. Now the architects danced to the tune of money-makers and the results were hardly better than those constrained by the public purse. A property boom that has continued ever since, with the occasional wobble, was underway. Peering through the fog, which still continued to blight London even in 1959, the urban sprawl continued unabated, but uglier now.

The fact that most British films made during the 1950s were shot in black and white accurately reflected the background to London life during that time. The buildings were grimy and blackened from decades of soot. Despite the gloomy buildings, life for most in London was far brighter as the decade drew to a close. We all live our lives to a background of great world events. Maybe we pause, perhaps read about them or watch history unfold on the television, but then we carry on with what is important to us in our private lives. Family rows or illness have a greater effect on us than any far-off war or disaster. The fifties offered plenty of conflict. For a time Korea dominated the news, to be followed by the Hungarian Uprising and the fiasco of Suez. When Harold MacMillan became prime minister in 1957, over forty countries were still governed by the Colonial Office. 'Super Mac' had little interest in the colonies, and Ghana and Malaya were the first to be granted their independence. Some regretted the breakup of the empire, but it was time to move on and in the early 60s a glut of countries broke away, including Kenya, Uganda and Tanganyika.

Few gave much thought about Britain's place in the world. Most realised that our time as a major power had almost gone. A new materialism was sweeping the country. The wish list had now extended to owning a car. Most British car manufacturers were booming, although their reliability was already a problem, even allowing for the fact that most models made had to be serviced every thousand miles. Front gardens were sacrificed for the new prized arrival. Privet hedges were ripped up, prize roses transplanted. A car offered a sense of freedom and luxury. The motorcycle with a sidecar 'for the wife' was an endangered species. Hire purchase was already popular in the buying of household appliances, but now half of all HP debt was attributed to car purchase. In 1950 only about one in seven owned a car. By the end of the decade this had mushroomed to about thirty per cent. A further boost was given in 1959 by the arrival of the Mini, which was also marketed as the Austin Seven. The designer, Alec Issigonis, created more interior space by the innovation of a transverse front-wheel-drive engine. With the price of the standard model at under £500, here was a genuine 'people's' car. With a family saloon such as the Hillman Minx costing almost £300 more, the effects on the competition was obviously going to be far reaching. With so many now striving to buy a car, the resulting congestion, particularly in London, was leading to long delays and frayed tempers. The second-hand car trade was also roaring ahead, as wealthy drivers sought the latest models, including the prized two-tone paintwork. The chairman of London Transport moaned that the enormous growth of car ownership had resulted in half of London's bus routes running at a loss. Another unwelcome consequence was the arrival of the parking meter and the dreaded traffic warden. The black day for motorists came in July 1958 and the charge was 6*d* for the first two hours, which then jumped

to a hefty 10s for the next couple of hours. The parking
restrictions helped redress the falling numbers using a bus.
The Routemaster double-decker introduced in 1956 replaced
London's trolleybuses and it soon became an iconic symbol
of London throughout the world.

By 1957 as many people crossed the Atlantic by air as
aboard ship. Within two years twice as many were choosing
to fly. London's Heathrow airport had to modernise. Until
1953 passengers had been housed in primitive conditions.
By now a million passengers a year passed through the
airport. Astonishingly, it was 1955 before the first permanent
passenger terminal was opened by the queen. The Europa
building eventually became known as Terminal Two. London
was drawing tourists and business visitors from around
the world. Britain had two highly respected state-owned
airlines. British Overseas Airways Corporation (BAOC)
handled long-haul flights, while domestic and European
destinations were serviced by British European Airways
(BEA). In 1952 BOAC was the first airline to introduce jet
aircraft. The British-built Comet was sleek and good looking.
It appeared to have stolen a march on its international
rivals. The first flight from Heathrow to Johannesburg went
without a hitch, but the Comet was hiding a hidden fatal
flaw. Two crashes in 1954 within months of each other
saw the plane grounded. Extensive tests identified chronic
metal fatigue. While the Comet was eventually successfully
redesigned, its absence allowed the Boeing 707 to dominate
the burgeoning passenger market. As so often, Britain led the
way in innovation, but saw its advantage being scuppered
by quality problems. By 1952 the first 'tourist' holiday flights
were introduced. This was an initial, faltering step towards
the package holiday, combining cheap flights with hotel
accommodation. Another British institution, the seaside

holiday, was about to become an endangered species. Who would want a holiday in Skegness when the delights of Tossa Del Mar were on offer? Now the car ferries were packed, with the Automobile Association reporting that two-thirds of their members had taken their cars abroad by 1959.

It was in the same year that C. P. Snow drew attention to a major problem facing Britain in his Rede lecture. While science and technology were opening up unforeseen opportunities for everyone, he maintained that scientists were being undervalued in Britain. Across the Atlantic and in Germany, engineers and scientists enjoyed real status and were seen as representing the future. It was galling to see British inventions not being followed through and subsequently being developed by our competitors. Worse, he detected a growing schism between science and the humanities. As both a novelist and a scientist, he was well placed to make this criticism. He maintained that science offered as much insight as any poetry or literature. Quite correctly, he argued that it was far more likely for scientists to offer solutions to the world's problems than some starry-eyed author or musician. Of course, some argued that science creates as many problems as it solves. Despite the intervening years, the old suspicions remain.

However mundane it appears to us now, it was the developing technology of television that most affected people's lives in the fifties. 1959 was really the first 'television election'. Previously, the BBC had been concerned not to deflect too much interest and debate from the traditional hustings. For the first time, public political meetings during an election campaign declined. Now the hustings were transferred to the nation's living rooms. The old embargo on political news was lifted. The camera reached into the very soul of the politicians trying to impress on screen.

Many appeared stiff, uncomfortable and shifty. They sweated under the heat of the studio lights and had difficulty in answering pointed questions. One man, although very much an Edwardian gentleman, took to the new medium with the aplomb of a leading actor. Harold MacMillan came over as relaxed, urbane and, importantly, reassuring. By contrast, Labour's party political broadcasts, which included animated cartoons and featured well-known supporters, were unconvincing. The general election TV campaign was likened to two detergent companies fighting it out for market share. Try as they might, Labour could not overcome the magic phrase 'never had it so good.' The Tories even featured a poster of a cloth-capped worker captioned 'You're looking at a Conservative.' Politics had not only given itself over to the hypnotic power of television, but also to the emergence of PR and focus groups. Despite *The Times* stating on the eve of the election 'that a great many people are summoned to yet another session in their endless appointment with history' it was difficult to avoid the thought that our politics were now just another marketing campaign.

Politicians in general were held in low regard by the public, not helped by two scandals, both involving Tory MPs. Peter Baker was at the time the youngest MP in parliament. He was an eccentric character who had won the Military Cross helping the Dutch Resistance during the war. Trying to run various business interests alongside his parliamentary duties proved disastrous. With a hyperactive personality, he was constantly at odds with the Tory whips who struggled to control him. He was running a raft of companies, including four publishing houses, and employing hundreds of staff. By the mid-fifties he was in deep financial trouble. Irregularities were spotted on a bill of exchange. He then forged the signature of the well-known and flamboyant industrialist

Sir Bernard Docker on a guarantee for £3,000 from the Bank of America. Subsequently, he obtained a sizeable loan from Barclays Bank based once more on forged signatures. With this money he paid off some of his creditors, but the net was closing in. In all, various banks lost over £100,000 as Baker tried desperately to keep his wide range of businesses afloat. Eventually, the MP was confronted by Bernard Docker and others whose signatures he had forged. His stuttered excuse 'that I have been ill for a long time' was unlikely to cut any ice. Arrested at Holloway sanatorium, he was sent for trial at the Old Bailey. Sentenced to seven years and packed off to the comforts of Wormwood Scrubs, he earned the unusual distinction of being one of the few to be expelled from the House of Commons. For a time he had employed Muriel Spark as his secretary, who based her eccentric fictional publisher Martin York on him in her novel *A Far Cry From Kensington.*

Financial jiggery-pokery by MPs allows the British public to castigate the whole political elite, but what they really enjoy is a good old sexual scandal involving one of their elected representatives. Comedy and tragedy mingled in the case of Ian Harvey, the Tory member for Harrow East. He was caught in the bushes with a nineteen-year-old guardsman in St James's Park. Ridicule was poured on him for attempting to run away while being escorted to Cannon Row police station. Hardly a honed athlete, he was quickly caught. He compounded his feeble attempt at avoiding publicity by giving a false name, but there was to be no escape. Later, Harvey admitted that the guardsman had been one of many he had picked up close to his house in Trevor Square. He had hidden his sexual instincts well enough by marrying the glamorous sister of Labour MP Christopher Mayhew. This enabled him to pass muster with the selection committee of his Harrow constituency who, in common with others, were suspicious of bachelors. A talented politician, he was promoted by MacMillan, but it seems extraordinary that he would risk his marriage and career by regularly pursuing troopers from Wellington barracks. Like so many, Harvey could avoid anything except temptation. Despite a general shift in public sentiment, homosexual acts were still illegal and liable to a lengthy prison sentence. Strings were probably pulled, as charges for gross indecency were dropped and the erring couple were only fined £5 each for breaching park regulations. The MP gallantly agreed to pay both fines. This was not to be the end of the affair. The establishment demanded proper retribution. Even in 1958 the 'abominable' crime had to be punished. The Carlton Club accepted his resignation without comment; Pratt's did offer him a social lifeline, but he declined anyway. Most hurtfully of all, he was given a dishonourable discharge from the Territorial Army, despite having had a 'good war'. His wife divorced him and he entered a period of social purgatory before finding some solace in his conversion into the Catholic Church.

The old guard still held sway in the corridors of power, particularly regarding sexual orientation. It seems likely that Terence Rattigan's CBE, awarded in 1958, had been downgraded from a knighthood. Paperwork relating to his recommendation referred to slight 'difficulties' and 'divided views'. Damningly, the word 'homo' was scribbled on the documents. It took until 1971, by which time opinion had softened, before his knighthood was forthcoming. By the late fifties a coterie of well-known personalities, including Noel Coward and impresario Binkie Beaumont, hardly bothered to hide their leanings. Politicians Tom Driberg and Tory peer Lord Robert Boothby also showed a confidence, or maybe it was arrogance, in pursuing their inclinations.

Despite the social changes experienced during the decade and the effects of the 'youth revolution', most still deferred to authority in a way that we would find strange today. This is illustrated by an unnamed partner employed at John Lewis writing to the chairman of the company in the mid-fifties and published in the John Lewis *Gazette*. It reads,

> After many years with the partnership I have been declared redundant and my engagement terminated. I personally can think of no organisation that creates such a wealth of good feeling and of helpfulness one to another that exists within the partnership of which you have the honour to be chairman and above this to have conceived such an outstanding experiment in modern history.

It is inconceivable that a modern employee would write in such terms unless they were being facetious, and it seems unlikely that the letter was. Among a certain class and age group who were brought up to respect their 'betters', it reflects an inbuilt reaction to defer to those in authority. This attitude was widespread. Policemen were still very visible on the streets and they were quite capable of clipping a cheeky youngster round the ear and generally would be supported in doing so. School teachers remained figures of authority, with doctors being held particularly high in public esteem. Society remained extremely judgemental. Shame was still very high on the agenda for any wrong-doing, either moral or criminal. Despite changing public opinion, divorce was still frowned upon. Children born outside marriage were still openly referred to as bastards. Looked at today all this seems difficult to believe, but underneath the continuing narrow-mindedness there was a basic decency to British life. For most it really was possible to go out of your house without locking the doors. Of course, crime existed, but most was confined to within the criminal fraternity or directed at commercial organisations. People were probably nosier sixty years ago. Neighbours talked to each other hanging over garden gates or on the landings of tenements. Strangers were watched with suspicion. In today's hectic world, it appears that many of us don't even know who our neighbours are.

As the decade drew to a close, shoppers thronged the West End. Unlike at the beginning of the fifties, shelves were now packed with an amazing array of tempting products underlying the growth of the consumer society. It was not just Oxford Street or Regent Street that drew the crowds. Many headed for High Street, Kensington. The attractions here were three stores all situated close to each other but with distinct differences in the prices on offer. Pontings trumpeted itself as 'the house of value'. At the other end of the scale was Derry and Toms. Upmarket maybe, but they were in urgent need of a new advertising agency, as they had to make do with a pathetic slogan 'A beautiful store selling beautiful things.' The middle market was catered for by Barkers. Most youngsters gave all three a wide berth while they headed for the Kings Road in Chelsea. Here, a young Mary Quant had opened the first of her two Bazaar Boutiques. What John Stephen was offering for young men in Carnaby Street was being complemented here by London's new fashion icon. Affordable, trendy and accessible, Mary Quant's designs were distinctive and came to define what was known as 'the Chelsea look'. Although very distinctive, the clothes represented a British style and fitted in perfectly with the new creative youth culture as represented by young authors, playwrights and musicians. It all seemed very exciting.

Food shopping had also gone through something of a revolution. Across London supermarkets were taking over from traditional grocers. Sainsbury's and Tesco had started their long-running battle for market share. By 1959 there were also seven Waitrose supermarkets trading. Always cautious in their development, they also had ten self-service stores and a further ten offering the traditional counter service.

With Christmas falling on a Thursday, shoppers were looking forward to a long weekend before having to return to work on the following Monday. Christmas Eve was the time to pick up a few bargains, particularly from the street markets. There was still the smell of fresh pine as the last Christmas trees were sold off at knock-down prices. If you were lucky there might also be one or two turkeys still for sale. Only a few years before turkeys were rarely available and even then they were out of most people's price range. By 1959 many of the birds on sale were frozen. It was to be some time before the novelty of frozen food wore off.

As the year ticked to a close, *My Fair Lady* was still playing to packed houses. The queen had been followed to the Theatre Royal by a string of other royals. The rich and famous also flocked to Drury Lane and Binkie Beaumont boasted that the show was fully booked for a year ahead. Over at Quaglino's, Hutch performed over twenty suggestive verses of 'Let's Do It' to a rather sad looking Cole Porter, who had one of his legs amputated the year before. Hutch was none too happy either as his career was going into a steep decline. A victim of the new obsession with rock 'n' roll. Both *My Fair Lady* and Hutch represented the past, but while the musical evoked nostalgia, Hutch had just become dated. A fine line maybe, but one being brutally drawn by a demanding public. Hutch was one of many performers, writers, artists and business organisations who were being left behind in the continual demand for change.

During the 1950s the country had moved from a time of austerity to one of conspicuous consumption. The effects of the war were fading as tower blocks and housing estates became part of London's skyline. New attitudes to life took longer to become established, but fresh perceptions were steadily taking root. The class void was less obvious, particularly among the young. This was as much to do with their dress as with any other factor. The tribal cloth cap had been discarded by working-class lads and left for their fathers to wear. The young of all classes now headed for the new trendy boutiques of Carnaby Street and the Kings Road. Meanwhile, the march towards women's liberation continued to be snail-like. While technology released them in part from the subjugation of the kitchen and housework, in other areas progress remained virtually static. Fridges and fitted kitchens satisfied some, but what of the workplace? In 1958 former suffragette Vera Brittain concluded, 'Women still occupy positions as substitute-delegates, vice-chairmen, sub-editors and assistant secretaries.' She was right. The first female branch manager of a bank was not appointed until 1958. A quarter of this country's doctors were women and yet most only held junior posts. Hundreds of women were employed in the civil service and yet they could boast only one permanent secretary. Lower down the ranks in offices and factories, women were paid substantially less than their male counterparts undertaking the same job.

The crowds gathered in Trafalgar Square on New Year's Eve in 1959. Their mood didn't reflect the gloomy, fog-bound image often levelled at the fifties. Many were optimistic and even a touch complacent. It was a time of full employment and increased disposable income. Life felt good and the future exciting. London had regained much of its old confidence and swagger. It remained edgy and a place of contradictions, but one willing to absorb and embrace new challenges.

London's population, although ever-changing, always seems to take on the characteristics of born and bred Londoners. They tend to be opinionated, noisy, garrulous and annoying to outsiders. Strangely, outsiders who come to live in London increasingly mirror the same characteristics that had previously irritated them. They, in turn, become 'bit players' in the cast of one of the world's greatest productions. London, that crazy, chaotic, exhilarating show that never ends.

Acknowledgements

My particular thanks to the following whose recollections made this book possible:

Michael Switzer, Jean Picton, Ann Spiers, Mark and Shirley Biggin, Jean Sporle, Roger Fry, Noel and Anne Cash, Marty Wilde, Doug Piller, Beryl Hart, Rochelle Venables (Managing Editor, *Good Food Guide*).

Also:

Judy Faraday, Archivist, the John Lewis Partnership; Susan Scott, Archivist, the Savoy Hotel; Francesca Bonnand, Assistant Editor, *Good Food Guide*; Rob Marriott, Archivist, Weatherbys; Andrew Thomas, the Crown Estate; staff at the Ritz, Grosvenor House and Dorchester hotels; staff at the Westminster City Archives.

Photographer Acknowledgements

The author is grateful to the following for permission to reproduce the illustrations used in this book:

The Crown Estate; the John Lewis Partnership; the Savoy Hotel; Getty Images; Mary Evans Picture Library; Soho Books; Jean Picton; Jean Sporle; the Windmill Theatre Company; Shirley Biggin.

Also to Joan Beretta for her invaluable help.

For more information about the author, visit www.mikehutton.org.uk.

Bibliography

Block, Michael, *Diaries of James Lees-Milne* (John Murray, 2007)

Breese, Charlotte, *Hutch* (Bloomsbury, 1999)

Burford, C. J. *The Orrible Synne* (Calder and Boyars, 1973)

Contarini, Paolo, *The Savoy My Oyster* (Robert Hale, 1976)

Day, Barry, *The Letters of Noel Coward* (Methuen, 2007)

Donovon, Paul, *The Radio Companion* (Grafton, 1991)

English, Alan, *The Sporting Century* (Collins Willow, 1999)

Feeney, Paul, *A 1950s Childhood* (History Press, 2009)

Foster, Andy, *Radio Comedy 1938–1968* (Virgin Publishing, 1996)

Gosling, Lucinda, *Debutantes and the London Season* (Shire Library, 2011)

Granger, Pip, *Up West* (Transworld Publishers, 2007)

Grosvenor House (James & James Publishers, 2009)

Hopkins, Harry, *The New Look* (Secker & Warburg, 1993)

Huggett, Richard, *Binkie Beaumont* (Hodder & Stoughton, 1989)

Jackson, Stanley, *The Savoy* (Frederick Muller, 1979)

Kynaston, David, *Austerity Britain* (Bloomsbury, 2007)

Laver, James, *Costume and Fashion* (Thames & Hudson, 2002)

Lees-Milne, James, *A Mingled Measure* (John Murray, 1994)

Linane, Fergus, *London Crime and Vice* (Sutton Publishing, 2003)

Marr, Andrew, *A History of Modern Britain* (Pan Books, 2008)

Masset, Claire, *Department Stores* (Shire Library, 2008)

Mitford, Nancy, *Noblesse Oblige* (Hamish Hamilton, 1956)

Montgomery-Massingberd, Hugh, *The London Ritz* (Aurum Press, 1980)

Morton, H. V., *In Search of London* (Methuen, 1951)

Morton, James, *Bent Coppers* (Warner Books, 1993)

Mosely, Charlotte, *The Mitfords* (Fourth Estate, 2007)

Moynahan, Brian, *The British Century* (Random House, 1992)

Porter, Roy, *London – A Social History* (Hamish Hamilton, 1994)

Sandbrook, Dominic, *Never Had It So Good* (Little Brown, 2003)

Sheran, Nina, *Tea Leaves under the Bed* (Pen Press, 2010)

Soames, Mary, *Speaking for Themselves* (Doubleday, 1998)

Stanley, Louis, *Sixty Years of Luxury* (Pearl Dean Publishing, 1991)

Tame, Richard, *Sporting London* (Historical Publications, 2005)

Willetts, Paul, *Members Only* (Serpent's Tail, 2010)

Young, Michael, *Family and Kinship in the East End* (Penguin Books, 1970)

Index